Iceland With Kids

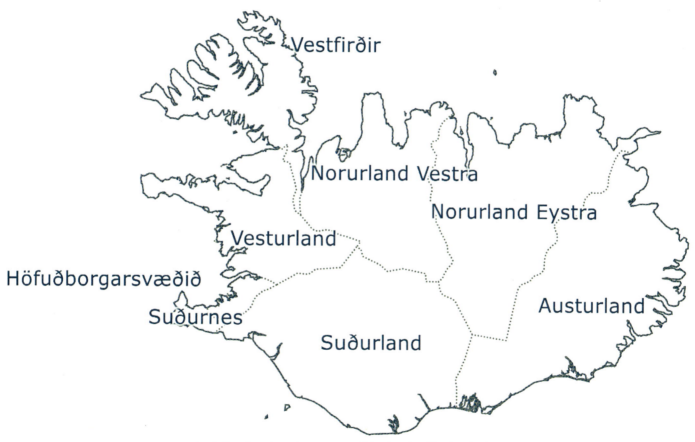

Just for fun, here's a map of Iceland with the Icelandic Province names. You won't see these words around much, and we'll use the English names for the rest of the book!

Suðurnes: Southern Peninsula

Suðurland: South

Austurland: East

Norðurland eystra: Northeast

Norðurland vestra: Northwest

Vestfirðir: Westfjords

Vesturland: West

Höfuðborgarsvæðið: Capital Region

About us: The Newman Family

That's us outside of Reykjavik in 2016. This was our second trip to Iceland; the first was in 2009 when we "only" had 3 kids, not 5. Eric took a sabbatical from work, and we spent the summer of 2016 traveling around Iceland.

We spent the first half of our trip traveling around Ring Road and experiencing all of the points of interest we could make it to, so we could let our readers know which ones we think are worth a look. In the second half of the trip, we settled down near Reykjavik and explored the more urban tourist attractions.

We wrote this book (and our web site: IcelandWithKids. com) to help families, or anyone, plan an Iceland vacation. We hope it helps you plan a wonderful trip! Reach out if you have any questions: Eric@IcelandWithKids.com

Why so dense?

This is a self-published book; self-publishing seemed like the easiest way to get it out quickly, and to be able to make revisions frequently.

It's also printed on demand; order a copy and it will be printed and shipped to you. That seemed like the easiest way to not end up with thousands of books in our garage! But, it's also expensive. We pay by the page. And so the pages are as large as standard book pages can be, and we've packed them with information and pictures. There's not much white space!

If you see a future book with more pages and white space, you'll know the first edition sold well. :-)

Creative Commons license

Most of the pictures in the book are taken by us, and we own the copyright. A few are from the web site Unsplash. com, which offers free photos for unrestricted use. Thanks Unsplash!

Any picture from Flickr is used under a Creative Commons

2.0 license. Please note that our use of these images from other people under this license does not imply their endorsement of this book. See the license here:

Liability

While we have made a good faith effort to ensure everything in the book is accurate, there may be errors. And while we hope you will have a safe and enjoyable vacation if you use this book, we are not guaranteeing that.

You are responsible for your own safety. Iceland trusts you to pay attention and be responsible for your own safety. In the United States (and other countries) when something is unsafe, you may find a barrier that is very difficult to cross. In Iceland, you may just find a sign that says "Don't go here." You are responsible for your own safety.

Maps

Any nice map you see was made by Eric Olason. (Boring maps were made by me, the other Eric.) His maps are the ones listed under the "List of Maps" on page 51. See lots of cool maps he has made at EricOlason.com. Thanks Eric!

A couple of maps made by me (Eric N) were made with Maptitude, and data is copyright Caliper.

Iceland With Kids
Part 1: Planning your trip

Table of Contents: Part 1

You can find the table of contents for "Part 2: Planning your Itinerary" on page 51.

Eric's dedication: Thanks to my wife and kids for not only putting up with a hectic style of travel, but also all of the time I spent writing the book, processing the pictures, making the (bad) maps, learning graphic design, and more.

Why Iceland?

As you may already suspect, this is a different kind of travel book. Instead of a paragraph about the airport, we're going to give you all of the details you need to get the best deal on your airfare. We'll tell exactly you how to get your cell phone working in Iceland with the least amount of effort. And we'll help you pick a reputable rental car company.

We'll help you get the most out of your whale watching boat tour or decide if you want to go on one at all. We'll tell you the attractions we enjoyed and the ones that might be best to skip. We don't cover everything there is to do in Iceland, but there should be plenty here to help you explore this amazing country.

The title of the book is Iceland With Kids, and the content is geared toward families with children. But, everyone visiting Iceland should be able to use this book to help plan their vacation. As long as you're not embarrassed to be seen reading a book called Iceland With Kids.

Before we start planning, let's take a minute to answer one important question: Why should you visit Iceland?

Iceland is Amazing

Throughout this chapter (and the whole book), take a look at some things you can see in nature. Glaciers. Waterfalls. Lava fields. Black sand beaches and volcanic rock formations. Now, you can venture far off of the beaten path; there are waterfalls that will be an hour hike each way, and there are roads that are only open in the summertime and only for 4 wheel drive vehicles. But everything in these images on the next few pages (except for one: Hengifoss) is within 10 minutes of a major road; some you can spot from the road.

It's pretty close

Iceland is northwest of the rest of Europe, meaning it's closer to the United States than the rest of the continent. How close is it? Well, it's about 2,600 miles away. That's almost exactly the same distance from New York to San Francisco. It's hard to see this from a flat map; it's clearer if you look at a globe.

This translates into shorter flight times. On the next page we list the average of the shortest scheduled flight times in both directions. (Without averaging, we are cheating: In the United States, flights from west to east are generally shorter than from east to west, because of the earth's jet stream.)

Seltún Geothermal area

Climbing Sólheimajökull glacier

Average flying time between New York and:

Reykjavik	5 hours, 42 minutes
Seattle	5 hours, 39 minutes
San Francisco	5 hours, 57 minutes
London	7 hours, 10 minutes
Paris	7 hours, 38 minutes

From New York, flying to Reykjavik is a few minutes longer than flying to Seattle, and a few minutes shorter than flying to San Francisco. And, flying to London or Paris is an extra hour and a half or two hours, respectively. That extra flight time might be a welcome addition on an overnight flight where everyone is sleeping. But it will make a difference if the kids decide they can't fall asleep on the plane.

It's very kid friendly

This is a difficult one to judge objectively. Some things we see in Iceland that make us think it is kid-friendly:

• Free admission for children to many museums. One museum let our kids in free even without a paying adult! At another museum, we were told that local kids frequently show up by themselves for a couple of hours after school.

• Free or discounted tours. It seems standard here to only charge half price for children on tours as well. And many tours are free for kids under about 6 years old, including whale watching trips.

• Well-priced restaurant options. Many restaurants in Iceland, fancy or not, offer kid's menus. And you won't just find macaroni and cheese or chicken nuggets on them—many offer fish, chicken, and lamb entrées. Restaurants that don't have a kids menu typically offer a half portion of any adult entrée for half price. And buffets can be a great deal too—often kids will pay half price, and younger children can be free.

• Breastfeeding in public doesn't seem to faze anyone here. And at pools, other women have offered to hold our baby while Lora was getting dressed or putting on shoes.

It's very safe

The US Department of State actually has fewer warnings about safety in travel to Iceland than about safety in travel to the UK! Iceland has very, very little violent crime. The BBC published an article in 2013 speculating on "Why violent crime is so rare in Iceland." More importantly for our purposes, Icelanders feel safe letting their children roam free: Our tour guide in Reykjavik (population 120,000) mentioned

Hengifoss waterfall

that she will sometimes pass her 8-year-old skateboarding in downtown Reykjavik when she is giving a tour. In how many big cities in the US would parents feel comfortable allowing an 8-year-old to wander alone?

It's not overwhelming

Iceland is pretty small. How small is it? It's about 310 miles across. It has about the same number of square miles of land as Kentucky. So, if you want to see much of the country in a week, you can. Note, though, that there aren't any 70 mile per hour highways in Iceland. That 310 miles is going to take you about 8 hours to drive, not 4. (And in much of the winter, it's not possible to get all the way to the east coast of the country at all.)

If we look at population, the numbers get even smaller. The population of Iceland recently surpassed 330,000. That's about the size of ... no state in the United States. Wyoming, the least populated state, has 584,000 people.

Driving isn't overwhelming either

For visitors from the United States, you will be happy to know that Icelanders also drive on the right side of the road. This is a major benefit over visiting the UK (though not so much if you are from the UK and visit Iceland- sorry!) Eric's

first experience with driving in a foreign country other than Canada was in a left-hand driving country. I think he still has nightmares about trying to go around a traffic circle the wrong way!

You may wonder about the signage, but the Icelandic Transport Authority has produced both a helpful brochure (in English!) and an accompanying 9 minute video that give you the basic rules and important signs. Go to www.icetra.is, and click on Road Traffic. You can read the information, and then you'll find links to the video and brochure at the bottom.

As a fairly sparsely populated country (about 1/200 the population of England), you are also much less likely to be caught in a traffic jam—though both in England and Iceland you may be delayed by sheep on the road!

Cheap airfare

Iceland can be expensive once you arrive; food is expensive, as are clothes and other necessities. But for a family group, airfare is often the most expensive part of the trip. With the introduction of a discount carrier (WOW Air) in the last 5 years, you can find airfare for under $400 per person, or even cheaper if you have some flexibility. This doesn't include luggage, but we'll cover that later on-- see page 13.

(Almost) everyone speaks English

One of the big fears for many travelers is "what if something is wrong and no one understands me?" Shouldn't a country where English is the official language be the first choice? Icelanders certainly do have Icelandic as their first language. However, their school system requires them (every single one!) to study English, usually beginning at age 8 and continuing until at least 16. The Icelandic national curriculum guide states as an objective: "[I]t is essential to have a good command of English right from the beginning of university studies as most study material in Icelandic universities is in English." So the goal is for all students to be competent in English by the end of compulsory schooling (age 16!). One tour guide asked our group if anyone had ever met an Icelander who did not speak English—she followed that up with "If anyone does, you should get their autograph because you'll never meet another!" In our experience, that has been true! Plus, because English isn't the first language here, your children will be exposed to a new language.

In summary: Iceland really is amazing

We'll be getting down to the nuts and bolts of planning your trip next. As you go through all of it, just remember that you're flying for less than 5 hours (well, from the east coast) to a very safe place where nearly everyone speaks English, and there's amazing nature around many many corners.

The harbor in Húsavík

Dyrhólaey

When to Visit?

Temperature

The time of year you visit Iceland will have a definite impact on your experience. Most people assume this is because of the temperature. And there is of course a difference in the temperature by time of year.

See the graph below, which shows average highs and lows in Reykjavik since 2002. As you would expect, July and August are the hottest months, and December and January are the coldest. But if you think about the numbers, the variation isn't all that dramatic. Those summer highs are only in the upper 50s! And the winter highs are all the way down to the ... well, the upper 30s. Yes, you can see some summer

Daylight

The bigger difference than temperature, especially in the summer, is in hours of daylight. In the middle of June, there are over 21 hours of daylight. In the middle of December, there are right around 4. Now, this is hours between sunrise and sunset. There is still some light outside of these hours. In fact, let's instead consider "Civil Twilight" which loosely translates to the time between dawn and dusk. Technically, it's the times when the sun rises above 6 degrees and sets below 6 degrees. Colloquially, it's the times when it's light enough to do stuff outside comfortably. Using this definition, the sun never sets (so it never gets below 6 degrees) from around May 20th until July 25th.

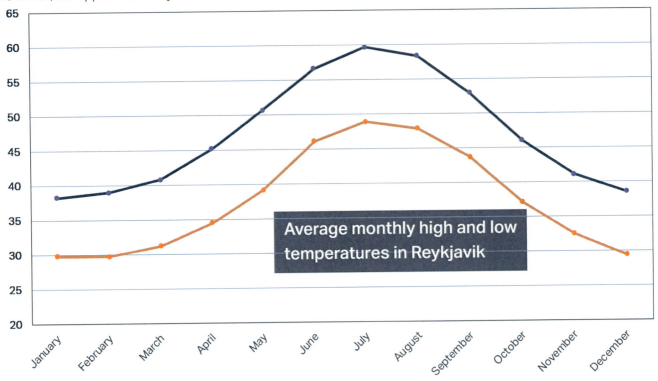

Average monthly high and low temperatures in Reykjavik

days in the 60s or (rarely) in the 70s. But most of the time, you're still wearing a jacket. Winter just means you wear an extra layer or two and a hat. And with the typical winds, you might be wearing that hat some summer days as well.

I don't want to downplay the difference between weather conditions in summer vs. winter. Conditions on the major roads can be bad between October and April, though conditions are usually fine at the beginning and end of that range. And you still need to be careful even in the good months, especially in higher elevations. At the end of May 2016 the mountain pass on the way to Seyðisfjörður was surrounded by snow. The road itself was fine, and the temperature stayed above freezing. But even two days before June, we had to think about snow. We'll cover a lot more about driving and road conditions later.

Hopefully the idea of the sun never setting for more than 2 months gives you an idea of how different this is from anywhere in the United States. You've seen temperatures like those in Iceland, but you simply haven't seen daylight like this.

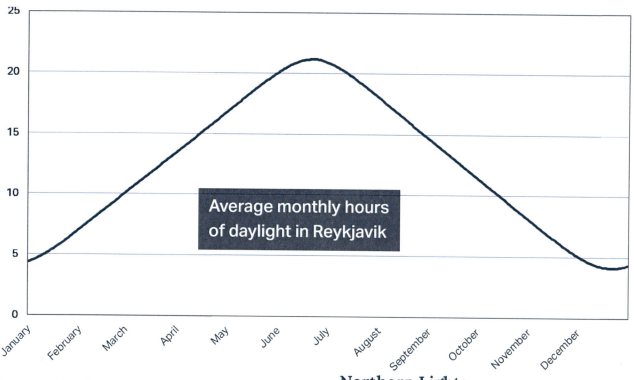

Average monthly hours of daylight in Reykjavik

So what does that mean for a family visiting Iceland? If you're there around spring (March or April) or fall (September or October), not much— the days will be about the same length as at home, give or take a couple of hours. You may notice that the CHANGE in daylight is dramatic, though, since you're on a steep part of the curves. From mid-February through mid-May, each day brings about 6 ½ minutes more of daylight. So on a week-long trip, your last day would have about 45 minutes more daylight than your first day. It makes sense-- the days have to go from 4 hours of daylight to 21 hours of daylight!

In the middle of winter, it means there will be usable daylight from about 10 AM until 5 PM or so. Now, "usable" is very subjective. Just remember that at the extremes of that range, a few bright stars and planets will still be visible.

In the middle of summer, there will literally be usable daylight for 24 hours a day. That's nice if you are a family of early risers; Icelanders seem to stay out late to enjoy the summer daylight; head out on a hike at 6 AM and you'll have the sunlight to yourself. But you may not appreciate 24 hour days as much if it's 11 PM, you've forgotten to eat dinner, and your hotel room is still bright as day.

You can check with your hotel or Airbnb rental and ask about blackout curtains. We found that most bedrooms in our rental houses had some attempt at blackout shades or curtains, but the quality varied widely. And sometimes, the lesser-used third or fourth bedroom didn't have any significant room darkening options at all. We actually ended up driving out to Ikea (page 157) in early July to purchase some throws and sheets to help cover up windows.

Northern Lights

One of the most common questions people ask is, "When can I see the Northern Lights?" You need three things in order to see them: Darkness, a clear sky, and the aurora activity to be happening at that time.

People seem to think that the aurora activity only happens in the winter. But it can and does happen year-round; you just can't see them in the summer because it's too light! If you look at the aurora forecast (en.vedur.is), they will predict how much activity there will be, even in the middle of summer. Ask yourself, are the stars visible during the day? Well, no, they aren't. But the stars are still there—it's just too bright to see them.

As soon as it is dark enough, you'll have a chance to see the Northern Lights. So you can only see the Northern Lights from late August until late April. But that sentence simply means, "The sky only gets really dark in Iceland from about late August until late April."

And if you're trying to see them at the ends of that range (August to mid-September, or mid-March through April), you'll need to be up between about 11 PM and 4 AM, which is the only time it's dark enough. And even then, you need strong aurora activity combined with clear skies. When you're visiting Iceland, especially with kids, you should view the Northern Lights as a potential added bonus, and not a reason to change your vacation to the off season.

Crowds

Tourism in Iceland is a booming industry. The population of Iceland is about 320,000, but about 2 million people visited in 2017! Not all at the same time, of course.

The off seasons are also much less "off" than they used to be. Of course, you will still find many fewer visitors in the non-summer months, but tourism is growing at a faster rate in those non-summer periods. The good news is that the summer months still don't seem overly crowded, with a few exceptions:

• You absolutely need to book lodging in advance, unless you plan to camp. An article on Iceland Monitor from January 2016 says: "According to managing director of Nordic Travel, tourists to Iceland have increased so enormously that finding accommodation for them all this summer could be very difficult."

• You also absolutely need to pre-book a visit to the Blue Lagoon. Try to book a week (or much more!) in advance, or else every entry hour may be completely sold out.

• Some restaurants may be too crowded. We weren't able to get a table at The Laundromat Café in Reykjavik, but there were many other options. A little more annoying was a 40 minute wait at Friðheimar, the tomato greenhouse in the Golden Circle area (page 63). But with a little flexibility, everything besides lodging should be fine in the summer months.

Overall, there's no bad time to go. Summer will bring more crowds but 24 hours of daylight, warmer weather, and mostly good road conditions. Winter brings more opportunities to see the northern lights, fewer people, and cheaper accommodations. If you are flexible, one of the shoulder months might be your best bet—April, May, September or October. You'll get plenty of light but not as many people.

Just for fun, below is a map that shows the population distribution in Iceland. Each bubble represents an area with at least 1,000 people living there.

Map data copyright Mapbox and OpenStreetMap.

How long to stay

So you're going to Iceland, and trying to figure out how to plan your trip. The internet is full of millions of pictures of thousands of things you can see and do. How do you plan your itinerary? What should do you do, and what will you need to skip?

Here are my brief recommendations for how you should structure your trip, based on the number of days you have. Note that the categories overlap:

1-5 days: Stay in Reykjavik, and do day tours
3-8 days: Cover one or two areas, but not the whole country
7+ days: Cover the whole country. Well, more of it at least.

I think that some people will find these surprisingly conservative. Why just stay in Reykjavik for 4 days? Why not try the whole country in 6 days?

The answer is this: No matter how much time you have, you won't see everything in Iceland. There is a main road in Iceland called Highway 1 (or Ring Road), that does circumnavigate the country. Ring Road is only 828 miles long. That gives you the sense that maybe you can see everything? 828 miles at an average of 60 miles an hour is under 14 hours of driving. But that doesn't work for three reasons:

First, the speed limit is never 60 miles per hour. The top speed limit is 90 km/h, or about 56 mph. These speed limits are more than just suggestions in Iceland. You can get a speeding ticket for going 6 km/h over the limit, or about 4 mph. And if you're going 101 in a 90 (or 63 mph in a 56 mph zone), the fine is roughly $300!

For many stretches, the speed limit is much less than 90. 70 km/h is common when entering or exiting a town, 50 km/h (in a town), or even an occasional 30 km/h (blind curves, 1 lane bridges, etc.) all occur. Remember that stretches of Ring Road are still gravel, and out east there are some serious hills.

Second, Ring Road doesn't cover the whole country. It totally bypasses the Westfjords (page 113), which are sticking up in the top left corner of the country. There, you will find The Museum of Icelandic Sorcery and Witchcraft, the town of Ísafjörður, the waterfall Dynjandi, and the Latrabjarg Bird Cliffs, which are the westernmost point in Europe.

Now, these aren't necessarily must-see attractions. They just serve to illustrate things to see and do that are an hour or more away from Ring Road. Ísafjörður (which is home to Tjöruhúsið (page 119), our favorite restaurant in Iceland) is 4 hours off of Ring Road. Seeing all of Ring Road doesn't mean you've seen all of Iceland. You can't see it all, so why not slow down and enjoy what you can see?

Even if you do pass through a part of Iceland on Ring road, attractions may still be a significant drive off of the main road. For example, as you head through North Iceland, you may want to go see Dettifoss (page 98), arguably the most powerful waterfall in Europe. You have your choice of 862, a newly paved road, or 864, an older gravel road that many people think provides a better view. Even the paved road will be an hour roundtrip from Ring Road, plus time to enjoy the views. Not to mention a hike to the other 2 nearby waterfalls, if you want. This is how Iceland seems to work.

And forget about trying to see the 67 (or more) named waterfalls or the 116 (or more) museums in Iceland. Given that you won't cover the entire country, I think it makes much more sense to slow down and enjoy yourself. Spend a few extra minutes lingering, and have time for unplanned detours if something catches your eye. (Or a nap if the kids need one.)

Hopefully all of that gets the point across: You can't see it all! With that out of the way, let's look at the choices I listed at the beginning in more detail.

1-5 DAYS: Day Tours in Reykjavik

The day tours are an important part of this plan. Reykjavik is a nice European city. But nature is a big draw as well. You'll want to take a day trip to see the Golden Circle, and at least one more to the South Coast (page 69) or the

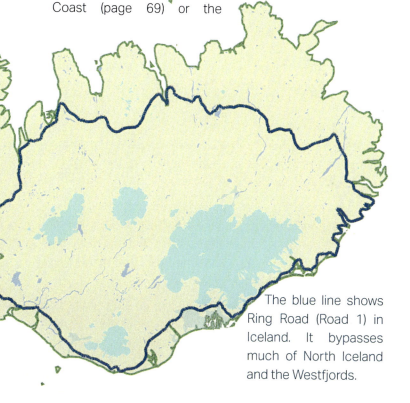

The blue line shows Ring Road (Road 1) in Iceland. It bypasses much of North Iceland and the Westfjords.

Snæfellsnes peninsula (page 124). Or do both! We'll cover the Golden Circle in great detail later.

Now, note that the next category starts at trips of 3 days. So I'm only saying that staying in Reykjavik is the best and only option for trips of just 1-2 days. You may end up with a 1-2 days trip if you take advantage of the stopover offers from Icelandair or WOW Air. If you are doing a stopover and flying Icelandair in the winter, see if Icelandair is having any fun Stopover Pass activities: Icelandair.com/en-ca/flights/stopover . (This link might not work in the future-- sorry!)

But I also think staying in Reykjavik is a fine option for slightly longer trips as well. If all of your kids are under 12, a big bus tour of the Golden Circle will cost under $200 for the whole family. A rental car will cost less (unless you get a full-sized 4 wheel drive vehicle), but you still need gas (which costs around $7 per gallon in Iceland right now!), and you need to think about insurance. Also make sure you understand F roads. And you need to worry about road conditions. There is something nice about having the details taken care of. Plus, a tour guide will provide you with more information than you will get on your own.

See a sample touring plan from Reykjavik on page 58. That plan is actually for a week!

3-8 DAYS: Cover One or Two areas, but not the Whole Country

Yes, there is also something nice about renting a car and having the freedom to explore at your own pace, and to not have to backtrack to Reykjavik every evening. That flexibility is especially nice when you're traveling with kids! (This book has pages and pages of details about driving in Iceland, starting on page 26.)

Renting a car and exploring is feasible with 3 or more days. But I think a week or more is the minimum to cover the entire Ring Road. And that's in the summer. There are going to be long stretches of road in the northwest and northeast that won't have many things to do, besides admire the stunning scenery, of course. But that's time you could spend seeing other things.

Here's a sample rough schedule:

• 1 day in Reykjavik. You could also explore a little of the area around Keflavik, where the airport is, or the amazing Reykjanes Geopark.

• 1 day exploring the Golden Circle area (page 61). Besides the main attractions, there are lots of other things nearby: Friðheimar, a tomato greenhouse that serves lunch; Raufarhólshellir Lava Tube Cave; the free Ljósafoss Power Station museum, and more.

• 1 day around Vik. See the black sand beaches (but first read the warning about Reynisfjara on page 73!), and try a glacier hike with Arcanum, if your kids are ages 10 and up

(page 82).

• 1 day around Vatnajökull National Park (see "Skaftafell" on page 76). Hike to Svartifoss, and see Jökulsárlón (page 77).

Then head back. This is just a rough idea-- see more sample itineraries with more details starting on page 55.

7+ DAYS: Cover the Whole Country

In the summer, you'll have lots of daylight, which makes driving much more enjoyable. A week in the summer is enough to travel the entire ring road, if you choose, with time to stop and see a lot of the country. You could start off with a similar itinerary as above, but then keep going on to East Iceland (page 85), Lake Mývatn (page 98), Akureyri (page 103), and back around. Or, since you'll see so many other amazing sights, you could even skip the Golden Circle, though Geysir (page 61) is pretty special.

But there's no reason you have to circumnavigate all of Ring Road. If you want to visit the Westfjords (page 113), or visit the Westman Islands (one of my favorite places for a summer visit; see page 79), even a week won't be enough to do that plus Ring road. I think people feel pressure to see "all" of Iceland; once you realize that's just not an option, it opens up opportunities to slow down. I promise you'll still see plenty of amazing things!

Icelandic Pronunciation

Even though Icelandic does technically use the Roman alphabet, there are many pronunciation differences- enough that you might have a lot of trouble making yourself understood without learning the rules. Here are some of the hardest letters, explained by wikibooks.org

A is like "a" in "Amish", "bar", "tar" and "car"

Á is like "ou" in "house", "about" and "shout"

E same as English except it's always short, like in "bed"

I is like the first "i" in "inside" and "impossible"

Í like an English "ee" and the "i" in "Maria" and the "y" in "diary"

J is like "y" in "yes", "Yoda" and "yikes"

O like "a" in British English "all" and "o" in "bolt"

Ó is like "o" in "sole" and like "oa" in "goat" and "soap"

Þ like English "th" in "thunder", "theatre" and "thong"

Ð and Þ are pronounced similarly. Also, Icelandic words never begin with Ð, and no words end with Þ.

Double LL is pronounced something like tl

Y is just like I, and Ý is just like Í

Licensed under Creative Commons 3.0 Share Alike (both theirs and my very shortened summary above.) Source: wikibooks.org/wiki/Icelandic/Alphabet_and_Pronunciation

What to Wear?

There was a point in our trip planning where we realized we had no idea what we needed to pack. We had plane tickets and lodging figured out. But what did we need to bring with us?

First, make sure you know what the average temperature is for the time of year you will be visiting Iceland. We'll copy the average temperature graph from the Hours of daylight section; see page 5 for the bigger version. You'll notice that it isn't as cold as you may fear, at least in Reykjavik—average highs are above freezing year-round.

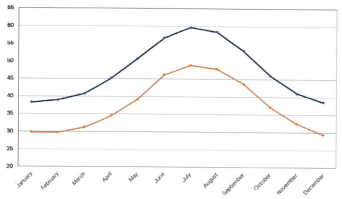

But, realize that Icelandic weather doesn't like to stick close to the average all of the time. There are summer days where the high will be 70, and summer days where the high will be 35. The 35 is somewhat unusual, though it does seem to happen occasionally. Iceland Review called the summer of 2015 the "Coldest Summer in Decades." Recently, Iceland Magazine said that "So far the summer of 2018 is the worst on record in Reykjavík." (It was cold and cloudy.) Also note that the wind in certain parts of the country can be much stronger than you are used to; a temperature of 50 degrees feels very different with a constant 30 mile per hour wind.

Next, think about what kind of vacation you plan to have. Will you be outside all day on a multi-hour hike with a picnic lunch? Or will you be wandering around downtown Reykjavik, spending time inside of stores and museums? In either case, you will still need warm clothing and layers, but you may not need to buy as much in the latter case.

Regardless, here are our three main points to remember:

• Layers are good, for both warmth and flexibility

• Cotton is bad, and wool is good, especially for the base layer

• A windproof outer layer is also good

Let's go over these in a little more detail.

Layers

When you need to dress warmly, just use more layers. The air trapped between your layers gets warm from your body heat, and acts as an extra insulator. Down jackets actually do this too, but they are bulky to pack. Also, if most of your insulation is coming from one jacket, you can't make yourself "just a little bit" cooler; it's all or none.

You're usually going for 3 or 4 layers in total on the top, and typically 1 or 2 on the bottom. Two layers on top can be fine for warmer days in Iceland, and a long hike on a freezing cold and windy day could call for 5 if you don't have a lot of wool.

The Base Layer in Iceland: Think Wool

Wool is amazing, and you should invest in some. Yes, I said invest, as wool is usually expensive. But a wool base layer- that is, the layer closest to your body- will keep you comfortable and warm. Wool is warm, it's breathable, it stays warm when wet, and it doesn't absorb odors. You'll want to wash your wool base layers eventually, but you really can hang it up unwashed and wear it again the next day. You can pack less and worry less about laundry during your vacation.

For adults, you'll typically pay $50 or more per piece (top and bottom) for a good wool baselayer. We bought sets made by Smartwool and Icebreaker. But, check out the Meriwool brand on Amazon (formerly called Elementex): They are selling 100% merino wool base layers for both men and women. They currently cost about $45 each (top and bottom), are a good weight, and have very good reviews. Wash them infrequently (and gently), and these should serve you well long after your vacation is over.

Some people worry that the wool base layer will be itchy. We didn't have any problems, though a very small percentage of people online (maybe 5%?) complain about itchiness. Some of those people say the problem goes away after a few wearings.

For our kids, we opted for the Helly Hansen wool base layer set, which have a layer of other fabric underneath the wool. Up to size 9 is called "Kid's HH Warm Base Layer," and larger sizes (actually 8 through 16) is called "Kid's Junior HH Warm Base Layer." These are NOT your typical sizes; it tries to stick closely to age, not the sizes you may be used to. See the size chart on Helly Hansen's web site—click on any product at hellyhansen.com and select the "size guide."

As mentioned above, these are not 100% wool, and I don't like that they don't seem to tell you how much wool is in them. They are actually 57% wool, and have a layer of wool on the outside: "Combining the unique Lifa® fiber technology next to skin to keep you dry, with a premium Merino wool exterior with superior insulating and wicking properties." What I like is that the elbows and knees are reinforced with fleece. Our kids must have worn their shirts 40 or more days while we were in Iceland, and many of them are still wearing them often at home. They are holding up very well.

The Middle Layers

I'm a little bit less concerned about the middle layers-- it seems silly to spend a lot on warm clothes that are just going to get sandwiched between your wool and your outer layer. I had a merino wool sweater that I brought and wore as a second or third layer. The only thing warmer than a layer of wool is two layers of wool!

The kids would usually just wear a regular long-sleeved shirt next, followed by a fleece jacket. And that was enough for most typical summer days for us. If it's winter, you could add an extra layer in there. Something like wool base layer--> shirt--> sweater--> fleece.

If you're going to be out quite a bit in very cold weather, you may want to learn layering from people smarter than me. Check out the layering guides from REI or Sierra Trading Post.

The Outer Layer for Iceland

If it wasn't raining, or even if it was just raining a little, most of us wore a fleece as an outer layer. This doesn't have to be anything fancy; we're not going for wool here. As an example, one of our kids wore a Columbia fleece jacket that cost about $25 on Amazon.

We also brought cheap rain gear with us. In fact, we bought the cheapest rain gear we could find. On the one hand, it worked well for the times we remembered to wear them. On the other hand, it kind of felt like wearing a few reusable bags that had been molded into the rough shape of a jacket. The sets we bought for the kids were called "Frogg Toggs Classic Pollywogg Kids Rain Suit"; they only cost $25 for the top and the bottom together. You'll find men's and women's sets from Frogg Toggs too. We only broke these out in heavy rain—a nicer rain set might see more use.

You could also wear a "regular" jacket as your outer layer, and this might be a better (warmer) idea if you're not going in the summer. Make sure it's large enough to fit over all of your layers that you'll be wearing underneath; you may even want a fleece below this in winter. You don't need a jacket rated to

any extreme temperature here. Since you have 3 or 4 layers underneath, it's less critical that this jacket by itself is super warm. Instead, look for windproof and waterproof properties. A "soft shell" jacket will do both wind and water well, though it might start to absorb some water in a downpour.

Here again, you need to think about your vacation plans. If you are planning an all-day hike, you need very a waterproof outer layer on the top and the bottom. If you're going to do shorter excursions, a soft shell or an inexpensive rain layer will be fine. And if you're willing to change your plans if it's raining, a fleece might be fine.

Boots or Shoes?

We bought hiking boots for everyone, for a few reasons. First, we did a couple of tours that required crampons to be attached to sturdy shoes: A glacier hike (page 82) and Into the Glacier (page 121). Second, some hikes had some slippery sections, and hiking boots provided modestly better traction.

If you're not planning a lot of long hikes, I think good shoes with good traction can be enough. And if you have older kids, they can rent hiking boots for the glacier hike, at least from the company we went with (Arcanum, page 82.)

While we're talking about footwear, wool socks can also help keep your feet warm. Just make sure your wool socks have a lot of wool in them: Look for 70% or more. The first result in a search for wool socks on Amazon says: "Made of 54% Nylon, 25% Merino Wool, 16% Polypropelene, 5% Spandex." Shouldn't those be called nylon socks?

What About Boat Tours?

Once you're out on the water for a whale watching or fishing trip, the temperature can drop and the winds can increase. It would seem you need to go all out and wear as many layers as possible. But, most boat tours provide you with insulated coveralls to wear.

You still need a layer or two underneath, depending on the weather. That wool base layer could be all you need for a summertime boat ride!

Be sure to bring hats and gloves, since the coveralls won't protect your head or hands. I don't think there's a magic formula for the right hats and gloves-- just buy something you and your kids will want to wear. I do find that many hand-knitted Icelandic wool hats are not as warm as a "regular" beanie, because

of the gaps in the fabric.

Bring options for warm weather too!

In the summertime, you can have days in the 60s, or even the 70s. It can happen. Surprisingly, it's more common in the northern or eastern parts of the country. That doesn't mean you necessarily need to bring shorts; just bring those layers and be ready to remove them as needed! Even a typical summer day in Reykjavik, with highs in the 50s, may only require a shirt and a jacket.

Icelandic Wool Sweaters: Lopapeysa

You may be planning to buy a traditional hand-knitted Lopapeysa sweater as a souvenir from Iceland. If so, buy one early and you can wear it on your vacation. One of these sweaters can easily take the place of two layers. You may not want to wear it in the rain, though; it can get a little smelly! Note that these sweaters can cost $200 or more. I think the best place to get a quality sweater is the Handknitting store in Reykjavik; see "Skólavörðustígur Road" on page 141.

That's it! If you come from a climate that gets cold in the wintertime, Icelandic weather might not be that big of a change for you. Just remember a couple of points:

1. The wind might be worse than you are used to, and you could be out on an Icelandic landscape with nothing to block the wind. If you park your car facing the wrong direction the wind can blow the door open with enough force to damage the hinges. (It's not that common, but it does happen. Park with the car facing into the wind—otherwise, the wind could grab the door right out of your hand and force it open.)

2. You may be outside a whole lot more in Iceland. At home, if it's a cold, blustery day with strong winds and maybe some sleet, you're probably not going to spend 3 hours outside hiking. That longer amount of time spent outside is where the wool and layers are going to benefit.

TF-FIP Icelandair B757
by Transport Pixels on Flickr

existent. Let's dig into the details.

Icelandair Kid's Fares

Children's tickets for ages 2-11 are offered at a 25% discount on Icelandair. But the discount is only on the base fare, and not taxes, fees, or fuel surcharges. The actual discount off of the total price was closer to 16%. Still, that can save $100 per child between 2 and 11.

Luggage Fees

Icelandair's new Economy Light

In October of 2017, Icelandair introduced a new fare class called Economy Light, which doesn't include a checked bag. It seems typical that the fare you find will be regular economy, but the below discussion doesn't apply if you found an Economy Light fare on Icelandair.

Airline Choices

Just a few years ago, there weren't too many options for flying to Iceland from the United States. You'd take Icelandair. But in 2012, discount carrier WOW Air started and suddenly things got a lot more interesting.

WOW Air has been rapidly expanding the number of US cities they fly from. In early 2016, they only flew from BWI (Baltimore Washington) and Boston. Flights from Los Angeles and San Francisco began in June 2016; Newark airport, 30 minutes outside of New York City, was added in late November 2016. Service from Miami began in April of 2017, and service from Pittsburgh begins in June 2017 and Chicago Midway in July 2017. (If you're in Canada, Wow also has flights from Toronto and Montreal.)

Update: Wow has had financial problems in 2019, and is contracting. See IcelandWithKids.com/wow for the latest.

Let's plan a trip to Iceland. Of course, your prices will be different, but this will give you a general sense.

Icelandair gives you a free carry-on and a free checked bag. With WOW Air, you can only get a free carry-on if it's small enough to fit under your seat; using the overhead bins will cost you around $45. And you can't get both a free carry on and a paid carry on—it's one or the other. Take a minute to really think about those severe restrictions. Unless everyone in your party just packs a backpack, you're paying an extra

WOW Air A330-300 on short final
by Nicky Boogaard on Flickr

Icelandair vs. WOW Air: Base prices

Limited cheap tickets

Note that there may only be 1 or 2 tickets available at the lowest price. When I upped my search to 4 people, some of the prices increased, by between $8 and $20 per ticket or so. WOW Air likes to advertise their low prices, but they may only have a handful of these cheapest seats on each flight.

From the US, your nonstop options will typically be from Icelandair and WOW Air. You can see an easy comparison on Google Flights. WOW Air will almost always be cheaper, and usually by several hundred dollars a ticket. $300 a ticket seems pretty typical-- maybe WOW Air is $400, and Icelandair is $700. For a family of 4, that's a $1,200 difference. But, surprisingly the true difference is much smaller, or non-

$90 per person or more for a roundtrip flight.

Note that these are the fees you pay WOW Air if you pay online. If you pay at the airport, they are more expensive. So if you show up at an east coast airport with a carry-on that's too big, you'd need to pay $50 instead of $45. Checked bags would cost $70 instead of $55.

WOW Air used to have weight restrictions on carry-ons, but those have been eliminated. Also, WOW Air tweaks their prices every few months (literally every few months). You'll have to check current fees on their web site: WOW Air.us/travel-info/optional-fees-and-charges.

WOW Air is now offering premium ticket classes, that

bundle checked bags and other options into the higher fare. "Wow Plus" gives you a carry-on, a checked bag, and cancellation insurance. "Wow Biz" adds food, an XXL seat with lots of legroom, and priority boarding. In most cases, though, I don't think the savings from the bundle justify the cost-- just picking the individual upgrades you want to pay for will often be cheaper.

Seats

Next, let's look at seats. With WOW Air, you have to pay to choose specific seats. Reserving a seat in the back of the plane cost $10, while seats in the middle cost $11, or $2 more each for flights from the West Coast. All of those seats have 30" or 31" of legroom.

Icelandair gives you 32" of legroom as their smallest option. If you want to reserve 32" seat on WOW Air, you'd need to pay an extra $40 for a group of 4 ($50 from the West Coast.) That's per ticket, each way.

Remember that you don't need to reserve a seat and pay any of these fees. But now you're involved in a game theory exercise. How many other people reserved seats? By the time you board, your options may be limited. Presumably, WOW Air would make sure kids aren't seated away from their parents, but theoretically families may be split up?

A new law would help with this. The LIFT Act, (Lasting Improvements to Family Travel) requires airlines to seat families together. As of late 2018, the FAA hasn't adopted any rules, so in rare cases airlines may not seat you together!

The bottom line

Let's go back to our hypothetical family of 4. Remember that WOW Air was $1,000 cheaper, and maybe $800 cheaper after the children's fare discounts. But let's assume each person checks a bag each way, with free small carry-ons. And let's assume you reserve $10 seats in the back of the plane. That's 8 checked bags (4 each way) at $50 each, and 8 seats at $10 each. Total incremental cost: $480, or more than half of the difference in cost.

If you decided you wanted 32" seats to match Icelandair, WOW Air is about the same price as Icelandair. And you don't get free drinks or an entertainment system.

The bottom line is that WOW Air can work well if you plan ahead. Maybe your family can get by with 2 large checked bags instead of 4 smaller ones?

There's one more type of seat on WOW Air that I didn't mention, and it may be a worthwhile splurge for some. There are "XXL" seats that cost an extra $50 ($05 from the West Coast), and give you at least 35" of legroom. For an overnight flight, paying the extra $200 for a family of 4 might be well worth it. Especially a tall family of 4.

Icelandair offers 33" seats in their economy comfort class, which will cost you at least $100 extra per person each way,

if not much more. That does give you meals and lounge access. But then the only option for more legroom beyond that is the 40" pitch offered in Saga business class. And now we're talking an extra $500 or $1000 or more per ticket.

Perks for kids: Icelandair vs. WOW Air

Besides qualifying for modestly discounted tickets on Icelandair, children 2-11 will get a free meal, free headphones, and some games, puzzles, and crayons. Besides the meal, everything was inside a bag our kids received. And the meal came in a cute cardboard box with activities printed on it.

Example Icelandair meals

The third option: Delta

A third (and I think final?) option from the United States to Reykjavik is Delta. For our hypothetical trip above for our hypothetical family of 4, the total cost is $2,629, or more than $300 more than Icelandair, and over a thousand more than WOW Air. Amenities are similar to Icelandair, though slightly worse. Legroom is 31" or 32", there is an entertainment system included, but you only get 1 free checked bag. You do get a meal included on each flight, which neither of the Icelandic airlines offers. If you find a competitive fare, Delta could be a fine option. Delta may also have a bassinet available for your infant. They call them SkyCots. But note that "SkyCots can be requested, but cannot be guaranteed." Otherwise, I think Icelandair or WOW Air will generally have better choices if you are booking several months into the future.

United also began flying from Newark to Reykjavik in May of 2018, though service is only offered in the summer.

Where to Stay

So far, you've decided how long you're staying in Iceland, and you've booked your airfare. Let's now take a look at lodging for your trip. We'll discuss four options: Hotels, camping, renting an apartment, or renting a house. And just to set expectations, you're not going to find a long list of recommended hotels; we're not even going to recommend one of these choices over another. There are simply too many different factors each Iceland traveler has to consider for that to make sense. Instead, we'll provide you with some specific tips and things to think about as you consider which option is best for you.

Whichever option you choose, you need to make a reservation ahead of time. The only possible exception here is camping, where you should be fine just showing up to a campsite. You may find some advice about Iceland that says you can just enjoy your day and then go find a place to stay. That might have worked 5 or 10 years ago. But tourism is booming in Iceland, and things are different now. Here's a quote from a January 2016 article in Iceland Monitor ("Iceland 'sold out' this summer?")

"According to managing director of Nordic Travel, tourists to Iceland have increased so enormously that finding accommodation for them all this summer could be very difficult. ... bookings started really early and if all hotels are booked up by the summer, some people may have to cancel their flights to Iceland."

South Coast Lodging

Lodging is especially tough to find on the South Coast. As soon as you know the dates you will be there, look for places to stay!

Hotels

My first thought when planning a vacation is to look for hotels, find one or more that are highly rated, and stay at one of them. But in Iceland, hotels seem small and very expensive, though that doesn't mean they aren't the right choice for your family or group. Here are some of the things to consider when looking for a hotel:

Location. Hotels are popping up all over Iceland because of the increase in tourism. Having more options is a good thing, but make sure you know where the hotel is. On the way from the airport to Reykjavik, we saw signs for new "airport hotels" that are being built. But some of these are 20 miles from the airport!

Similarly, just because a hotel claims it's in central Reykjavik doesn't mean it really is. Let's pick on a perfectly nice hotel: The Icelandair Hotel Reykjavik Natura. The first feature listed on their web site is "Central, Reykjavik location." But this hotel is right next to the Reykjavik City airport. (Note that this is

The well located Black Pearl Hotel

not the airport in Keflavik that you will be flying into.) But if you want to get to the main tourist areas of Reykjavik, you're looking at a 15 or 20 minute walk. And the walk to the old harbor area would be over 30 minutes.

That's fine if you were expecting that, and these trips would be just a few minutes by car. Just make sure you know what you're getting into. As a quick check, I typically use Google Maps or another mapping program to see the distance to Hallgrimskirkja (close to lots of shopping) and/or Icelandic Fish and Chips (close to the harbor area).

The one downside to good location can be noise. If you are right in the downtown area, you may end up hearing music from a local bar well past midnight, especially on weekends. Check reviews on TripAdvisor.com or another site to see if people complain about noise.

Breakfast. Breakfast buffets can be quite impressive in Iceland. You can easily pay over $20 per adult and half that for children. Hotel Reykjavik Natura, who I picked on above for their location, charges 3000 ISK for adults for breakfast, or about $26. So, if your hotel includes a free buffet with your room, that can be a valuable perk. For the most part, hotels are the only type of lodging that have the possibility to include free breakfast.

Let's pick out another hotel here as an example. CenterHotel Thingholt (which is also in a good walkable location) includes free breakfast with its rooms. The buffet includes eggs, meats, smoked fish, Skyr, pastries, and more. You probably wouldn't pay for such a fancy breakfast every day, but it's nice to not have to think about how to feed your family in the mornings.

Blackout curtains. As noted earlier (page 5) it never gets dark in Iceland from late May until late July. We found that the quality of the blackout curtains varied widely in our rental houses and apartments. (We have too many kids to make staying in a hotel worthwhile—we'd need 2 or 3 rooms!) Some places had good curtains that fit the windows well. Some had good curtains that didn't fit well, and let in a lot of light around the edges. And some had non-blackout curtains that left the room light enough to read in all night!

The benefit of hotels is that you can read reviews and get

a sense of whether the blackout curtains are high quality or not. If you're going during the peak summer, search reviews for blackout or curtain and see if people generally have a favorable or unfavorable opinion.

TripAdvisor ratings. You will find reviews of houses and apartments on Airbnb or Booking.com. But hotels usually have the largest quantity of reviews on sites such as TripAdvisor.com. Don't just look at the ratings (number of stars, 1-5) or rankings (4 of 25 hotels in a town). There are two reasons for this. First, you may find some one-star reviews that don't seem quite reasonable. Someone gave Hótel Óðinsvé one star because they arrived at 7:30 AM but weren't allowed to get into their room until noon. But check-in time at this hotel is 2 PM. Read the negative reviews and see if the issues people cite are issues for you.

Second, try to ignore the rankings. Seriously. The ranking algorithm is a combination of average star ratings and popularity (and maybe other factors)? Take Hótel Óðinsvé again, for example. Its average rating as of September 2016 is 4.20 stars, based on over 800 reviews. Hotel Hilda has an average star rating of 4.39 based on 98 reviews.

Óðinsvé: 4.20. Hilda: 4.39. But Óðinsvé is ranked much higher than Hilda. Óðinsvé is 15 out of 59 hotels, while Hilda is 44 out of 59. 44th place out of 59 hotels sounds terrible, but you need to simply ignore it and read the reviews.

Number of people a room. In the United States, I expect nearly every hotel to have a room with 2 double or queen beds, which would hold 4 people. In Iceland (and in many other European countries) you have to be more careful, as some hotels may only have rooms that hold 1 or 2 people. The new and highly rated Skuggi hotel in Reykjavik is an example; The CenterHotel Thingholt, whose breakfast we discussed above, is another. We estimate that about a third of the hotels in Reykjavik only have rooms that hold 1 or 2 people, and half can only hold a maximum of 3.

But there are some hotels that offer room for 4 to 6 people. Here are a few options in Reykjavik:

• The Black Pearl is an all suite hotel. Each room holds at least 4 people, and some hold up to 6. It's one of the top-rated hotels in Reykjavik, but it doesn't come cheap.

• The Grand Hotel Reykjavik has family rooms, some with 3 double beds. This is a good budget option, and it includes a breakfast buffet. Just don't expect a massive suite.

• The Icelandair Marina Hotel has Studio 6 rooms, which hold up to 6 people. They have a king sized bed, bunk beds, and a pull-out couch.

Camping

Camping is the cheapest option for lodging in Iceland. You can bring (or rent) camping gear, or rent a campervan, and stay at campsites throughout Iceland. Note that the rules for tent camping are a little different from capervans. But we recommend treating them the exact same way.

Many people seem to assume that you can camp in a tent just about wherever you want. Drive around, find some land that doesn't seem to be owned by anyone, set up your tent, and camp. You can argue this is true, based on a literal reading of the law. But it's also one of the best ways to offend and upset Icelanders.

Here is the rule for tents, as interpreted by the Environmental Agency of Iceland (ust.is):

"Camping with no more than three tents is allowed on uncultivated ground for a single night, unless the landowner has posted a notice to the contrary. However, campers should always use designated campsites where they do exist. Do not camp close to farms without permission. If a group of more than three tents is involved, these campers must seek permission from the landowner before setting up camp outside marked campsite areas."

The idea here is that, if you're on a multi-day hike through the highlands (the center of Iceland, where there are very few if any facilities), you are absolutely allowed to camp in the wild. This is a fundamental right of exploration that Icelanders cherish. But we were driving with an Icelandic tour guide through Þingvellir National Park, and saw campers with a tent literally right next to the road. Our guide shook his head; I asked if they should be camping there. "Absolutely not," he responded. "There's a campsite 10 minutes from here!"

Campervans must use campsites. You may be told otherwise, but this law was changed in 2013. Your only two options are to stay at a designated campsite, or have permission from the land owner.

You can find a list of campsites at tjalda.is/en/. Note that some of them are open year-round, but many are only open during the summer. You may still be able to camp at a "closed" campsite, but there won't be any services. You'll need to plan ahead and contact the campsite if you'll be there outside of their season.

You can purchase a camping card at campingcard.is. The card works at many campsites, but not all (or even most) of the ones listed at Tjalda. But for about $120, you get 28 nights (units) at campsites. A typical campsite might cost

Campground near Lake Mývatn

$10 per adult and $5 for older kids. So you might end up spending $25 or $30 for a family of 2 adults and 2 kids. That same stay would only cost 1 unit on the camping card—each of the 28 units can be used for 2 adults and all of the children in a family. So as long as you are staying fewer than 28 nights, and you plan to stay at campsites that accept the camping card, all of your camping will be covered under the $120 card. For a family, it pays for itself at about 5 nights.

If you're camping in a tent, you'll of course need to either bring or rent a tent and sleeping bags. And make sure you understand the weather—it can be very cold and very rainy at any time of year. You can rent equipment from places like Gangleri Outfitters or the plainly named Iceland Camping Equipment Rental. Expect to pay around $40 a day to rent a tent and 4 sleeping bags with mats.

A campervan can save you money vs. renting a car and staying in hotels or rental houses. A 5 person camper van can cost around $200 a night if you plan ahead. Companies that offer a 5 person campervan include Kuku and Go Campers; even for 4 people, a 5 person camper gives you a little bit of space for luggage.

We didn't do any camping on our Iceland trip. (You may be sensing a theme, since we didn't stay in any hotels either! We'll have a lot more advice once we get to renting houses and apartments.) You can save some money if you prepare. Just make sure you'll have enough room in your tent or campervan, and that everyone will be warm enough.

Apartments

It's tough to decide if some lodging options are hotels or apartments; the classifications aren't perfect here. For example, The Reykjavik Residence Apartment Hotel even defies classification in its name. You may consider this particular property to be a hotel because it includes amenities beyond those you might find apartments: daily housekeeping and a 24-hour check-in desk. Here are some reasons who you might give up on those amenities, as well as a possible free breakfast, to stay in an apartment:

You want more space. When you have kids, the novelty of all being in the same single hotel room quickly wears off. You can get 2 connecting rooms, or at least 2 rooms next to each other, but that can get expensive. Apartments have kitchens, living areas, and possibly multiple bedrooms.

There aren't many choices for families with kids. We just gave a few examples on the previous page. But very few hotels in Iceland have rooms that hold more than 4 people. When you search for a family of 5, most of the options all seem to have "apartment" or "guesthouse" in the name.

You can hardly find any available hotel rooms. Many hotels may be completely sold out, or are selling out quickly, especially in the summer. With the number of visitors to Iceland increasing at 30% - 40% a year, it might be a couple of years until the construction of new hotels catches up.

Booking.com

If you are looking for an apartment or guesthouse for your stay, you may end up looking at Booking.com. Booking.com, which is owned by Priceline, dominates the European travel market. According to a July 2016 survey by HOTREC, a European Hospitality organization, Booking.com controls about two-thirds of the online lodging market in Europe (source: seekda.com. Search for "booking portals gain market share"). Often, searching on Google or Bing, or browsing TripAdvisor, will end up taking you to Booking.com at some point.

For our summer trip, I booked many rooms using Booking.com. Here are some tips and tricks I have learned that may help you use the site.

Most reservations on Booking.com allow free cancellation. But the cancellation windows vary. Here's an example:

👥	$140 included: 11 % VAT, € 2.70 City tax per night	• ☕ Breakfast included ❓ • **Low rate** – no money back
👥	$155 included: 11 % VAT, € 2.70 City tax per night	✔ **FREE cancellation before 11:59 PM on February 13, 2018** ❓

Note that you have two options for the same room: you save $15 if you waive the cancellation option. (I'd pay more to increase flexibility.) This is for Kvöldstjarnan Gistiheimili guest house, which is typical: there's no fee if you cancel up to 1 day before arrival; cancel with less 24 hours remaining, and they will charge you for the first night.

You need to pay attention to the cancellation time frame. Many offer free cancellation up until a day or two before your stay, but some require notice of a week or more. And without reading the fine print, you won't necessarily notice the difference. Hover over that question mark before you book; some may require you cancel 5 or 7 days before your stay.

And some properties on Booking.com simply don't allow free cancellation. You won't see that second option, just the "low rate" version.

You are taking on currency risk in exchange for the free cancellation.

Most properties are booking your reservation in Euros or

The unique Hotel Reykjanes Apartments. There's a thermal pool in the background-- and geothermal steam rises up from the mat by the front door!

Icelandic Krona. For example, when we stayed at Lónsleira Apartments, the price was quoted at $339, but really I am paying 304 Euros. If the exchange rate changes, 304 Euros will be valued at more or less than $339, and that's what I will pay. Look for the fine print:

"The amount displayed in $ is just an estimate. You'll actually pay in ISK, according to the exchange rate on the day of payment."

So how much will the Euro fluctuate vs. the US Dollar, or the Canadian Dollar, or whatever your local currency is? If I knew, I'd be a currency trader!

See the current exchange rate in US dollars by searching for "USDISK" in your favorite search engine. Try "EURISK" for Euros, or "CADISK" for Canadian dollars.

There have been some unusual moves in currencies recently, but far from unprecedented. A 10% change either way if you book a few months ahead can happen. You'll need to leave some money in your budget for fluctuations, or book immediately but lose the free cancellation benefit! That is another small advantage for booking without the cancellation option, but it free cancellation still seems much better!.

Make sure you aren't booking shared accommodations or tons of rooms (unless you want to).

Booking.com's search engine tried to put our family of 7 into some interesting configurations. For example, a search turned up accommodations in Selfoss Hostel, but it was a twin room plus 5 beds in a shared dormitory space. While Selfoss Hostel may be lovely, I'm not looking to have that configuration. Other times, Booking.com will try to book 4 separate 2-person rooms for our family.

At the top of your search result, there will be a sentence you can click on that says "Show me private rooms only."

Booking.com does charge a commission, and may not always be the cheapest option.

The consensus is that Booking.com charges a commission of up to 15%. (Search for "commissions Booking.com" on Google, without the quotes.) You may be able to find the

The cottage Thormodseyri

same property at a cheaper price on other sites; try Airbnb too. (See next page.) This doesn't seem typical, though; more often, I found that Booking.com was the only option.

Booking.com tries to create the impression of scarcity.

Everywhere you click, you are bombarded with messages that you'd best book RIGHT NOW. "Just booked!" will be highlighted in red. "We have 2 rooms left!"

"We have 1 room left!" appears in red when I looked at Lambanes Reykir Holiday Home. But this is a single house, and so it only offers one "room" to book. They always have one room left (at most).

One more example. On February 4th, I was looking at rooms in Kvöldstjarnan Gistiheimili. Two messages tried to convince me there was scarcity. The first said that the latest booking for this property, was on January 28th, almost a week before. The second message said "It's likely that this guesthouse will be sold out within the next 3 hours!" Is it really likely that it will sell out "within the next 3 hours?" when no one has booked in a week? There were at least 4 rooms left.

Two days later, I went back to look. The same rooms were still available. "It's likely that this guesthouse will be sold out within the next 3 hours!" (As an aside, the exchange rate had changed slightly, and so the booking was $8 more expensive when I went back to look again.)

Booking.com does a nice job of telling you what you are getting.

When I'm booking a place for my family to stay, I want to make sure we will be comfortable. (Or, I guess if it's cheap enough, I want to know how uncomfortable we will be.) How many kids will have to share a bed, and how big are those

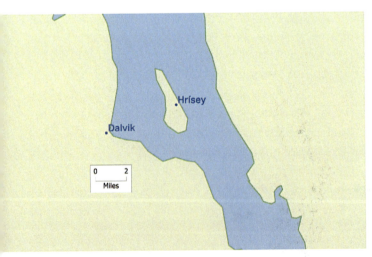

beds? Will the parents get their own room? Will we have to sleep on a sofa bed?

Booking.com usually does a very nice job of telling you exactly what you are getting. How big the space is, how many beds, etc. An information box for the cottage the cottage Thormodseyri says it is 1668 square feet, has a dishwasher and free Wi-Fi, and the configuration of the 4 bedrooms.

It's a nice layout that shows you exactly what you are getting.

Read the fine print, if there is any.

Some properties will have a fine print section at the top, and some will not. It's just one of the options on the menu bar below the name and address of the property.

Always read the fine print! (I guess that's good advice for life in general ... It may just provide information about check in times, or other informational items. Other times, there may be additional fees. For example, the Fine Print for Vestri Pétursey specifies a bed linen fee. "Bed linen and towels are not included. You can rent them on site or bring your own." At $10 (or 10 Euros?) a person, that fee could make the difference in your decision to book this property.

Beware the Booking.com measure of distance.

I've saved my favorite tip for last. This may just be an Iceland thing, but I find it really funny. Suppose you are looking for a place to stay in Dalvik, Iceland. Dalvik is up in the north, and offers some whale watching trips.

Booking.com doesn't have any places to stay in Dalvik, at least not on the dates I was searching. But the first result it recommended was Visithrisey Holiday Homes, a mere 4.3 miles from Dalvik.

Looks lovely, so let's go ahead and book it! But let's first figure out how to drive from Hrísey to Dalvik.

Turns out that the drive involves a ferry (www.hrisey.is). The ferry does run every 2 hours, and will take your car. But I'm guessing that wasn't what you were signing up for when Booking.com told you the towns were less than 5 miles apart.

Booking.com can be a great web site for the family traveler, especially if you have a lot of kids like us. It offers larger accommodations than you may find at sites that primarily offer hotels, and free cancellation on most bookings. Just make sure you understand the ins and outs, including fine print, currency risk, some unjustified pressure to book now, and some "nearby" options that aren't so nearby.

Airbnb

My path to lodging for our trip to Iceland follows the layout of this section of the book, though I skipped camping. I started by looking at hotels. Many were already sold out for the summer, or the rooms were too small. And getting two rooms would be prohibitively expensive.

Then I started looking for cottages and apartments to rent, and ended up at Booking.com. Then I landed on Airbnb.com, and ended up making a majority of our lodging reservations there. If you are traveling with kids, renting an entire house is very appealing. Here are some tips and tricks I learned along the way.

There are other sites you can use as well: VBRO.com and Homeaway.com, for example.

It's important to know that the Icelandic Government has passed a new law aimed at limiting Airbnb rentals. (Source: Grapevine.is. Search for "Airbnb law Iceland" without the quotes.) Starting in 2017, homeowners in Iceland will only be able to rent out their properties for up to 90 days a year, unless they purchase a license.

In June of 2018, the Icelandic government began allocating money to crack down on property owners ("Iceland's Parliament To Begin Cracking Down On Airbnb " in the Grapevine newspaper). They are making sure properties are registered and owners are paying taxes on rental income. You shouldn't have any problems as a tourist, though the new laws and crackdown may limit availability and possibly raise prices.

On with the tips:

Don't expect the same level of service with Airbnb.

First and foremost, remember that you are dealing with an individual person renting out their property to you. Property owners are referred to as "hosts." Airbnb is just a platform that connects you to individuals who want to rent out rooms or houses to you.

Have you ever had a hotel cancel your reservation because they charged you the wrong price? This happened to me. First I saw a message from Airbnb: Your host has canceled your reservation. Then I saw the comment from the owner: The discounted price for a weekly rental was only available in the winter. The owner had made a mistake when entering the price levels.

Maybe this bullet point should be called "If it seems too good to be true, it probably is." So what happens if the owner / host cancels on you? Airbnb offers you the option of a full refund, or they will give you a full credit PLUS about a 10% bonus to book somewhere else on their platform.

In some cases, there may be plenty of other options, and rebooking with a slight additional credit will be just fine. But what if you booked months ago, and there are limited options remaining? Anecdotally, you may be able to escalate a complaint to Airbnb and receive a much larger credit. There is a story on Reddit.com where a user says they were eventually able to get a substantial credit after the host canceled their booking months after they made it. (Search for "reddit Airbnb canceled reservation" without quotes.) But there is no guarantee this will work.

Airbnb does discourage hosts canceling, and there are some minor penalties for a host who cancels your reservation. Airbnb will automatically post a feedback entry on your behalf: "The reservation was canceled 54 days before arrival. This is an automated post." So you can scroll through the feedback and see if the owner has a history of cancellations, but it's rare to find one.

In addition, if a host cancels within 7 days of your reservation, they are charged $100, or $50 if it's more than 7 days out.

Cancellations aren't the only time the level of service is not up to that of a hotel. Here are some other issues I ran into:

• I had host ask me to change my dates, because they had accidentally double booked.

• I had a host decline my booking request without giving me a reason.

• I had a host decline my booking request because I wanted to stay on Thursday and Friday nights, and they wanted someone to stay the entire weekend.

• I had a host simply not respond to my request (which expires in 24 hours.)

Now, I'm not listing all of this to steer you away from using Airbnb; I would definitely use the site again. But there are some extra hassles that come along with the benefit of a larger space at a potentially cheaper price.

Only some Airbnb reservations can be canceled.

Airbnb lets the host choose from 3 main levels of cancellation policies: Flexible, moderate, and strict. If the cancellation policy is "flexible", you can get all of your money back, probably less the service fee, up to 24 hours before your check in time (default is 3 PM).

If the cancellation policy is "moderate", you can get all of your money back, (probably less the service fee,) up to 5 days before your check in time.

If the cancellation policy is "strict", you CANNOT get all of your money back. You will only get a 50% refund if you cancel a week or more before your check-in date.

Airbnb service fees are not always refundable.

Even the "Flexible" level above does not automatically refund your service fee; this is a fee of about 10% that goes to Airbnb. Unless you cancel within 48 hours of making the reservation, you will forfeit the roughly 10% fee that goes to Airbnb.

Guests are charged a service fee of between 6% and 12%; the more you spend, the lower the percentage gets. The service fee is clearly listed right below the rental price. If your request to book is accepted, and you later cancel, the service fee will not be refunded unless you see the little piggy bank.

Essentials might not be included.

Most listings will have an icon showing that essentials are included; click to expand the "Amenities" and see all of the details. It will list whether or not the rental has a kitchen, Internet, TV, heating, etc. One of those will be called Essentials: towels, bed sheets, soap, and toilet paper. Most rentals will include these, but a few do not.

For example, at the Cabin in the Lava, Essentials is crossed out and (in a different section) the details say: "Guests have to bring their own towels, bed sheets, and bed linen." This is likely a dealbreaker for most people, so make sure you confirm that essentials are included.

You'll pay right away.

There are two booking options hosts can select: Instant book or ... not instant book.

"Instant book listings don't require approval from the host before you can book them. Instead, you can just choose your travel dates and discuss check-in plans with the host."

If a listing does not offer instant book, the host first decides whether or not to accept your reservation. With an instant book reservation, your credit card is immediately charged the full amount of the reservation. Without instant book, your credit card is charged the full amount as soon as the host accepts your reservation, which may just be a few minutes later.

The only good news with paying when you book is that you do get to lock in your exchange rate. So if the value of your local currency weakens before your trip, you won't pay any extra.

The Airbnb cleaning fee can be pricey for short rentals.

Most, but not all, rentals include a cleaning fee. This is a fee that is charged one time per rental, regardless of the length of your stay.

Take a cottage in Arnarstapi as an example. The fee per night is $227, but the cleaning fee plus the Airbnb service fee increases this to $358. The $93 cleaning fee, charged once per stay regardless of length would be much easier to stomach for a rental of a few days or more.

Airbnb is charging you a 3% exchange rate.

"If you're paying in a currency different from the default currency of the country where the listing or experience are located, we also charge a 3% conversion fee on your total cost; the conversion fee accounts for Airbnb's holding costs and foreign currency risks." That's a stretch—they're really just taking the 3% conversion fee your credit card might or might not charge you. It's more revenue for them.

You won't see the local currency as you browse listings; everything is listed in dollars (or your local currency) so the fee is somewhat hidden. But as you go through the booking process, the fine print will tell you that Airbnb is adding a 3% fee. It's built into the exchange rate and the price you see listed.

The good news is that your credit card will be charged in dollars, and so you won't pay a foreign exchange fee. And that foreign exchange fee can total 3% on some credit cards, so Airbnb is just taking this money instead. But if your card doesn't have a foreign transaction fee, Airbnb is taking an extra 3% from you.

Airbnb can be a great tool for a family visiting Iceland. In some cases, I was able to book an entire house for less than a cramped hotel room would cost. In the picture below, you'll see had an apartment on the top floor of the building to the right; you can see our giant white van parked out front!

So go ahead and give Airbnb a try- just know what you are getting into!

Our Airbnb apartment rental in Djúpivogur

Car Rental

I don't know how many car rental companies there are in Iceland- 100? It's tough to tell, since some of them are just agents and don't have their own fleet of vehicles. Choosing one is really hard; there are a lot of horror stories out there. People who were asked to pay hundreds of dollars for damage they didn't do. Or people who were asked to pay thousands of dollars for seemingly minor damage. If you want to see some examples, find an article online called "Are the horror stories about car rental in Iceland true?"

There are two things we recommend you do to minimize the chances you will have a bad experience. First, choose a reputable car company. We used, and recommend, Blue Car rental. (They did give us a discount on our 45 day rental, but we still paid a lot of money for the car, and the opinions here are our own.) But we'll offer some tips below to help you evaluate other car rental companies in Iceland.

Second, you can buy inexpensive third-party insurance; that is, insurance not directly from your car rental company. What costs $50 a day in extra charges from the car rental company will end up costing you about $8 a day from a third party. But more on that later.

Before we look at choosing a company, let's take a minute here look at how to choose a rental car. Here are things to keep in mind:

Transmission

The default rental car will be manual transmission. You'll save money with a manual, and have a wider choice of cars. But you probably don't want to be learning how to drive a stick shift on your vacation. (I did exactly this, and it was kind of fun, but stressful. I did have a few hours of experience. 20 years ago …)

Vehicle Size

If you will need a third row of seats for a larger family, the default 7 passenger car is going to have almost no room for luggage in the truck area. Literally almost no room. Let's pick the Kia Sorento as an example, which can be equipped with either 5 seats (2 rows) or 7 seats (3 rows). With the third row in use, total cargo space behind that third row is 11.3 cubic feet. In theory that will hold several suitcases, but in practice none of your suitcases may actually fit. The Toyota Sienna minivan, in contrast, has 39.1 cubic feet of space.

4 Wheel Drive

We'll cover this later in the section about driving (page 30). If you are going to drive on F roads, which are only open in the summertime, you need a 4 wheel drive car with good clearance. If you are going in the winter, 4 wheel drive may help you have extra traction when starting on snowy or icy roads. But all cars have 4 wheel braking; 4 wheel drive doesn't make you invincible on winter roads. And 2 wheel drive cars with good snow tires can still handle winter weather in many cases.

To be clear, there are tons of amazing things for families with kids, or anyone, to see and do in Iceland without venturing onto an F road. Even roads that are not F roads offer plenty of adventure. Many are gravel. Some wind along cliffs right next to the ocean. Some have one lane tunnels where traffic going one direction has to yield to oncoming cars in occasional pull-off areas. Avoiding F roads may mean you miss out on some of the remote interior highlands, but it doesn't mean you miss out on Iceland. I strongly recommend you skip the F roads. But for more details about F roads, see page 30.

You may be more comfortable on bumpy gravel roads in an SUV with higher clearance. And some people may substitute "4 wheel drive" for "SUV." In general, though, you don't need a 4 wheel drive car.

Our recommendation rental car company: Blue Car Rental (BlueCarRental.is)

Here are our questions that will help you evaluate a car rental company. We'll tell you why Blue stacks up well in many of these categories, but other companies can also be good choices.

• Will the company guarantee you a new rental car? When I rent a car in the United States, this isn't really a consideration- I just assume I'll be getting a car that's less than 3 years old. But in Iceland, you could be getting a 10-year-old car; the slightly cheaper price may not be worth it. Some companies even embrace older cars as part of their brand: You'd never see companies called Sadcars or Cheapjeep in the United States. But these are actual options in Iceland.

• Make sure the model year is specified on your rental. If you look at the list of all of Blue's cars (BlueCarRental.is) they list one older model 4X4, which they will only rent in the summer. Just about every other car is from model year 2018 or 2019.

• How much insurance is included? Almost all rental car companies in Iceland include basic CDW insurance. That stands for Collision Damage Waiver. This is a limit to how much money you would have to pay out of pocket for damage to your rental car.

Some companies may limit your liability to $1,000; others may limit your liability to $2,800. If you have to pay either of those, you're going to be sad. But I think this is a nice, though not critical way to see if the car rental company is trying to do right by their customers. (Note that this included insurance may void your credit card insurance; see page 24 for all of the details.) Blue includes a damage maximum of around $750 for 2 wheel drive cars and about $1,000 for 4 wheel drive cars.

• How much do child car seats cost? In an effort to advertise the lowest base car rental price, companies may charge high rates for car seat rentals. You may find a company that charges $16 a day per child seat for short rentals; that can end up increasing your rental cost dramatically.

Blue provides booster seats for kids free of charge. (These will be high back boosters unless you ask for a backless one.) And safety car seats for younger kids cost a fixed fee of 4000 krona, or around $35. For a short rental, that car seat cost could be expensive. But for a longer rental, which I think is more common, this can be cheaper than a per day fee.

• How is their customer service? I recommend sending an e-mail to a company you plan to rent from, just to make sure you hear back. For a week-long trip in the summer, you could be spending $1,000 for a full-sized automatic transmission car. It's worth making sure you'll hear back from the company if there are any issues.

• Blue has been responsive to all of my e-mails, which I appreciate. But how do they respond to a customer with an issue? Lucky for you readers, we did have an issue, because I didn't take my own advice. And they took care of it. If you have a big family, as we do, remember that many 7 or 8 passenger vehicles will have almost no trunk / storage space behind the third row of seats. I knew this, and ordered a roof rack for our Land Cruiser. But even with that, there was no way we were all fitting in the car with our luggage. Blue found me a car that worked for us- – and it's not an easy feat to change the vehicle type for a 45 day rental on the spot.

• Are studded snow tires included? Okay, we didn't have snow tires on our summer rental. But if you rent in the winter, Blue guarantees studded snow tires. By law, they have to give you regular snow tires. But guaranteeing the studs gives you an extra layer of safety. Blue doesn't have to do this, but it's nice to know they do; it makes me think they strive to make sure their customers have a positive experience.

Just to be complete in our discussion of Blue, here are a few things that could be improved, or really just things to know:

The infant car set we received did not use ISOFIX, so we had to attach it using the seat belt. I haven't seen other rental car companies in Iceland offering ISOFIX either, and we were able to install the car seat safely. (Update: Blue has told me that they recently purchased new Britax car seats.)

You will have to do about a 4 minute walk to their office from Keflavik airport. (They say 3, but I'm adding a minute to walk over with kids and luggage.) To their credit, Blue has a nice video that shows you how to walk to their office from the airport. (Search for "Blue Car Rental - Airport walk to office" on YouTube.) There is also a free shuttle service, but the walk is usually faster.

You are still responsible for damage. This is specific to Iceland, not to Blue at all. But you may be used to rental car returns where they don't really even look for damage. Damage to the car is much more likely in Iceland, and they will do a thorough inspection when you return the car. Make sure you note any damage when you pick up the car; it seems prudent to take some photos or a video. Like any other car rental company in Iceland, Blue will charge you for damage not covered by the insurance. We'll look at insurance next.

But those are minor quibbles. There is no additional fee to walk to the rental office; if you have a lot of small kids and multiple adults, you can send one adult over to pick up the car.

Overall, Blue will rent you a newer model car at a reasonable price. It may not be the cheapest option in Iceland, but it's not that far off. And you'll have extra insurance built in, a new car, and a very high likelihood of a pleasant experience.

Of course, there are other options out there that will provide you a good experience. Ask yourself the questions above and see how your options stack up.

Blue Car Rental 5% Discount Code

We've been recommending Blue Car Rental for about 2 years, and we continue to think they are a top choice for a rental car in Iceland. We're happy to announce that we've partnered with Blue to offer you a 5% discount on your rental with Blue. Here's how to do it:

Browse Blue's web site. See what they have for the dates you are traveling, and (hopefully) find the car you want to rent.

E-mail them your booking request at blue@bluecarrental. is. Here's the key: put the code #BlueIWK in the subject line. (Yes, the IWK stands for Iceland With Kids!)

And that's it. Blue will respond with confirmation, as well as a link to a payment page. And that payment will be 5% less than what you saw on their web site.

In the winter, it can be tough to tell if the road is covered in ice or water. See "Winter Driving Tips" on page 29.

Car Rental Insurance

Car rental insurance is baffling, and it seems to be even more baffling in Iceland. CDW. Super CDW. Grand CDW? Premium CDW? Sand and Ash? Gravel? Note that, while the information below is customized for Iceland, much of the information can apply to other countries as well.

Collision Damage Waiver

Almost all rental car companies in Iceland include CDW. CDW stands for "Collision Damage Waiver." So it's not really insurance at all- it's a liability waiver. The rental car company agrees to not charge you more than a certain amount of money for any damage to the car when you return it, no matter how much damage there is. How much can they still charge you? A lot-- many limits are $2,000 or more.

You will find CDW included with just about every rental from a reputable company in Iceland, with no extra fee.

But if you return the car with damage, limiting your maximum out of pocket to $2,000 isn't going to matter much. You're still leaving Iceland with a bitter taste in your mouth.

Super CDW (SCDW)

You can pay for additional coverage to limit how much you will be responsible for out of pocket. SCDW will lower those limits, and some of those limits start to look much more tolerable. If you damage your 2-wheel-drive rental from Geysir, you're only out $250. But you're paying about $10 a day for the privilege of paying $250 (at most) at the end.

Note that you can keep going at some companies, to pay more and more so you can be responsible for less and less. Saga offers two more expensive levels: Grand CDW ($16 a day, adds windshield and gravel protection, limits liability to $250 or so) and Premium CDW ($38 a day, $0 liability, adds Sand and Ash protection). So at least at $38 a day, you have no worries.

Gravel insurance may be a nice add-on.

Gravel insurance protects you against damage on the front of your car caused by gravel (usually kicked up by other cars.) All of the companies here charge about $5 a day for it. Blue, our recommended company, includes it for free, which is nice; some companies may include it as part of the Grand CDW or Premium CDW packages. For a few extra dollars, this seems like a good option. But again, if you opt for third-party insurance (see next page) this may be redundant.

Sand and Ash insurance is probably not necessary

Besides a total loss of the car, sand and ash damage seems like the most expensive damage you can do to a car. In effect, the car is "sandblasted" by the small sand particles, which are driven into the car by high winds. Costs can be $5,000 or more, and are NOT covered by CDW or SCDW.

But here's the important part about sand and ash: It is predictable. If you check the weather conditions at road.is and en.vedur.is and avoid high winds and storms, you should never have a problem with sand and ash. I guess you need to avoid erupting volcanoes too.

Theft Protection just seems silly

I like Blue because theft protection is included in the base rental price, so it's one less thing to worry about. (As noted above, they also include gravel insurance.) But paying for theft protection seems excessive. I apologize in advance if you take my advice and your car does end up being stolen. But Iceland is arguably the safest country in the world, and I have never heard of a rental car being stolen.

If you have a large group, be aware that many 7 passenger cars have almost no trunk space! We ended up with this giant Renault Trafic with seating for 9 (and a manual transmission.)

You are more likely to have a problem with damage to your rental car in Iceland.

I don't have anything more than anecdotal evidence. But there are dozens and dozens of stories online about minor damage turning into charges for hundreds or thousands of dollars. When there is a blog post out there with the title of "Are the horror stories about car rental in Iceland true?" you need to really think about this. Most of the stories are about two things. One, people got an old car, and the check engine light came on, or the car broke down. Or two, people were charged outrageous amounts of money for either minor damage, or damage the renter didn't think he or she caused.

In my opinion, very few of these cases are deliberate attempts to take advantage of tourists, though some of them certainly are. But a careful inspection for scratches or dents just seems to be much more likely in Iceland than it is in the United States. Make sure you take pictures, or a video, of the car when you receive it to make sure you aren't charged for damage you didn't cause. And rent from a reputable company.

Your credit card insurance probably will NOT cover damage

Many credit cards provide car rental insurance when you charge the rental to their card. There are some exceptions. But, it seems pretty clear: Visa and Mastercard will generally NOT cover damage unless you waive all rental car insurance. That is, you have to turn down the free CDW coverage your rental care company provides.

Visa says: "To activate coverage, complete the entire rental transaction with your eligible Visa card and decline the collision damage waiver (CDW) coverage if offered by the rental company."

And Mastercard says something similar: "How to get coverage ... Decline the Collision/Damage Waiver offered by the car rental company." Check the terms of your particular card, though.

American Express SHOULD work, though I'm not positive. Their policy implies some wiggle room: "Coverage for theft of or damage to a Rental Auto is activated when the Cardmember declines the full Collision Damage Waiver or similar option (CDW), or pays for a partial collision damage waiver, offered by the Rental Company." But note that there are some exclusions that could impact you: Cars must cost under $50,000 new, so they won't cover a Toyota Land Cruiser or Range Rover. And, the terms say "Compact sport/utility vehicles, including but not limited to Ford Explorer, Jeep Grand Cherokee, Nissan Pathfinder, Toyota Four Runner, Chevrolet Blazer and Isuzu Trooper and Rodeo are covered when driven on paved roads." There are lots of gravel roads in Iceland; will they not cover your SUV when driven on a gravel road, or especially an F road? (See page 30.)

You can decline CDW coverage from the rental company, but ...

Your Visa or Mastercard insurance WILL most likely cover you if you decline the CDW provided by the rental car company. Several commenters online have said they were able to do this with Sixt (not a recommendation!) But when I imagine myself in this situation, it's just not something I want to do. Try this thought exercise yourself: You decline CDW coverage, which the rental car company was willing to give you FOR FREE. Okay, not actually free, but the company won't give you a discount if you decline it. Then, something happens to your car, and it causes $15,000 worth of damage. Now, you are on the hook for $15,000 worth of damage and worry the entire flight home, and maybe for many weeks after that, if your credit card will reimburse you or not.

Instead, you could have paid the maximum out of pocket with CDW, which is around $1,000 for a 4WD car from my recommended company, Blue Car Rental. Then you can hope that the rest is covered by your excess insurance company (see below). The excess insurance costs about $8 a day. So for $5 for a week's rental, you avoid the $15,000 out-of-pocket hassle.

Many third party rental insurance policies also will not work in Iceland.

But third party excess insurance options still will not work. For example, Insure My Rental Car has language similar to the credit card companies, though only for some states. The travel policy document may say, "... the Covered Person must have rejected at the time of the rental any waiver of liability for Loss Damage available from the rental agency."

The company I used to recommend, Worldwide Insure, no longer issues excess rental insurance for Iceland. (If you're going to a different country, check out Worldwide Insure!)

The answer for Iceland: Excess car rental insurance from a few select companies.

For citizens and permanent residents of the United States, my new recommendation is Roamright. They have been reasonably responsive via e-mail and Facebook, and their policy doesn't require you to decline other coverage. The cost is $7.99 per day; choose "Car Rental Insurance" (the last option) from the drop down box under "Coverage for".

Allianz could also work for people in the United States, though they haven't been as responsive to my e-mails.

Recommendations for car rental insurance in Iceland

If the maximum out of pocket is reasonable for your car company (say under $500 or so) you may consider just paying for SCDW and gravel insurance, for about $15 a day.

If the liability limit is closer to $1,000 or more, you should consider Roamright to insure the out of pocket amount. You can also just decide to self-insure up to the CDW limit, especially since paying for SCDW and Roamright can cost $20 a day or more.

The big downside of insurance from Roamright or another excess insurance company is that you have to pay the full price for any damage, and then wait to get reimbursed. It won't be much fun to have to put $1,000 on your credit card (or possibly more for sand and ash) and then hope to get a check in the mail. Besides that, the excess insurance seems like a good option.

Many people still opt to go with their credit card insurance by declining the CDW. If you do this, which I don't recommend, make sure you understand your credit card insurance policy clearly. Is it primary or secondary coverage? Does it cover the type of car you are renting? (Many exclude cars over a certain value.) How do you prove you declined the CDW?

If you have a premier travel credit card with an annual fee and no foreign transaction fee, you may want to research the rental car insurance and see if the fine print works for you.

And no matter which way you go, take pictures of the car when you get it, and also of any damage during your rental!

Driving in Iceland

For many years, I had a rule for international travel: I wouldn't drive in any country besides the United States or Canada. It made vacations less stressful if I didn't need to deal with unfamiliar cars, roads, and signs. For our first trip to Iceland in 2009, we stayed in Reykjavik and took guided tours from there. (This works fine, by the way! You lose a lot of freedom, but I do still think it's more relaxing for the adults in the family. See "Sample touring plan: Reykjavik as a home base" on page 58.)

Then my wife and I headed to Ireland, and I decided to drive. Yes, for my first experience driving outside of North America, I chose a country that drives on the left side of the road. Then I drove in Iceland during our most recent trips, and in a manual transmission car for a good portion of the time. So I guess my driving rule is a thing of the past.

Driving in Iceland is fairly simple, at least as simple as driving in another country can be. You drive on the right side of the road, which is good for those of us from the United States. The signs are mostly understandable from the picture, even if there is no English. And traffic is usually minimal, though you will find traffic in Reykjavik and nearby towns. The only real traffic jam we found ourselves in was just before Iceland was playing a historic soccer international soccer match, and nearly everyone was heading home to watch the game.

Let's start with some tips, and then head into a discussion of the road signs.

Driver's License

You don't need to bother with an International Driver's License or anything else: "A foreign driver's license is valid in Iceland for those who stay here on temporary basis." Source: Icelandic Multicultural and Information Centre.

Weather and Road Conditions

Check the weather and road conditions every day. Make this a part of your morning routine, and check again if there are any possible issues. Get up, get dressed, and check road.is (road conditions), safetravel.is (safety warnings), and en.vedur.is (weather.) And if the forecast for road conditions don't look good, change your plans.

You're mainly looking for alerts that will be prominent on those pages. You'll find a lot of overlap in the alerts, though safetravel will have most of them. You may want to start with the weather; they provide a nice summary of any "yellow alert" areas. See the examples on page 28.

These alerts are less common than I'm making it seem here, especially in the summer. And many of these just cover small regions of the country. But it's easy to check and reduce the chances of driving into a potentially dangerous situation.

Speeding

Go the speed limit. Speed limits in Iceland are exactly that: maximum speeds. Don't assume you have a "grace period" of 5 or 10 km. These speed limits are more than just suggestions in Iceland. You can get a speeding ticket for going 6 km/h over the limit, or about 4mph. For example, suppose you are caught speeding on a 90 km/h zone; this is about 56 mph, and is the highest speed limit you will find in Iceland. You'll be fined for going 96 km/h, or just 4 mph over the speed limit. That fine is 10,000 krona, or roughly $100. But the fine jumps to 30,000 krona, or around $300, for going 101 km/h or more. That's still only 7 mph over the speed limit!

If you are interested, you can calculate your theoretical fine at the Icelandic Transit Authority's web site. Google "sektarreiknir", and the first result should be for "Sektarreiknir | Samgöngustofa." It's in Icelandic, but the page should be easy enough to figure out. (Or if you are using Google Chrome, right click and choose "Translate to English.")

Just to summarize in miles per hour: If you are traveling 60 in a 56 zone, you can get a ticket for about $100; your rental car company will most likely send you a bill a few weeks after your trip. If you are going 63 in a 56, that fine triples.

Also see "Speed Limit Signs" on page 31, and "Speed Cameras" on page 33.

There are only a few speed cameras that will catch you, but still, don't speed. The cameras and potential speeding tickets aren't really the reason you shouldn't speed. The speed limits in Iceland are there for a reason-- you'll find sheep in the road,

A lovely road in the Westfjords

drink with dinner, and you are planning to drive to your hotel afterwards. Nevertheless, this is still my advice: Don't drink any alcohol until you are done driving for the day.

Cell Phones

By now you're probably sensing a pattern. Don't speed. Don't drink. And so you may be able to guess the policy for cell phone use: Don't hold a cell phone while driving. From the brochure above: "The use of hands-free equipment is an obligation when talking on a mobile phone and driving at the same time."

Headlights

You are supposed to have your headlights on whenever you are driving, day or night, light or dark. I forgot this a lot, though since my car had daytime running lights, it didn't seem to matter much. But try to remember to turn your lights on when you start the car. And test to make sure you can't leave them on by accident once you turn off the car.

Gas Cards

Your credit card will work almost everywhere in Iceland, though we'll cover all of the exceptions later (page 45). But one major exception is automated gas pumps. You'll likely need a PIN to go with your chipped credit card. And even though all United States credit card companies will send you your PIN through the mail, this PIN may or may not work. (It may just work for cash advances, or as a security measure on your account.)

Happily, this is starting to change. See "What about a PIN for chip and PIN in Iceland?" on page 45.

Still, make sure you have options. If the gas station is open, you can just go inside and ask them to activate the pump, or you should be able to use your debit card with its PIN. But I felt more secure when I had some gas cards with me. These are gift cards that will only work at one brand of gas station. N1 is the brand you will find the most consistently in the more remote parts of the country. There's an N1 in the town of Keflavik less than 10 minutes from the airport, though it's

for example. I have a collection of pictures of different sheep on different roads. Also, you may also find tourists stopped by the side of the road to take a picture, and they often block a good portion of the lane. This is something you probably won't see on highways at home.

Alcohol

Don't drink and drive. At all. A brochure from the Icelandic Transport Authority says: "It is against the law to operate a vehicle in Iceland after having consumed alcohol or other intoxicants and penalties for violations of these laws are severe." Find the brochure from icetra.is, and click on "More on Road Traffic"

Note that it doesn't mention a specific blood alcohol limit. It says don't drive after having alcohol. It seems like you will get a fine for driving after consuming any alcohol, and many sites claim that the maximum blood alcohol level is 0.05. That's lower than the legal driving limit in many places in the United States.

Let's think about this. In many states in the US, the blood alcohol limit is 0.08. Just to be clear, that means if you drive with a blood alcohol level of 0.06 in the United States, you are doing a perfectly legal (though arguably dangerous) thing. In Iceland, at a blood alcohol level of 0.06, you lose your license.

Or at least Icelandic citizens do. And I've seen sites claim that a level as low as 0.02 can result in a fine.

I'm not much of a drinker. But it seems like it could be difficult advice to accept if you are used to having a

Watch for sheep in the road!

a couple of minutes off of the road to Reykjavik. Or you'll pass more on your way to Reykjavik. You can see the locations at n1.is/en - click on "Stations" at the top.

Roundabouts

Finally, my most obscure tip: roundabouts. This section may seem silly if you live in an area with lots of roundabouts (sometimes called traffic circles). Drive on these counter-clockwise, and yield to traffic already in the roundabout. That part is pretty intuitive, I think; the road onto the roundabout will steer you the right direction, and it seems reasonable to wait for an opening.

But, have you ever driven in a two lane roundabout? You'll find them in Iceland; you'll get to a few pretty soon after leaving the airport. Here's the part to remember: the INSIDE lane has the right of way. So, we already know that vehicles outside of the roundabout have to yield to traffic already in the roundabout. But if you're in the outside lane, you need to make sure someone in the inside lane isn't trying to exit. If so, you need to slow down to let them exit.

For me, the answer was easy: if I'm taking the first exit in a two lane roundabout, I would use the right (outside) lane. Otherwise, I used the left (inside) lane, so I had the right of way. In Hafnarfjörður, a town just outside of Reykjavik with lots of busy two lane roundabouts, the locals tend to wait for the inside lane too. You may see a much longer lineup of cars waiting for the inside lane.

A sample warning from safetravel.is

⚠ **ALERTS**[3]

Alerts & warnings

South Iceland Dec. 30th
Limited visibility on the roads around Vík today due to snow blowing over the roads. Strong wind gusts in the area! SLOW DOWN!

Road closures!
Roads 862 and 864 towards Dettifoss in North Iceland are CLOSED due to bad conditions.

Avalanche risk!
Considerable avalanche risk (level 3/5) in mountain areas of Tröllaskagi peninsula and in the East fjords! Fresh and unstable snow so study avalanche safety before heading to the mountains!

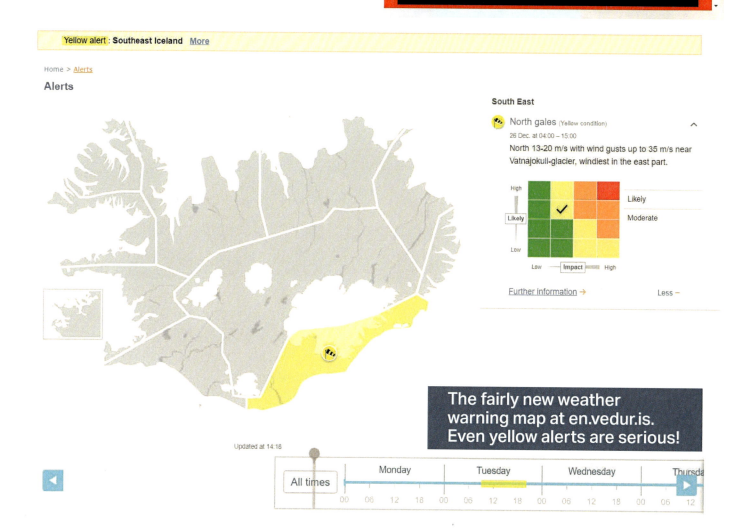

The fairly new weather warning map at en.vedur.is. Even yellow alerts are serious!

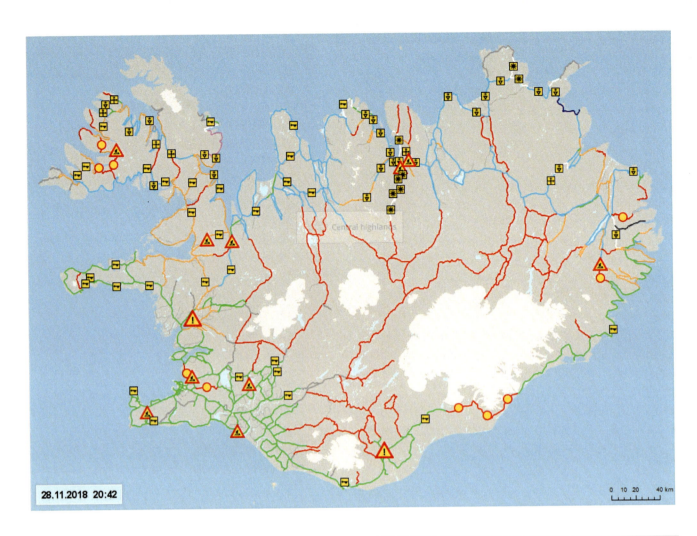

——— Easily passable	——— Difficult driving	Snow showers	Storm conditions	Winter service
——— Spots of ice	——— Difficult condition	Snowfall	Fog	Mountain vehicles
——— Slippery	——— Impassable/Closed	Blowing snow	Blowing sand	Closed
——— Extremely slippery	——— No winter service	Blizzard	? Unknown	Driving prohibited

The road condition map at road.is. You can click through to see details on the region you are in (or will be traveling to.)

Winter Driving Tips

• Check safetravel.is, road.is, and en.vedur.is at least every day. (This is good advice year-round.) Be ready to change your plans.

• Watch for black ice. Just by looking, it's tough to tell if it's water or ice. Hopefully it will be marked in dark blue on road.is.

• Snow tires do help a lot. 4 wheel drive only helps a little. All cars have 4 wheel braking, so don't assume 4 wheel drive will give you better traction. Studded snow tires will help even more. One of the reasons we like Blue Car Rental (page 22) is that Blue provides studded winter tires on all cars during winter (October through early May.)

• You may not have many hours of daylight. See page 5. But just remember that in the heart of winter, you might only have usable daylight from about 10 AM until about 5 PM. And about 3 of those 7 hours are going to be dusky.

• Be aware of the wind. Wind is strongest in the winter, and can blow snow on the roads, or blow your car door open. See page 78.

• Leave extra time! Don't assume Google Maps or your GPS program will give you accurate driving times in Iceland.

F Roads

If you are planning to drive in Iceland, you need to understand F roads. F roads are mountain roads; Fjallið means mountain in Icelandic.

Some F roads are hardly roads at all-- you might consider them mountain tracks. Here is a picture of F210, for example:

These F roads are only open in the middle of summer; the exact date varies every year based on the weather. And you need a 4 wheel drive car to drive on them; some F roads may also require sufficient ground clearance, and possibly river crossings.

The most important thing to understand is that some maps and mapping programs are not aware of these limitations of F roads, and will not warn you about them. Let's look at an example.

Suppose you would like to go see Þórsmörk, sometimes written as Thórsmörk. It's a beautiful protected valley in South Iceland, covered in lush green vegetation. Google Maps tells you it's a reasonable 2 hours and 20 minutes from Reykjavik, and the map makes it look like a nice day trip to Þórsmörk. But what you can't see until you zoom in is that the last road is F249. You **can** see the F road on the map from the Icelandic Road Association (http://vegasja.vegagerdin.is/eng/)

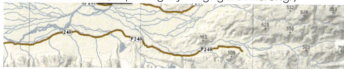

Once the road name changes to F249 heading east, it crosses 3 rivers. The 3rd of these crossings is over the river Krossá. Oh, did I mention that F roads typically do not have bridges? Take a look at this part of F249 (right side of page.)

If you really want to try and cross this, and it's one of the 2-3 months where the road is even open, you need:

- A 4 wheel drive vehicle
- Significant ground clearance. How significant? It depends

on the day. You need to watch other vehicles cross, wade in the water yourself, or talk to someone who knows the conditions today. There are rangers in the area who can help.

- To make sure nothing has changed. For example, rivers fed by glaciers tend to get deeper later in the day, as more ice melts.

- To drive downstream if possible, so you aren't fighting against the current

- To keep a constant slow speed

- To realize that your rental car insurance more than likely doesn't cover damage due to river crossings.

But the mapping programs don't tell you any of this. I think the title of this article in Iceland Magazine says it best (though this is talking about West Iceland): "Police constantly assisting travelers stuck on impassable roads which they thought were shortcuts."

If you do plan to drive on F roads, check road.is to see which roads are open. Go to road.is and click on "Road Conditions and Weather" and then "The entire country".

Most F roads are in the interior of the country, and you'll see they are all red (closed!) until maybe late June. Then some will start opening, until they start closing again in the fall.

Road.is also has other resources if you plan to tackle F roads. From the main page, scroll down and click on "Mountain Roads" on the right, under Shortcuts. Here you will find a list showing the typical opening dates. (Closing dates are less predictable, as they generally close with the first major storm. This can happen in late September or October.)

Iceland is stunningly beautiful, but it is also natural and untamed. You'll have an amazing experience. Just make sure you understand the roads. To be fair, most F roads don't have water crossings, but they do require a 4 wheel drive vehicle. And, unless you plan carefully, avoid F roads. There's plenty to see without them!

Road Signs

Let's cover signs you may see while driving. We're not covering every single sign, but just the most common and/ or most important.

Speed Limit Signs

Here is a speed limit sign (with a no parking sign below it). This is 30 kilometers per hour, or about 18 miles per hour. You may see this when you are inside a big town.

30 is somewhat uncommon; the default speed limit in a town is 50 kph. In fact, sometimes you won't even see a speed limit. Instead, if you see the sign that indicates you are entering city limits, you need to slow down to 50. Here's what you'll see through your dirty windshield:

To make things a little more confusing, you will also sometimes see signs that just say "this restriction has ended." And you'll have to figure out what the speed limit is now. So for example, the parallel diagonal lines (above right) just mean "end". So this means that the 30 kph speed limit has ended. In this case, you're still in a town, and so the speed limit goes back to 50.

You will also see signs that say you are leaving a town:

The stripe is almost always red; this one may have faded / worn off? This means the speed limit is no longer 50; assume it goes up to 70 unless you see a sign that indicates 90. You will nearly always see a sign just past the end of the city limits that steps you up to 70, and then sometimes up to 90 very soon after that.

If the speed limit sign is blue, this is a temporary reduction in speed because of a hazard; usually a sharp curve. (Below)

You may or may not see and end speed limit sign for these; you just have to assume that the limit goes back up once you are past the curve.

A normal speed limit can also be reduced if there is road work:

Once you are out of the work area, you may just see a sign that indicates the end of the road work. (That is, a road work sign with a diagonal line through it, or sometimes just a black sign with a diagonal line through it.) Again, you have to remember what the speed limit was. If you're on a highway far from a town, the limit is most likely 90.

One Lane Bridges and Tunnels

This is probably the most important sign you will see, as it is a sign you simply cannot ignore:

This sign doesn't indicate that the road narrows—it indicates that you are approaching a one lane bridge on a two way street. You have to slow down and watch for oncoming traffic. If traffic from the other side is already on the bridge, or will get there before you, you must pull over to the side; there will be a place to do so before the bridge on both sides. Sometimes the pullover location is marked with an M:

Supposedly the "M" is for the word Mæting, as in meeting; it's a place to go when cars meet.

Very rarely, you will find yourself on a longer bridge or tunnel where you cannot see the other end. There will then be pull off places built into the bridge or tunnel. I think we only came across one bridge and one set of tunnels like this.

What's important is that only one side of the road may have the pull off places. If the pull off areas on your side, then it's your job to pull over when the time comes. If they aren't on your side, then you still need to watch out for tourists who haven't read this book!

Below is a picture from a one lane tunnel. This tunnel is on the way up to the town of Siglufjörður (page 107). There's a nice Herring Museum there, but it's fairly far away from the Ring Road, and so you may not run into it. And there's another one lane bridge, up in the Westfjords (page 113), that actually has an intersection in it. That one is also in an area most travelers won't get to.

But there is a long one lane bridge is in South Iceland. (See "One lane bridges" on page 97.) You won't really know you're on it until you're on it. If the pullover areas are on your side, use them if you see traffic coming. But most of the one lane bridges are extremely short—we're talking 50-100 feet. So it's easy to see if anyone is coming well ahead of time. It's not so bad once you get used to it. I'm not sure I could get used to the one lane tunnels, though.

Yielding

This is a yield sign. In some parts of the United States, yield seems to mean merge. That is, people won't slow down as they look for an opening in the highway traffic. In Iceland, there are very few stop signs; you'll see a yield sign almost everywhere outside of big cities. Yield means "stop unless there's no one coming". You will see yield signs at a T intersection where the other traffic does not stop. Don't treat these as merges! Stop until the road is clear.

Animals on the Road

I didn't take any pictures of these signs. But you'll see a sign with a picture of an animal and a distance. For example, you might see a cow, and below it will say "0.0 – 10.6 km". That means you should watch out for cows on the road for the next 10.6 kilometers. You'll see these for sheep (everywhere) and reindeer (in east Iceland). We only ever saw sheep on the road, but we definitely saw lots of sheep on the road. Obey the speed limit and watch out.

Speed Cameras

You get a warning about most speed cameras, but not all. The warning signs look like this:

And the cameras that follow soon after look like this:

If you're going more than 5 kps over the limit, your rental car company will get a ticket which they will helpfully pass along to you. See "Speeding" on page 26 for the details.

Points of Interest

The best kind of sign you can watch for is the point of interest sign. The symbol is called a "looped square"; you may know it as the command key on an Apple keyboard: ⌘

That happens to be a really nice playground up in Súðavík (page 118) in the Westfjords. If you have some free time and a sense of adventure, follow one of these signs and see where you end up. Remember, though, that it could be a half hour drive, and you could end up on an F road; see (page 30) for more information about F roads. But sometimes you'll discover something new!

For the record, Apple didn't invent the looped square; the symbol is well over a thousand years old:

Traffic Lights

I don't want to spend much time on traffic lights, since they work pretty much as you expect them to. The one exception is the red / yellow combination. Just before a red light turns green, you get about a second when both the red and yellow lights are on.

I think this is more common in countries where people drive manual transmission cars; this gives you a second to shift into gear. So the order goes red, red/yellow, green, yellow, and then back to red.

Other Informational Signs

You may sometimes see a blue arrow. There's one in the picture above, below the traffic light. That's just telling you where your lane is, or where it goes.

In the background of that picture you can maybe make out some yellow signs that indicate the height of the bridge; these shouldn't matter to you if you're driving a normal sized truck or van.

Here's a better view of a different one. This one says that the height of the tunnel is 4.2 meters. You may also see a similar sign before a one lane bridge, except the little triangles will be on the left and the right. This will show you the width of the bridge. Again, none of this should be an issue for you.

Other signs

Let's run through some other signs and their meanings:

Blind hill. You won't be able to see cars coming from the other direction. But stay in your own lane, and maybe slow down a little; as long as everyone stays in their lane, this is a non-issue.

Don't go off road-- it's super illegal.

There are paved roads in Iceland. And gravel roads. And F roads that are rocky, and F roads with river crossings that would ruin most vehicles (page 30). But all of these have one thing in common: They are all roads!

In the US and maybe in other countries, people talk about "off roading"-- driving on unsurfaced areas. Do not do this in Iceland. It's illegal to drive on any surface that is not a road, and Iceland doesn't mess around with this. In August 2018, a group of tourists were fined $13,000 for driving on a flat non-road area. ("Fined 1.4 Million [Krona] for Off-Road Driving.")

(above) This just means caution. Slow down, but there was probably a construction speed limit sign around this one.

Dangerous intersection. The X may make you think you shouldn't be going this way, but it's just a warning sign. Use caution.

No stopping. Once again, you may think you're going the wrong way. But one line means no parking, and 2 lines mean no stopping.

Now this sign above is do not enter. Now you really are going the wrong way!

Loose gravel / stones. Slow down, and hope a car around you doesn't kick up a stone.

Pavement ends. Slow down—it's easy to lose traction when you transition from nice pavement to gravel.

Road narrows. You may need to pull over when traffic is coming from the opposite direction; there may or may not be "M" pull over areas (see page 32.)

Slow driving. The picture shows a normal car, so all cars can go on this road. But it's a rough road, and it might not be much fun.

Uneven road. This was not placed on the road—this is a place on the road that is in bad shape. It could have been damaged by passing water.

Speed hump coming up, in this case in 9 meters. This was placed on a nice road to slow you down.

You may also see a larger version of the sign above. It shows you the temperature and wind speed. But it isn't the weather information for where you are now, but rather a known trouble spot that you are approaching. Often this is at the top of a mountain pass up ahead. So the temperature may be much colder than where you are now. Use caution if the temperature is below freezing or the wind is extreme. Note that wind speed is measured in meters per second; 10 meters per second equals just over 22 miles per hour.

The sign above says that Reykjavik is 202 km to the left, and Búðardalur is 48 km the same way. Note that the 60 on the bottom right has a solid outline; that means you are turning onto Road 60. But the 1 is a dotted line; so you're heading toward 1, but not actually getting on to Road 1 right here. If you're looking for 1, turn left here and keep looking for signs.

Other driving topics

Let's quickly cover a few scenarios you'll run into driving around Iceland.

Getting Gas

We'll look at credit cards a little later (page 45), but the short version is that your credit card will work just about everywhere, except possibly at a gas pump. (But things are getting better-- see "What about a PIN for chip and PIN in Iceland?" on page 45.) Some gas stations are unmanned, and others may only have people working certain hours. (For both of these, you can get gas even if the station is closed, as long as you have a way to pay!)

Here are your options. If you have a PIN number for your credit card, give it a try. But don't expect it to work- that pin may only be for cash advances. Next, try it without a PIN at all-- this is starting to work more and more. If not, your debit card and its PIN should work, though you may want to call your bank before your trip to notify them of your travel plans.

If the gas station is open, you can go inside and pre-pay for gas. Just give them an amount of krona you'd like as your maximum; if you use less, you're only charged for what you use.

You can also just go inside, buy some prepaid gas cards, and use one or more of them to fill your tank. This is what I did—buy a few extra cards so you'll always have. N1 is the most prevalent gas station around the country. If you have money left on a gas card at the end of your trip, you can use it for hot dogs, or anything else in the gas station.

If your credit card works, or if you use a debit card, you'll be asked how much gas you'd like.

Actually, this isn't how much gas you want; this is how much you are authorizing them to put a hold on your credit card for. If you choose fill up, they will just authorize 20,000 krona or so. (In other words, "Fill up" is just a bigger number than all of the others. See the picture at top right.) That hold can stay on your card for a day or two, but you will only have to pay for the gas you actually

pumped.

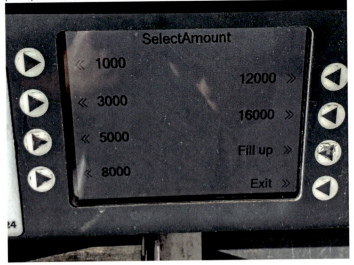

Parking Meters

In Reykjavik, many parking areas have metered parking. There won't be a meter next to your car; rather, you'll have to walk to the nearest ticket printing machine to buy a slip to put on your dashboard. See a typical machine below.

To use this machine, put your credit card in and leave it in. Push the language button (the gray button at the top right) and wait for English to appear. The machine is pretty slow to respond, so push the button and wait a second. Then, push

the plus until your desired end time shows up on the screen, and press the green button to print. Don't forget to take your credit card!

Note that if you keep adding more time, you may at some point cycle to the next morning. That is, suppose you pay enough that you can park until 6:55 PM. But you may only have to pay for parking until 6:00. In that case, the machine may say that you can park until 9:55 AM the next morning. This can be confusing, so be sure to watch as you add more time.

There are 4 zones of parking in Reykjavik, called P1, P2, P3, and (you guessed it) P4. P1 are the premium spots, and cost 320 krona per hour, though they are free on Sundays. Not surprisingly, all of the parking close to popular areas (the main shopping area of Laugavegur, and right on the harbor), is the most expensive category, P1. Even crossing the street can be enough to get to P2 or P3 parking. The blog "I Heart Reykjavik" has the best parking map I have found; just search for Parking in Reykjavik online and you will find it.

P2, P3, and P4 all cost 170 krona per hour, but with some tweaks. P3 only charges 170 for the first 2 hours; after that its only 50 krona per hour. And P4, strangely, is free on Saturdays as well as Sundays; the others are only free on Saturdays.

There seems to be an inefficiency if you park in parking garages. Some parking garages cost 80 krona for the first hour, and 50 krona each additional hour. So 4 hours in a parking garage is still cheaper than just 1 hour in a P1 zone. And, there is a cheap parking garage right at the edge of Laugavegur! Park at the garage at 94 Laugavegur, called Stjörnuport. You'll only have to drive on Laugavegur for a block, and you won't have to worry about getting a parking ticket if you stay past your estimated time. My guess is they will raise the rates in the parking garages at some point, so enjoy it while you can. See the latest prices at bilastaedasjodur.is. Click on English at the top.

The best option for truly free parking in Reykjavik is just west of Hallgrim's church (Hallgrimskirkja). Spots might be limited during the busy summer season, but you should be able to find a spot early to mid morning.

Using a GPS app on your phone

F roads (page 30) aren't the only way you can have issues with navigation in Iceland. Icelanders have been having fun recently laughing at tourists who are misled by their GPS devices. One guy drove 5 hours up to Siglufjörður instead of 45 minutes to Reykjavik (We are happy to hear that while he was there, he visited the excellent Herring Era Museum. We really liked it too! See page 108.) There is also the story a tourist was invited to a family BBQ when their GPS led them astray.

We relied on Google Maps almost exclusively for our journeys around Iceland. We have gotten slightly lost, but nowhere near enough to become famous; the guy who drove 5 hours became quite the celebrity for a few days. Here are some of our experiences and recommendations.

Using Iceland Maps Offline

Some mapping programs can be used offline. Maps. me, Here maps, and Navmii are three programs that can easily download the entire map of Iceland to use offline.

Google Maps can also download portions of the map for offline use, though it is a little more cumbersome. After you install the Google Maps app, search for Iceland. Click on the "hamburger" menu (3 lines at the top), and it will bring up a menu. Choose "Offline maps."

Click "Custom Map" and choose your region:

You'll have to divide the country into multiple sections, and you won't be sure you got them all. But these offline areas will be stored for 30 days, so you can download them before you leave for Iceland.

Google Maps in Iceland

Other mapping programs have a better process for getting offline data, but we still recommend Google maps. Maps. me charges money if you want to add navigation, and Here maps had some trouble finding some less popular points of interest when I tried it.

We had Icelandic SIM cards, and so just used Google Maps without downloading the maps. There were a couple of times where we lost data (not Google's fault, of course), and we stop getting directions. But these were few and far between, especially when we were using Siminn data. (See page 27 for information about cell phones in Iceland.)

No, We're Not Off-Roading!

A more persistent issue, especially in East Iceland, was Google Maps thinking we are ever so slightly off of the road. When this happens, the mapping program won't prompt you to make a turn. You'll need to pay attention and make turns to stay right next to the blue line.

Should We Go to Reykholt, or Reykholt?

There are lots of towns with the same name in Iceland. The one that actually caused us some confusion were the two Reykholts:

The Reykholt at the bottom right is in the Golden Circle area, and is home to Iceland Riverjet (page 66). The top left Reykholt is in West Iceland, and is home to Snorrastofa cultural museum.

I could fill this post with other pairs– Vik to Vik, Hof to Hof, Grimsey Island to Grimsey Island (seriously! the main one is north of Akureyri, but there's another one outside of Drangsnes), Húsavík to Húsavík and on and on. You get the idea. If you see a town labeled on the map, make sure you verify that you have the right place!

Guessing at Icelandic Landmarks

Google Maps doesn't like to say it can't find a destination you entered. For example, when you type in "Snæfellsjökull visitors center", it will take you to Hotel Hellnar. But when you arrive at Hotel Hellnar, the sign on their door will convince you that you´re not the first person to be led astray by your mapping program:

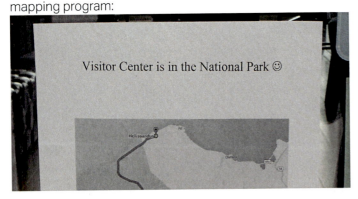

Visitor Center is in the National Park ☺

(Note that it looks as though this particular example may have been fixed recently.)

I'm picking on Google Maps in this post (and on Iceland a little, with its multiple city pairs that share a name.) For the most part, we had no issues using Google Maps to navigate. Once you're aware of these issues, and learn not to blindly trust your GPS directions, you should have very few problems navigating the country.

Child Car Seats

One of the struggles of traveling with children is lugging car seats everywhere you go. So the question is, when you travel to Iceland, do you bring your own child car seats? I think, for the most part, the answer is no.

As you would expect, Iceland has its own rules about car seat safety. While they are similar to what is in effect in many US states, the rules are not the same. The Icelandic Transport Authority publishes an English-language brochure on Child Safety in Motor Cars that you may wish to read. Head to icetra.is and click on "Car Seats for Children" at the bottom.

The main difficulty is that the US organization that certifies car seats has different (not necessarily better or worse, but different) standards than the European one. There is no exception in Icelandic law for visitors, so car seats in Iceland are required to be approved by the European rules, not US rules. That said, many anecdotes suggest that no one will be checking to see the approval sticker on your car seat. But I don't know that for certain. And there could be issues with rental car insurance coverage if you get into an accident and are not using legal child safety equipment; US-approved would not be legal! The other issue you may encounter is that while the US uses the LATCH system, Iceland uses a similar-but-not-the-same system called ISOFIX, so you may have to fasten in your car seat using belts—Cars equipped with ISOFIX attachments don't necessarily have a place to attach the top tether. If you need to use the seat belts, don't forget a belt clip for non-locking belts. My recommendation would be to stay on the side of legality and, in most cases, just rent seats!

Let's look at the different types of seats, starting with what Iceland considers "baby seats."

Baby Seats (some double as carriers)

Iceland requires this type of seat until 13 kg (29 lbs.), but some may go up to 18 kg (40 lbs.).

This is the most difficult situation. The problem is that infant seats sold in the US all have chest clips. European regulations forbid the use of a chest clip. So far as I can tell, that means that if you bought your infant seat in the US, that seat will be illegal to use in Iceland! The gist of the disagreement in regulations is whether the extra safety provided by a correctly positioned chest clip is worth the danger of an incorrectly positioned one, coupled with the extra seconds an additional fastener requires when removing the child in an emergency.

What this means is– if you don't plan to break the law, you must either rent or buy a baby seat in Iceland (or elsewhere in Europe, I suppose). It also means that when you are looking at whether to rent a car or to just take day tours, you should not forget to include the rental costs and availability of car seats in your calculations. The cost of renting a child seat can vary wildly from company to company. (See page 23.) Of course, the quality may vary as well!

We rented a baby seat with two rental car companies in Iceland and have had mediocre experiences. If your child requires a cushy, top of the line seat, rental seats from the rental car companies aren't going to cut it for you.

The first car set we rented (from Blue, page 22) was a bare-bones model. But it was clean–it looked as though the cover had been washed between rentals. And it had a locking clip (which was good, because we needed one!). This was the larger size seat acceptable for infants, which was nice.

The second experience was slightly different, since we ended up with the smaller size seat, which was more difficult to deal with. It is also a "carrier," but because it does not come with a base, it certainly would not be convenient to use as a carrier. Strapping it into the car without the base also makes it more difficult to put the child in, as the seatbelt has to go across the car seat! This car seat was also very clean, and the cover looked freshly washed. However–and this is a big deal–this was the second seat from this company–the first one had a crack in the styrofoam shell that we noticed as we tried to install it! The rental company was very courteous about replacing it immediately, but a broken seat shouldn't have been issued in the first place! As you can see, we had a mixed bag of experiences with renting from car companies.

Then, if you are going to rent an infant seat in Iceland, what do you do on the plane? It appears that neither Icelandair nor WOW Air have bassinets available on their planes. (Delta might; see page 14.) That means holding the baby. For the whole flight. Unless you plan to take your infant seat on the plane and then store it somewhere until the return trip, which is not practical for most people. Both WOW Air (to Iceland) and Icelandair (from Iceland) gave me a child lap belt for our baby (3 mos. old). This belt attached to my seat belt, and just wrapped around her waist. It didn't seem as though it would protect her much except for maybe from falling off my lap if I fell asleep! But maybe it would also help in case of unexpected turbulence?

Child seats (rear- or forward-facing):

From the time a child outgrows the baby seat (at 13 or 18 kg (29 or 40 lbs.) depending on the type of baby seat) until heavy enough to ride in a booster, Iceland requires that he or she ride in a child seat with a five-point harness. Further, the child seat must be rear-facing until the child is 1 year of age; they recommend rear-facing seats until age 3.

With this size car seat, you run into the same problem as with the infant seat: US seats all have chest clips, EU-approved ones cannot. I have seen some manufacturers claiming to sell a seat that is approved in both places, but it looks as though you have to specify which place you want it to be approved by–in other words, it isn't the same car seat;

A rented infant seat, installed with a seat belt.

they just make two slightly different versions. We haven't yet found a seat that is approved by both set of regulations (FMVSS 213 and ECE R44-04). For now, my advice is to rent a seat when you get there.

Then there is the question of what to do on the plane. If you do plan to bring your seat on the plane, check first to make sure it is allowed—the seat must be approved for air travel and different airlines have different rules about age/approval/seat availability/location for car seats. If you are planning to rent a car seat once you get to Iceland, you probably do not want to also bring a separate car seat for the plane. (But that means your child will not be in a car seat during the flight; that could be good or bad, depending on your child!) One option is to get a special device called a CARES safety restraint just for the plane ride, but those look to be about $60-$70, and are only for aircraft use, so probably not worth it for most families. (We have no affiliation with this product and have not used it.)

Older kids in the front seat

The hard rule in Iceland is that you must be at least 150 cm (4" 11') to sit in a front seat that has an airbag. In the US, rules vary by state, so make sure to let your child know beforehand if they will have to be "demoted" to the back seat again for the trip! (And no, I don't know what that means for an adult with a driver's license who is under 4" 11'.)

Booster seats

Iceland says that your child should not ride in a booster until at least 18 kg (40 lbs.) and should be in a booster until 36 kg (80 lbs.) or until they are too tall for the booster. High back boosters are recommended, but not required.

Don't let the belts twist when you strap your children in, even though you'll see that in one of our pictures! The photograph (top of next page) shows a good quality high-back booster that was provided to us on a tour bus in 2009:

Unlike with the other categories of child seat, it is possible to find dual-approved (US and EU) boosters, so you may want to bring your child's booster seat. However, do note that the vast majority of booster seats sold in the US are not EU-approved, so check on your specific booster. And do consider the next paragraph before deciding whether to bring one—boosters have different airline rules than car seats do!

The car seat options at Blue Car Rental, though blue told me they have sinced purchased new Britax seats!

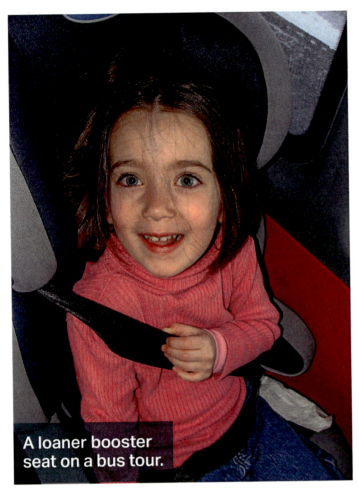

A loaner booster seat on a bus tour.

Another option, if you have space left in your luggage, is the Bubblebum inflatable booster seat (backless), which is certified safe by both US and European regulations (this is highly unusual), costs around $30, and gets good reviews on Amazon. (We have no affiliation with this product, and have not yet used it, but may in the future.) One perk of this product is that it is only 13 inches across, so that you can fit three across a back seat if you need to. If you are taking a bus to Reykjavik instead, and not renting a car at all, most tour bus companies should provide a booster. The ones we were provided on tour buses and taxis (request the seat when you call for the taxi!) in 2009 were mostly good quality- not as good as what you may use at home, but we thought they were good enough.

That seems to be the general theme if you're renting a car seat in Iceland: They won't be great, but they will usually be good enough.

If your child uses a booster, he/she cannot use that on the plane, so it will have to be checked (or counted as a carry-on). On Wow Air, the booster (or other car seat) can be checked for free, as long as the child is no older than six—and you aren't also checking a stroller for that same child. (My soon to be seven year old and my ten year old both still sit in boosters, so that would be paid checked baggage for us!) On Icelandair, you can bring a car seat and stroller for free, but only if the child in question is under age 2 (so no free boosters). You will need to check with your specific airline to see whether this is an option for you, remembering that your boosters are probably not legal in Iceland anyway!

Renting a booster from your car rental company can be a reasonable option-- Blue even offers them for free. We also did find a store (Rúmfatalagerinn) that had $20 very basic backless boosters, so you could also buy your own in Iceland. (See rumfatalagerinn.is, though the web site is in Icelandic!)

Unfortunately, the closest Rúmfatalagerinn to the airport is in Reykjavik, which would be an awfully long drive when you are very tired (45 minutes each way!) just to buy a booster seat.

Drive carefully!

There really are sheep on the road. (This picture came from up in Northern Iceland; see "Kolugljúfur" on page 111 to see the waterfall they were near.

Power Converters and Adapters

There are 2 major differences when comparing power outlets in Iceland vs. those in the United States. First and most obvious is that the outlets are shaped differently. For example, an outlet in Iceland can look like this:

Photo by
Alex Harden (aharden on Flickr)

Second, in Iceland, the power that comes out of an outlet is 220 Volts, as it is in most of Europe. In the United States, it is 120 Volts.

To solve the first issue, you just need to use a power **adapter** to change the shape of the plug. If you also need to change the voltage. you need a power **converter**.

Power Adapters in Iceland

So a power adapter just changes the shape of the plug allowing you can plug in your device.. BUT—and this is really important—**you need to make sure the device you are using is capable of handling the higher voltage**. (For what it's worth, the frequency of the Alternating Current is also lower—50 Hz vs. 60 Hz. But the point is that it's different stuff coming out of those holes.) You don't want to send 220V into a device that is expecting 120V.

Now for the good news. In my experience (which includes nothing that makes me qualified to answer this question definitively), any device with a battery that charges will be fine; the "wall wart" AC adapter functions as a converter to make sure your device gets the right voltage.. Take a look at the fine print on your cell phone or laptop charger now. I have yet to find one which does not also work at 220 V. See example above (right.)

Note the "Input" line specifies that this device (which is a 5 port USB charger) can handle inputs of between 100V and 240V. Power in the US is about 120V, and in Iceland it is about 220V. Both of those fit nicely in the range above, and so we can use this device in Iceland without converting the power to a lower voltage. You'd just need a simple adapter to

change the shape of the plug.

USB ADAPTER
Model: K-5B25
Input: AC 100-240V 50/60Hz 650mA
Output: USB*5 5V===5A(Max)
  USB1 5V/2.1A(iPad)
  USB2 5V/1.3A (Samsung Tab)
  USB3 5V/2.1A(iPad)
  USB4 5V/1A (iPhone)
  USB5 5V/1A (Android)
CE · PSE · FC · CCC · RoHS
MADE IN CHINA

But, PLEASE check your device. Don't assume that your cell phone, laptop, tablet, camera, etc. will be fine just because it has a battery. In my experience it will work fine, but I'm really not qualified to tell you it will be fine. Look at those voltage input ranges in the super small print on your charger.

Devices that Need a Power Converter

Devices that use power directly, and don't store it in a battery, may not work if you give them 220V of power. And there are some things you might take with you that fit into this category: direct plug shavers or hair dryers come to mind.

For example, my (corded) Wahl beard trimmer says: "120 VAC 60HZ 12W." This needs 120 Volts, period. Do not plug it into an adapter and send it 220 Volts. You will need a converter; more on that in a minute.

But some plug-in devices can handle the higher voltage. Here is a fun little feature on our hair dryer:

On the bottom is a somewhat cryptic built-in voltage converter. The hair dryer doesn't require precise voltages, so you just need to give it a sense of the range it should expect. In this case, that would be 125 for the US (which will give it about 120 volts) and 250 for Iceland (which will give it about

220 Volts). Turn the little white circle with a screwdriver, or maybe just a dime, and then don't forget to turn it back when you return home. But this hair dryer will work with a simple adapter, because you can tell it to expect a higher voltage.

See the next section for a warning about using converters with high voltage appliances, like hair dryers.

Buying a Power Adapter or Converter

So now you know whether you will need just an adapter, or a converter too. Adapters are very cheap. You are looking for a Type F. Some may say they are for Germany in the description, but a standard Type F adapter that will work in Iceland too.

The grounding pins are at the top and the bottom; see the image on the previous page on the left. Your adapter can be plugged in either direction; that is, up and down doesn't matter.

You can also buy 2 prong, ungrounded adapters. They will just use the middle two holes, and not have anything touching the outer grounding connections. These are Type C adapters. They look almost the same, and still fit just fine in the grounded outlet. Why get the 2 prong instead of the 3 prong, since they are about the same price?. The only reason is that the 2 prong adapter is more widely used, and is likely to work in many other countries. But unless you're looking to travel to other countries besides Iceland that only use type C, just go ahead and get the type F listed above.

Remember that these adapters are nothing more than small metal conduits that take your plugs and connect them to other plugs. There's nothing in here that requires power; it's a very simple device. Unless the connector breaks, and as long as you're using a device that can handle 220 Volts, there's little that can go wrong here.

Converters are significantly more complicated, and, surprise surprise, significantly more expensive. Be careful when you're looking for one. If you search on Amazon for "power converter", you just get the simple adapters that will not help you. Search instead for "voltage converter" and you will have more luck.

Note that it's totally fine to use a voltage converter with devices that just require an adapter. If the device knows how to handle either 120 V or 220 V, it doesn't matter which you give it. So if you have some devices that need a voltage converter, you may want to invest a high quality converter.. See icelandwithkids.com/power for our recommendations.

High voltage appliances: warning

Let's get back to hair dryers. Here's a typical disclaimer for a power converter:

"Please don't use this power converter to charge your hair dryer, hair straightener, and curling iron."

Why are we singling out hair care products here? Simply,

they use significantly more power than anything else we're dealing with here. My beard trimmer uses 10 Watts (which are roughly volts multiplied by amps, but you probably don't need to know that). Most of your chargers for cell phones or cameras will draw somewhere between 2 and 10 Watts; a laptop charger may draw 60 watts, or even 90 at the top end.

But a hair dryer can use 1600 watts. The most popular hair dryers listed on Amazon draw 1875 Watts, and one that claims to be "powerful" uses 2200 watts. We're in a totally different class of power usage here; ever see your lights dim when you turn on your hair dryer?

So what do you do if you want to have one of these high wattage devices in Iceland, and yours can't handle the higher voltage? Buy one that says it is "dual voltage" before you go (or in Iceland if you'd like a unique souvenir) and use it with a cheap and simple adapter. You shouldn't have to spend more than $40, which is around the same price as the fancy voltage converter above. I think the rule of thumb here is that any device that uses more than 100 watts should not be used with a power converter (aka voltage converter).

Power summary

- Outlets in Iceland are shaped differently than those in the United States, and they provide a different voltage.

- Most devices with a charger should work just fine, but check the label on the "wall wart" adapter.

- Assuming your charger can handle 220 Volts, just buy a simple adapter that solves the physical outlet shape issue

- If your device can't handle 220 Volts, and uses under 100 Watts, you can buy a voltage converter and use it.

- If your device can't handle 220 Volts and uses over 100 Watts, don't bring it. Either buy one that can handle 220 Volts, or do without it.

Passports

If your country is part of the Schengen agreement, you can stay in Iceland for up to 90 days without a visa. (The US, Canada, and most of Europe are included in Schengen.)

From the US, you want to make sure your passport will expire at least 3 months beyond your return date, and 6 months is better. The US Department of State says: "Three months required, six months recommended beyond your planned date of departure from the Schengen area."

If you're from the EU, your passport just needs to not expire during your stay.

Cash, Credit Cards, and PINs

Here's our second to last topic before getting to the maps and touring plans for Iceland. Let's dive in!

Do I Need To Bring Or Get Cash For My Trip To Iceland?

There is no need to purchase Icelandic Krona before your trip. Typically you will pay a hefty premium to purchase Krona in your home country-- up to 10%. Most currency exchange places (AAA, TravelEx) don't even offer Icelandic Krona.

If you do find a place that will offer an exchange for Krona, look carefully at the exchange rate. There may not be any fees, but they may offer you a very poor rate. Compare the rate to what you find online; search for "USDISK" to see how many Icelandic Krona your US dollar should buy. That rate can often be 6% or more lower than the true exchange rate.

So don't bring any cash, unless you happen to have some from a previous trip. The next question is whether you even need any cash at all? A credit will work in just about any situation for purchases large and small. In fact, there are only a handful of reasons you would ever need cash:

Bus fare in Reykjavik. To pay for a bus fare in Reykjavik, you need exact change. I guess you don't need exact change, but you need cash and you won't get anything back if you overpay. You could buy several bus tickets at a convenience store, and pay with a credit card. You could also get a Reykjavik City Card (page 58), which includes unlimited bus fare for the

"179/366 Kronur" by Danny Nicholson (dannynic on Flickr)

EITT ÞÚSUND KRÓNUR

Brynjólfur Sveinsson 1605-1675

length of the card. This can make sense if you will be visiting several museums; the bus fare would be a nice bonus. And it avoids the issue of paying cash for bus fare.

Avoiding credit card transaction fees. More on this n the next page. But many cards charge you 3% per transaction. You can maybe save a little bit if you exchange cash at an ATM, but very little. And that's assuming you won't get any miles or cash back.

Emergencies when your credit card is declined. Or when the credit card machine isn't working. It happens!

Farm stands. We've found several self-service stands selling fruit, jelly, and banana bread. There is a box there to put your cash in.

It's fun. Look at that money! It's cool. It's different. And, especially if you're traveling with kids, there's something nice about having some cash. It lets the kids pay for things in Iceland. And it helps to make the trip feel a little more "exotic."

Kids. Iceland is a very safe country; we let our kids walk to the local hot dog stand by themselves, and we gave them cash to buy lunch.

So I think it's nice to have some cash, but for the most part, it's just for fun. But you never know: We did need some cash to pay for a house we rented on Booking.com, and I was fortunate I had enough!

Where Can I Get the Best Exchange Rate on My Cash?

Again, skip the currency exchange stations, and head for the ATMs. Unfortunately, you'll likely pay a fee both to your bank as well as the bank that operates the ATM. For your bank's fee, see their web site, or the Nerdwallet article online (Google "foreign ATM fees" without quotes.) My bank charged me a flat $5, which is 1% for a large $500 withdrawal.

Here's what you'll pay the Icelandic banks, though these can and do change over time:

Landsbankinn will charge you a minimal exchange rate (about 0.3%), but I don't know if there is any way to actually get this rate. Maybe if you walk into a bank branch with US dollars? But if you use an ATM, they charge you a 0.75% fee for "Withdrawal from ATM, with card issued by another bank."

Arion Bank charges 2% ("Debit card withdrawal from foreign bank or ATM.")

Íslandsbanki looks like they only charge a flat 165 ISK ($1.50 or so) fee, which could be a real savings.

Here's a real-life example from our trip: I took out cash from an Íslandsbanki ATM. I was charged a 165 krona fee. And, as far as I could tell, the exchange rate looked very good. I certainly didn't pay 1% more than the actual exchange rate. Given that rates fluctuate in real-time, I can't swear that I wasn't charged a 0.25% fee or something. But from what I could tell, I only paid an extra 165 krona. That's a great deal on a large withdrawal! Then, when I checked my bank statement, Wells Fargo had charged me $5 for a foreign ATM withdrawal.

What do I Need to Do to Use My Credit card in Iceland?

You should call your credit card company and provide them the dates for your trip. This decreases (but does not eliminate) the chances that your card will be flagged with a fraud alert. Some companies have an automated system for this, or a mobile app; others will have you speak to a representative.

You can also ask them about the foreign transaction fees you will pay. There are two separate fees here: The bank that issues your card (Bank of America, Barclays, etc.) can charge 1% or 2%. And both Visa and Mastercard charge a 1% foreign transaction fee. (We're ignoring American Express and Discover here, as they are much less used in Iceland. You'll want to have a Visa or Mastercard card.) If your credit card doesn't advertise its low foreign transaction fees, or if it's not advertised as a travel card, odds are you will pay 3% total: 2% from the bank and 1% from Visa or Mastercard.

Which Credit Card is Best to Use in Iceland?

Credit card companies are slowly eliminating foreign transaction fees; a July 2016 article on Marketwatch.com was titled: "Credit-card issuers are ditching foreign transaction fees to attract big spenders." You can call your credit card issuer to find out what the terms are on your card. But it seems that, if your card is advertised as a "travel" card, you're in luck. Not only will most of these cards not charge a foreign transaction fee, but they also don't pass along the 1% fee from Visa and Mastercard. You'll end up paying no fee at all. But be careful; some of these cards will just say "you won't pay us a foreign transaction fee" but they still pass along the 1% from Visa or Mastercard.

Again we'll look to Nerdwallet for their article "Best No Foreign Transaction Fee Credit Cards" (Scroll about halfway down the page to see "Major issuers' foreign transaction fees.") Capital One is a major outlier here- they don't charge a fee, AND they don't pass on the 1% fee from Visa and Mastercard. USAA is another company that doesn't charge a foreign transaction fee, but they may still pass on the 1% from Visa and Mastercard.

What about a PIN for chip and PIN in Iceland?

Now things get complicated. Credit card companies in the United States are switching over to a "Chip and signature" system, where your credit card has a small smart chip embedded in it. In Iceland, they use a "Chip and PIN" system, where you need to enter your 4 digit PIN during each

transaction. In nearly all situations, your old magnetic stripe card, or your newer chip and signature card, will work just fine. You'll stick out as a foreigner because you'll have to sign the receipt, but your card will work.

The exception can be situations where you are purchasing gas in an unattended transaction. Gas stations outside of the Reykjavik capital region are the most commonly cited example. (The automated parking machines in the Harpa Concert Hall also don't work with cards that aren't chip and PIN.) Without the PIN, you may not be able to get gas. If you find yourself in this situation, your only option may be to hope someone else drives by, have them pay for your gas, and then pay them in cash. Hey, a good reason to have some cash!

You can try to call your credit card company and ask them for a PIN. Every credit card company I have called will happily offer to send me a PIN in the mail. But, critically, I am not convinced that all of these PINs are actually a PIN for chip and PIN. I fear that some credit card companies are just offering a PIN that serves as a password to enhance security when you call in to customer service. Unless the letter you receive with your PIN clearly says this will work for chip and PIN foreign transactions, you should assume you can't get gas at an unattended gas station.

This is starting to change. From CreditCards.com in March of 2018: "Both Visa and Mastercard changed their rules in 2015 to require unattended terminals worldwide to accept cards without requiring a PIN. While some merchants have been slow to adapt, Conroy said, issuers are now reporting a 95 percent acceptance rate abroad, up sharply compared to previous years." Try to enter a blank PIN-- press enter or cancel when prompted for a PIN.

Your best bet here is to buy some prepaid gas cards. You'll need to choose a specific brand of gas, and then make sure you find a gas station that matches. Or, buy a couple of different kinds, each enough for a tank (or a half tank) of gas. If you haven't used them toward the end of your trip, you can spend them on snacks or souvenirs, or let the kids binge on some gas station hot dogs.

N1 is the most recommended brand, and as we drove through more remote parts of Iceland, N1 was definitely the brand we saw the most. So the first time you come across an N1 station, or if you see prepaid gas cards anywhere else, go ahead and buy a gas card. Worst case, you can use it to buy some hot dogs or Icelandic candy for the kids at the end of your trip. See n1.is/en for a map of locations.

Your debit card and PIN should also work; you may want to call your bank to notify them of your travel so you don't trigger any fraud alerts. I still recommend you have a prepaid gas card on hand until you can confirm that your debit card does indeed work at an unmanned gas station. But we had no problem using my debit card for gas.

Getting to Reykjavik from the Keflavik Airport

Later on in Part 2, we'll show you lots of interesting things to do with your family close to the Keflavik airport (see "Keflavik" on page 164). But whether you visit these attractions or not, at some point you will probably be looking for the best way to get from the airport to Reykjavik. As with most other decisions you'll make, you have to balance price against time and convenience. A taxi that picks you up and shuttles you directly to your hotel is convenient, but not cheap. And a bus that forces you to transfer to a smaller shuttle to get to your hotel is cheaper, but not as convenient.

If you're renting a car, skip this age! Otherwise, here are some options.

Large busses

Let's start with the buses. The two biggest bus companies are **Flybus**, run by Reykjavik Excursions, and **Airport Express**, run by Grayline. Both will offer Wi-Fi on the bus, and both will require you to transfer at the BSI bus terminal in downtown Reykjavik to get to your hotel.

The good news is that both should provide car seats for children, and the journey is free for small children.

We'll look at a one way fare; roundtrip fares offer about a 10% discount. But, you'd want to book a different trip one direction if you wanted to stop at, say, the Blue Lagoon on the way back.

	Adults	Older kids	Kids 11 and under
FlyBus	3950isk	1975isk	Free
Airport Express	2900isk	1450isk	Free

(Flybus considers older kids to be 12-15; Airport Express gives you the discount for ages 12-17.)

So Airport Express is substantially cheaper-- this difference used to be smaller, but FlyBus has raised their prices by 30% recently.. Both companies do offer a cheaper option that just gets you to the BSI Bus Terminal in Reykjavik, but I'm assuming you want to get to your hotel. Reviews for each are comparable, so Airport Express seems like the way to go, though for most families the difference will not be overly significant.

Assuming you have 2 adults and all kids 11 and under, you're only paying about $60 for the whole family to get to your hotel on Airport Express.

Each company will run a bus approximately 45 minutes after an international flight lands. Still, I think it makes sense to make a reservation through the company's web site. You can also make reservations when you buy your airline ticket. WOW Air allows you to reserve seats with Flybus, but you'll still pay the 3950 krona.

Private minibus / taxi options

If your family happens to be the right size, you may benefit from private service from a private company like Back to Iceland. Oddly, they charge a lot more for leaving the airport than for going back at the end of your vacation. Here are the options:

	Airport to Reykjavik	Reykjavik to airport
1-3 people	19000 kr	12000 kr
4-8 people	25000 kr	18000 kr
9-13 people	35000 kr	30000 kr
14-17 people	45000 kr	40000 kr

If your group size is at the top end of one of these ranges, this can make sense. For example, 8 people at 25000 krona is 3125 krona per person. Of course, you're not getting a discount for kids, though. Though you get a 5% discount for booking online. Back to Iceland also offers Wi-Fi on all of their buses.

Another high-rated option is Iceland Taxi Tours, which offers a fee of 19700isk for up to 3 people in a taxi. That's after a 10% online booking discount. The price goes up to 25600isk for 5-8 people.

These expensive options definitely save some time. With Flybus or Airport Express, you'll be waiting for the rest of the groups to board the bus, and you'll have to either transfer at the BSI bus station. You're buying a private service just for your party—you should even get a driver with a sign waiting for you. And you're going straight to your hotel.

So which is the best option? As with most choices, it depends. If you have a lot of kids 11 and under, one of the big bus companies may still make sense. If you are a family of 8, with lots of older kids (or maybe grandparents), a private option may not be much more expensive than the bus options.

Stories online talk about hassles and long waits when making the transfer at the BSI bus station with the full-sized bus companies. Your mileage may vary, and this may be the exception. But you may want to save the big bus tours for when you don't have to deal with luggage, and probably sleepy children after an overnight flight.

Using your Cell Phone

For the last couple of years, I have been recommending visitors to Iceland purchase an Icelandic SIM card, even if it meant you had to purchase a new unlocked cell phone. In 2018, that's still a pretty good option, but other options have improved for travelers wishing to use their cell phones in Iceland or other countries. All major US carriers now have options for service that are somewhat reasonably priced, and Sprint and T-Mobile now have totally free choices. (But be careful—if you're on AT&T or Verizon, you'll need to do a little bit of work to make sure you don't get charged what I consider to be exorbitant data rates.) And the option of renting a mobile hotspot has gotten less expensive and more convenient. We'll walk through all of the details below to help you decide whether a cell phone from an Icelandic company like Siminn, Vodafone, or Nova makes sense for you.

Before we dive in, let me note that this information is specific to people from the United States. If you live in an EU country in Europe, there's no need to keep reading: The new "Roam like Home" law implemented in June of 2017 allows you to use your plan in any EU country just as if you're still at home. (No word on what will happen if the UK leaves the EU.)

Don't forget that you'll need a power adapter to charge your phone! See page 42.

The four options

If you are from the United States and visiting Iceland, you have several options for cell phone service; let's look at the major four.

Option 1: Becoming a Wi-Fi nomad

First, you could disable roaming and just use your phone when you have Wi-Fi; most hotels and restaurants will have free Wi-Fi, though it will be harder to find when you're driving. There are mapping programs that store all data on the phone (like Maps.me) you could use for navigation. Google Maps will also save portions of the Icelandic map for offline use. But you might have to pay a dollar or two a minute to send or receive phone calls, unless you call over Wi-Fi, or use a service like Skype. Texts might also be expensive. And unless you know you have free international data on your current plan, turn off cellular data on your phone just to be safe. (iPhone: Settings–> Cellular. Android: Settings–> Data Usage) Your AT&T and Verizon plans won't have free data; Sprint will, and T-Mobile might. See details starting on the next page.

Option 2: Adding an International Plan

The second option is to pay for an International plan with your cellular provider, or use one is included with your current plan (Sprint and T-Mobile only.) Do not just start using data when you arrive in Iceland. For example, AT&T will charge you $2.05 per megabyte of data you use while roaming internationally, unless you have an international data plan. How much is $2.05 per megabyte? Well, the homepage at IcelandWithKids.com is about a quarter of a megabyte, so it would cost you 50 cents to load. Our article about planning your trip would cost about $1.50. If you're browsing a lot of web sites and maybe doing some video chat with people back home, it would be easy to burn through a gigabyte of data in a week. Cost: over $2,000. Verizon charges the exact same rate.

On the other hand, if you have Sprint or T-Mobile as your carrier, international data might be free (depending on which plan you have) though at slow speeds. But that's much better than an expensive bill. We'll cover all of the specifics for each of the major carriers starting on the next page.

Option 3: Buying an Icelandic SIM card

The third option is to buy a SIM card from an Icelandic company. This will give you lots of high speed data for less money than just about any international plan (well, except for the free but slow ones.) The downsides: You need to have an unlocked phone, and you'll have an Icelandic phone number instead of your own.

None of these 3 options matters if your phone doesn't work on the cellular network in Iceland. Iceland uses the GSM network protocol, which is also what AT&T and T-Mobile use. But Verizon and Sprint use CDMA. Most modern phones (and all modern iPhones) can use both, but check your Verizon or Sprint phone at WillMyPhoneWork.net to make sure. An older phone like the iPhone 4S may not work if it was a CDMA model.

If you won't have an unlocked phone that will work in Iceland, you can buy one for as little as $60. That gives you a competent Android phone that is already unlocked. See IcelandWithKids.com/cell for our latest recommendations. When you get back home, put it on Sprint's 1 year free program if it's still around, or T-Mobile's low usage $3 a month plan as an emergency phone for the kids. (As of February 2018, the Amazon Prime phones no longer have any ads.)

Option 4: Renting a Wi-Fi hotspot

This is probably the simplest option you have. You can pay a daily fee to rent a MiFi device from a company like Trawire; some rental car companies offer this as an add-on, or you can arrange for a rental yourself. Here you are paying for convenience. Your phone just sees the device as a Wi-Fi hotspot, so you don't need to unlock your phone, swap SIM cards, or sign up for international plans. (Phone calls and texts would still use your home cell phone plan, though.) And multiple people in the same family or group can share a single hotspot.

Trawire has improved their service in recent months, and I can now recommend it. The device is now $9 a day (with a minimum of 3 days), down from $10 in 2017. And you can now pick up the device in the 10/11 store in the Keflavik airport when you arrive in Iceland. (You used to have to pick it up at a local gas station.) They will provide you with a return postage paid envelope; just drop the device in the mail on your way out of the country. There is a mailbox by the oversized luggage area in the airport before security:

From: isavia.is

There should also be a mailbox past security in the airport. (The airport has confirmed there's one past security, but they didn't know where; I think it's near the Blue Lagoon store.) But you may want to mail it before security, since you could be less rushed. The airport offers free Wi-Fi.

Trawire offers service from Siminn, the best carrier in Iceland. And you can share the service with everyone in your family– up to 10 devices. You do all have to be in the same place, though. Still, for a family with many devices, this can be a real bargain. Just make sure you're always connected to the Wi-Fi device, and not using data through your carrier's plan! Turn off cellular data on your phone just to be safe. (iPhone: Settings–> Cellular. Android: Settings–> Data Usage)

Options 3 and 4 might have you at the 10/11 convenience store in the Keflavik airport. It's past security and to your right as you leave the secured area. It's the yellow circle #2 on the map above. Here's what it looks like:

What's the best option for you?

Below you'll find information specific to each of the 4 major carriers in the US: AT&T, Verizon, Sprint, and T-Mobile. After that, we'll cover the details of purchasing an Icelandic SIM card, should you decide to go with that option. On our recent trip, we chose to purchase Icelandic SIM cards so we didn't have to worry about data usage.

AT&T in Iceland

Will my phone work in Iceland? Almost definitely. AT&T uses the GSM network, which is also what Iceland uses.

How much will I pay without a plan? A lot. $2.00 a minute for calls, $0.50 for each text sent, and $2.05 for each megabyte used.

International plans: You have two options to add an international plan and avoid the outrageous data fee. First, you can pay for a Passport plan for a month. $60 gets you 1 Gig of data, or $120 gets you 3 GB. Calls would cost 35 cents a minute, and texts are free. You can make a one-time purchase of a Passport plan, which will be good for a 30 day period of your choosing; no need to worry about your billing cycle.

Second, you can purchase an international day pass. For $10 a day, you can use your existing plan as if you never left home. So if you have a good data plan and a trip that isn't several weeks, this can be a good option.

Unlocking your phone: If you purchased your phone from AT&T, it is almost certainly locked. That means you can't use the phone with another carrier until AT&T unlocks it. AT&T won't unlock a phone until you have finished paying for it; your monthly bill may include an installment payment for the phone itself, separate from the cellular service charges. Once the phone is paid off you can request an unlock.

If you have a prepaid plan and purchased the phone from AT&T, you can unlock the phone after 6 months of usage on AT&T.

Recommendation: Unlock your phone if you can, or buy an inexpensive unlocked Android phone, and use an Icelandic SIM card. Or pay the $10 a day to AT&T and keep your current plan.

Sprint in Iceland

Will my phone work in Iceland? Probably, but you should check at WillMyPhoneWork.net, especially if your phone is a couple of years old and is not an iPhone. Sprint uses the CDMA network, but Iceland uses GSM. Most newish phones can handle both, though.

How much will I pay without a plan? Almost nothing! Calls are $0.20 a minute, and texts and (slow) data are free.

Free international plan: Sprint's Global Roaming plan includes free international data; texts are also free, and calls are $0.20 per minute. Sprint is clear that "all sprint plans include" Global Data, so this should work in a prepaid plan as well.

So what's the catch? The speed is 2G; given that 5G is going to become more common in 2018, 2G is several generations behind. The speeds may be as slow as 64 kbps.

Not only is that not fast, it's probably about 15 times slower than something you would consider fast. I've seen mixed reviews from people who tried it; it's probably enough to send and receive e-mails (and texting should be great), but it might be frustrating for web browsing.

You may consider trying it for yourself, and then purchasing a data plan if you find it unbearable.

Paid international data plan: Sprint should hopefully send you a text when you first turn on your phone in Iceland, though it may take a few minutes or hours. It will provide instructions for how to activate high speed data. (They assume you'll hate the free plan, and will pay to upgrade!) But the price is very reasonable: Pay $5 a day, or $25 a week for unlimited high speed data. This is the best option you'll find among the major carriers. Pay $25 for a week for unlimited data and texts; calls are 20 cents a minute. That's even better than an Icelandic SIM card.

Unlocking your phone: You can of course still consider an Icelandic SIM card. Sprint has a baffling page describing their phone unlock policy, and a separate page listing the unlock requirements. That second page boils down to "We'll automatically unlock your phone once it's paid off."

Unfortunately, the special option for customers traveling internationally is now gone. The unlock policy used to say "For Sprint customers traveling abroad for a short period of time, often their Sprint service can be provisioned to allow for international roaming." but that language was removed in August of 2017. You can always call and ask if they can "provision" your phone to allow you to use an international SIM card, but that doesn't appear to be an official option any more. Let me know what happens if you call and ask, though!

Recommendation: Try the free slower speed option, and pay Sprint the $25 for high speed data if it's not good enough.

T-Mobile in Iceland

Will my phone work in Iceland? Almost definitely. T-Mobile uses the GSM network, which is also what Iceland uses.

How much will I pay without a plan? It depends. If you have a T-Mobile ONE, Simple Choice, New Classic or Select Choice plan, calls are $0.20 a minute, and texts and (slow) data are free. On any other plan, you'll pay $1.49 a minute for calls, $0.50 per text sent, and $15 per megabyte of data; that data rate is so high that in my opinion, it should be illegal. **Make sure you check which plan you have!**

Free International Plan: Included ONLY with T-Mobile ONE and Simple Choice North America plans. If you have one of those, you get free sow data (though at 128kbps, it's not as slow as Sprint's free offering.) Otherwise, you pay the absolutely outrageous cost of $15 per megabyte. Make sure you are absolutely certain you have the right plan!

Paid international data plan: You have one option for a

modest speed boost. For $15 a month (or $10 a month if you upgrade more than one line), you can pay for T-Mobile One Plus. One of the features included boosts your international service to 256 kbps. Let's not call that fast, but rather less-slow. You'll have to add this to your plan and then remove it once you get home.

Surprisingly, T-Mobile has told me that there is no way to boost your speed beyond 256 kbps in Iceland, even though they do offer high speed data passes for other countries. You can pay $15 for 265 kbps, but that's it. You can of course get an Icelandic SIM card for much faster speeds, if you have or decide to buy an unlocked phone.

Unlocking your phone: In general, a device you bought from T-Mobile is probably locked. Once your phone is paid off (or after 18 months of service under some plans) T-Mobile will unlock it for you. You'll have to contact support.

Recommendation: If you're not a heavy data user, and just want e-mail and occasional web browsing, try the 128 kbps data for free and see what you think. Otherwise, use an Icelandic SIM card; unlock your phone or buy an inexpensive unlocked Android phone.

Verizon in Iceland

Will my phone work in Iceland? Probably, but you should check at WillMyPhoneWork.net, especially if your phone is a couple of years old and is not an iPhone. Verizon uses the CDMA network, but Iceland uses GSM. Most newish phones can handle both, though.

How much will I pay without a plan? A lot. Calls are $1.79 a minute, sending a text costs $0.50, receiving a text costs $0.05, and data costs $2.05 per megabyte.

International plans: Just like AT&T, if you don't sign up for a plan, you'll pay an offensive $2.05 per megabyte used. And (again just like AT&T) you have two options here. First, you can add an International Plan. $40 a month gets you 100 minutes, 100 outgoing texts (incoming are all free) and 100 MB of data. Or pay $25 a month for 100 MB, but no voice minutes.

A second option seems better to me. You can pay $10 a day for a TravelPass, and use your data allotments from your regular plan. The first 512 MB per day will be at 4G speeds. You'll be downgraded to 2G after that. But 512 MB is a lot of data per day, unless you're streaming lots of video.

You need to activate TravelPass on your account; log in online or use the Verizon app. You'll only pay for days you use data in another country. It might be best to just leave it active on your phone to avoid the possibility of a huge data charge in the future.

Unlocking your phone: Some good news for Verizon customers: Your phone is probably already unlocked. Which means you can pop a SIM card in it once you are in Iceland it will work. Verizon generally doesn't lock devices. If you have an older Verizon phone and you are prompted for an unlock code, it's either 000000 or 123456. If you have prepaid service, you need to call Verizon after 12 months and they can unlock your phone.

Recommendation: Buy an Icelandic SIM card, since your phone is likely unlocked. Check to make sure it handles GSM by looking at WillMyPhoneWork.net. Or pay $10 a day for TravelPass.

Icelandic SIM Cards

Let's take a look at the logistics if you've chosen to use an Icelandic SIM card in your unlocked phone. This is the option we chose for our 2016 trip, and we didn't have any issues. Make sure you know how to remove and reinsert a SIM card into your phone. Most iPhones require a small paperclip (or SIM card removal tool, which is just a thin metal rod, like a paperclip) to be inserted in order to pop out the SIM card slot.

The three main Icelandic carriers, sorted from best coverage to worst, are: Siminn, Vodafone, and Nova. Of course, that's also sorted from price, highest to lowest.

If you are flying to Iceland on Icelandair, I think the choice is easy. Buy the Vodafone Starter Pack from sagashop.is. Click the flag at the top right to switch to English, and then search for "Vodafone". You can order it ahead of time—give them your flight number and they'll bring it to you on the plane. For 23 Euros ($27 or so) you'll get "2 GB of data, unlimited Talk&Text domestically and 50 minutes for overseas calls." It also includes unlimited calling and texting within Iceland. It's a good deal, and you can install it in your phone while you're still on the plane. Once you land, you'll be good to go.

All SIM cards kits from all companies here can be adjusted for the size your phone needs. So don't worry if you need a micro or nano-sized SIM card. The cards in the kits are perforated so you can "punch out" the size you need. Take the card out of your phone to see what size you need; then be careful to create that same size with the Icelandic SIM card. And don't lose your original SIM card!!

If you're not flying Icelandair, then you can buy a Siminn SIM card from the 10/11 store in the Keflavik airport. You should also be able to get them in the Elko electronics store. But Elko is in the secure area, and 10/11 is outside of the secure area. I didn't even think about buying a SIM card until we had already passed through security and customs.

There should be two options at the 10/11, though check siminn.is/en/prepaid to see the latest offerings. The main card is the Prepaid Starter Pack. For 2900 krona (around $29) you get 5 GB of data, 50 minutes of calling and 50 texts. The calling and texts are good for Iceland or International calling to 54 countries. That should be plenty of data for most trips, though you can always add more.

The other option is a Siminn Prepaid Data card, which gives you 10 GB for the same price. But you don't get voice minutes or texting options, and there is no way to add them. This could be a valuable option for some travelers, but it's a whole lot of data. You could use it as a hotspot and stream video to use up some data! (If this is the only card you can find, you can use Skype to make calls and other apps such as Whatsapp to fill in for texts.)

If you are flying Wowair, the Duty Free catalog used to sell Nova SIM cards, but I don't see them anymore. All they have now is an ad that says you can buy a Sinimm card on board the Flybus that takes you from the airport to Reykjavik. For $30 USD, can buy either of the same two Siminn cards discussed above on the bus. It's not a terrible option, but the same cards are for sale in the airport for $6 or so less. Don't forget that paperclip!

Problems with your Icelandic SIM card

When you put in an Icelandic SIM card, your phone should just work, as long as it's unlocked. If your phone doesn't connect, you may need to update your settings manually. Check out the APN Settings web site for Iceland: **apnsettings. org/iceland**. Click through the carrier you're buying a SIM card from (Siminn, Vodafone, Nova, etc.) and print out the instructions, or save them to your phone. It's unlikely you'll need to do this, though anecdotal evidence suggests Verizon users are more likely to have an issue.

Summary

A few years ago, getting the Icelandic SIM card was the best choice in many cases. And you still can't go wrong with any of the Icelandic SIM card options, should you choose that option. But all of the major US carriers have improved their offerings for international travel. On Sprint in particular, I think I would pay the $25 for high speed data. If keeping your phone number during your vacation is important, you now have options. And Trawire has improved their offering as well, and it's now a viable option that doesn't involve messing with your phone.

Part 2: Planning your Itinerary

Overview of Itinerary planning

Part 1 of this book focused on the nuts and bolts of getting to Iceland. With our advice, you'll have a plane ticket, lodging, possibly a rental car, a working cell phone, power adapters, and everything else you'll need for your trip.

Part 2 will cover what you should do and see once you get here. Let me be clear right now: We are not going to cover every attraction in Iceland! And, to be honest, we skip more than most guidebooks. You won't find anything about the Latrabjarg bird cliffs, which are stunning and filled with puffins in the summer. But they are also in a remote part of the Westfjords, and only accessible by a very bumpy and narrow cliffside road. We'll tell you how to get to some stunning cliffs, and we'll tell you how to see puffins. Just not Latrabjarg.

And we won't cover the highlands, the central part of Iceland that is only accessible on f roads in the summertime in a 4 wheel drive vehicle with sufficient clearance. (See F roads on page 30.) We think planning for travel on F roads isn't worth it for most families.

Tell us if we missed something you were hoping for-- e-mail me at eric@icelandwithkids.com. We'll tell you what we know, and maybe consider it for the next edition!

Tips for creating your itinerary

You can follow our itineraries exactly. Or you can add to them. The next few pages offer some sample touring plans. Suppose you want to follow the first one ("Sample touring plan: The South Coast" on page 55.) One of the days is on the Golden Circle.

Then, you can build your Golden Circle day using the Golden Circle section, starting on page 61. E-mail us if you get confused!

If you find something online that you want to add, go for it! Just remember to:

1. Make sure it's not on an F road! See page 30.

2. See how far off of the road it is. A destination that's a half hour off the road can easily take 2 hours or more to visit. Dettifoss (page 98) is a good example of this.

3. Try not to pack your days full. This may just be a personal preference of my family, but we had more fun doing less and leaving more time to explore and relax.

Fun Fact:

The Icelandic word for stupid is "heimskur." Heima means home, and so heimskur literally means "who has never been from home". See: http://wiktionary.org/wiki/heimskur

An unexpected surprise: Feeding lambs at Sheep Farming Camp. See page 116

List of Maps

Table of Contents: Part 2

The table of contents for Part 1: Planning your Iceland trip can be found at the beginning of the book, before page 1.

All of Iceland

Hestyri

Reykjafjörður

Bolungarvik
Suðureyri
Flateyri
Ísafjörður
Melgraseyri
Árneshreppur

Siglufjörðu
Fell
Ólafsf

76

Dvergasteinn
Þingeyri
WESTFJORDS

HÚNAFLÓI

Sauðárkrókur
Blönduós
75
76
Varmah

Bíldudalur
63
Patreksfjörður
62

60

61

61

61

61

60

60

Hólmavík
Drangsnes

Thingeyrar

1

BREIÐAFJÖRÐUR

Kleifar

Hvammstangi
Laugarbakki

1

NORTHWEST

Borðeyri

Staður

Stykkishólmur
54

Búðardalur

54

60

IC

Hellissandur
54
Grundarfjörður
56
Ólafsvík

55

54

WEST
1

50

Reykholt

Hellnar
54
Akrar

50

Borgarnes

FAXAFLÓI
Akranes

1
47

GOLDEN CIRCLE

So

36

37
30

REYKJAVIK
Reykjavik
Mosfellsbær

Reykholt
Skálholt
Flúðir
32

Gardur
Garðabær
Kópavogur

36

Stóri Núpur

Sandgerði
Hafnarfjörður
1
Hveragerði
30
26

Keflavík
42
Selfoss

Hella

43
38

425
427
Eyarbakki
Stokkseyri

Grindavik
Strandakirkja
Þykkvibær

Hvolsvöllur

**Start here! The International
Airport is in Keflavik.**

Ásólfsskáli
1

Vestmannaeyjar

**WESTMAN
ISLANDS**

Sample touring plan: The South Coast

Good for: Families with small children, or anyone looking to explore some highlights of Iceland without having to drive several hours each day.

Here's a rough outline for a week-long trip with minimal driving. Lots of Iceland tourists might be surprised by how little ground this trip covers. This plan was built specifically to minimize driving time. There's less time in the car, and plenty of time to explore. Some of the best experiences our younger children had were getting an hour or so to just explore a beach or a waterfall.

This trip could be shortened to 5 days-- You could cut a day in Reykjavik and a day in the Westman Islands.

Let's orient ourselves a little bit: You'll be starting from the airport in Keflavik, in the lower left corner of the country; find Keflavik just below the Reykjavik labels. See the previous page.

Day 1: Two options

Option 1: Reykjanes Geopark. This will get you to some amazing sites on your first day. See page 161.

Option 2: Reykjavik. Relax, walk around if you're not exhausted from the flight. Take a nap early if needed, or try to stay up until 6 PM and then crash. Consider the Laugardalur area (page 146): Reykjavik Family Park and Zoo, Ásmundur Sveinsson Sculpture Museum, Laugardalslaug thermal pool. Those are all just a couple minutes drive from each other, but it's about 10 minutes away from the main downtown harbor area.

Stay in Reykjavik.

Day 2: Golden Circle.

See what sounds good from our Golden Circle plan on page 61. The Golden Circle section there is organized as a tour.

Day 3: Westman Islands (Summer only)

This is an unusual recommendation, but I loved the Westman Islands. I think the 35 minute ferry ride is a great adventure for kids. This can be a day trip, or you can stay overnight.

See our Westman Islands information on page 79.

Be sure to visit the aquarium to meet and pet the puffin. Or consider the bus tour with Eyja tours, which includes a visit to the aquarium.

Day 4: East toward Vik.

Seljalandsfoss waterfall, Skogafoss waterfall (both right off of Ring Road), Reynisfjara and Dyrhólaey. Stay in or around Vik. See our South Coast plan on page 69 for more details.

And read up on the "sneaker waves" at Reynisfjara! (See page 73.)

Day 5: Drive back.

See The Icelandic Horse Center (page 175), and Kerið crater (page 66) or anything else you missed in the Golden Circle area. Stay in Reykjavik.

Day 6: Reykjavik Harbor area.

Do a Whale Watching trip. (See our tips for whale watching in Iceland on page 173.) Visit the Whales of Iceland museum beforehand (page 106). (Be sure to consider the family ticket!) Icelandic Fish and Chips for dinner; explore the little Volcano House attached to it. Maybe a hot dog at the hot dog stand. See "Reykjavik Old Harbor" on page 132.

Day 7: Visit the Blue Lagoon and Keflavik.

The Blue Lagoon (page 169) is on the Reykjanes Peninsula along with the Keflavik Airport. They are about 20 minutes apart.

If you have time, see Keflavik (the town near the airport). Visit the Viking Museum, and the settlement zoo next door. And check out the Keflavik harbor area, including the Giantess in the mountain and the sculpture by the water. See page 166.

Then back to the airport- it's only about 10 minutes away from these parts of Keflavik.

South Coast Lodging

WOW Air and Icelandair have both expanded the number of flights they offer to Iceland. More hotels are being built to handle the influx of travelers, but this takes time. The south coast of Iceland has been hit the hardest: Lots of tourists head there, but there is very little lodging. I recommend you book for accommodations as soon as possible—maybe even before your airfare is confirmed. If you can find a place on Booking.com (page 17) or another site that offers free cancellation and works for your family, go ahead and reserve months and months in advance.

Sample touring plan: Around Ring Road

Good for: Families comfortable with more driving who want to "see it all" (which is, of course, impossible.) But there is something satisfying about not backtracking at all, and making a big loop around the country.

Your lodging options may very well dictate what you end up doing each night. This is a very rough outline—I really liked the towns of Djúpivogur and Seyðisfjörður out east, but it might be easier to find a place to stay in Egilsstaðir.

Day 1: Golden Circle

Visit the Golden Circle attractions (page 61), and stay in Selfoss.

Day 2: South coast

Stay wherever you can between Vik and Höfn . See "Vik" on page 73, and "Höfn" on page 85.

Day 3: Drive east

Stay in Djúpivogur (page 86) or Breiðdalsvík (page 89) or Egilsstaðir (page 91) or Seyðisfjörður (page 95). The first 3 are all right along Ring Road, and Seyðisfjörður is half an hour each way over a remarkable mountain pass. If you have the time, I think it's a worthwhile detour.

Engine Braking

There were a lot of stretches of time where we were going down a mountain at relatively slow speeds. Engine braking comes in handy: This is when you keep the car in a lower gear in order to keep from accelerating, instead of riding the brake.

Almost every car I've seen, even if it's an automatic transmission, can do this. You should be able to shift into numbered gears, or (rarely) "L" gear. It's a little tricky if you've never done it before, but it can keep your brakes from overheating. Read about "engine braking" in Wikipedia.

Day 4: Head to the North

Stay in Mývatn (page 98) or Akureyri (page 103) or Húsavík (page 101). We had a wonderful and memorable whale watching experience in Húsavík (page 102), but that's another detour. Mývatn and Akureyri aren't much out of the way. Mývatn might be the best bet here, if you can find a place to stay: There's a lot to see in this area. But if nothing else, Akureyri should offer plenty to do, and plenty of places to stay. You could even spend 2 nights in one place here, just to take a break. Sometimes it's nice to not have to pack up every single day.

Day 5: Driving Day

This is probably going to be a driving day. You can go whitewater rafting or horseback riding in Varmahlíð (page 109), The Icelandic Seal Center in Hvammstangi (page 111) and maybe take a detour to Eiríksstaðir the Viking Longhouse (page 112), but otherwise you're just trying to cover some ground. Look to stay somewhere along Ring Road, or up by Snæfellsnes if you have time to head there.

Day 6: Snæfellsnes (page 124)

This is out of your way, and should be skipped if you don't have time. But the south coast of the peninsula can make for a great day: Rauðfeldar Canyon (page 124), the hike from Hellnar to Arnarstapi (page 124), Djúpalónssandur black pebble beach (page 125), and Vatnshellir Cave (page 125).

Day 7: Reykjavik Harbor area.

See plan on previous page. Or, more Reykjavik plans on the next page!

Day 8: Reykjanes Geopark

Blue Lagoon, Keflavik. See previous plan.

Cell phone carriers

Siminn support:

8007000@siminn.is
www.siminn.is/en/prepaid
 +354 800 7000

Vodafone support:

vodafone.is/english/prepaid/
1414 (dial if you are using a Vodafone SIM)
twitter.com/vodafoneis (Honestly, this is the best way to reach them)

Nova support:

https://refill.nova.is/#/
+354 519 1919 nova@nova.is
Message on www.facebook.com/novaisl/

Sample touring plan: Snæfellsnes and the Westfjords

Good for: Avoiding the touristy areas and trying something different. Most tourists don't make it to the Westfjords. There's a lot of driving, and I don't think it's a good option outside of the summer. But if you want to take a few days and try something (just slightly) off the beaten path, the Westfjords are a great option.

Day 1: If you're not in a hurry, you can take some time to see the Reykjanes Geopark (page 161) by the airport or spend some time in Reykjavik (page 127); you'll be passing just outside of Reykjavik to head to the Westfjords. Or stop by Borgarnes (page 123) to see a museum or stock up on supplies. Stay near Búðardalur (page 114) if you can.

Day 2: Take Road 60 to Road 61. This will keep you on paved roads the whole way. We're bypassing the western portion of the Westfjords to stay on better roads. Spend some time in Hólmavík —have the kids spend an afternoon at the camp at the Sheep Farming Camp (page 116) if it fits in your schedule. Or explore the Museum of Icelandic Sorcery and Witchcraft (page 116) if your family would be into it.

You could stay in Súðavík (page 118) and let the kids play on the playground there. Or just go the extra 20 minutes or so to get to Ísafjörður (page 119).

Day 3: Explore Ísafjörður. It's a great town that will have some tourists in it, but it still feels like Iceland. Explore the shops and restaurants in town, and then a tour provider such as WestTours.is could help you plan some adventure. To really get off the beaten path, have them take you to Hornstrandir Nature Reserve. I don't recommend heading there yourself, though-- it's very remote and dangerous if you're unprepared.

Please eat at Tjöruhúsið (page 119)!

Day 4: If you're up for some adventure, you can make a circle west of Ísafjörður to see the southwest corner of the Westfjords. Check out Dynjandi waterfall on the way, and head to Rauðasandur beach. We didn't make it that far on our trip, so I can't give you details—we retraced our path back down to Hólmavík. The route toward Dynjandi has a fair bit of bumpy gravel roads that we wanted to avoid. Past this, you can also consider a ferry to the north part of the Snæfellsnes, though you'll have to check the schedule at seatours.is.

If you have time left once you leave the Westfjords, explore Snæfellsnes (page 124, which outlines a good itinerary for a day or two there) or Reykjavik (page 127) or the Reykjanes Geopark (page 161) and Keflavik (page 164). Oh, and the Blue Lagoon (page 169) too!

The Domestic Flight

Good for: Minimizing driving but still getting to see more of Iceland

We'll touch briefly on flights within Iceland again when touring the Westfjords ("A domestic flight?" on page 114). There are two domestic airlines in Iceland; note that nearly all of their flights are from the Reykjavik City airport and not from Keflavik. Eagle Air (eagleair.is) flies to some great destinations, including the Westman Islands and Húsavík, but their flights always seem very expensive to me. Air Iceland Connect (airicelandconnect.com), on the other hand, has some online prices that can make a flight to Ísafjörður or Akureyri pretty reasonable.

Air Iceland Connect does offer a flight from Keflavik to Akureyri, but only if you're flying internationally the same day. The web site gives you a clear warning: "Please note: This flight route is only for passengers arriving with an international flight the same day." For even more savings, search Google for "light fares Air Iceland Connect" without the quotes. You'll have to only have hand luggage, though so each person would be limited to a backpack.

Otherwise, you have to get to Reykjavik for the second flight. A couple of quick examples:

Fly from Keflavik to Akureyri

Fly straight from Keflavik to Akureyri right after to flying into Reykjavik. Be sure to look at the flight times; you cannot go through customs in the airport, so you're stuck in the airport until your departing flight.

Rent a car, and spend a few days exploring Akureyri (page 103) and Húsavík (page 101) and Mývatn (page 98) before heading back. If you have some time, book a one-way car rental and head to the Westfjords (page 113) or Snæfellsnes (page 124) before heading on to Reykjavik (page 127)and back to Keflavik (page 164).

For the one way rental from Akureyri, two options are Budget or Europcar (also known as Holdur). We recommend Holdur.

Fly from Reykjavik to Ísafjörður

Or spend a day in Reykjavik, and then fly from the Reykjavik City Airport to Ísafjörður. Explore that city and take some day trips to the remote areas of the Westfjords.

Again, fly back or drive one way. Holdur car rental works from Ísafjörður as well.

Note that if you're renting from Reykjavik or Keflavik, stick with Blue Car Rental (page 22)

Sample touring plan: Reykjavik as a home base

Good for: Families that don't want to rent a car, or that rent a car but want to stay in the same place every night

On our first visit to Iceland in 2009, we stayed in one apartment in Reykjavik and didn't rent a car. We missed a lot of the country, but we also saw a lot and had a great time!

Day 1: If you're renting a car, consider exploring the Reykjanes Geopark while you're nearby. Otherwise, take one of the buses to Reykjavik (page 46) and spend the day exploring. Perhaps start with the walk up Skólavörðustígur Road (page 141) to Hallgrim's Church (page 141). Or consider a guided walking tour (see below).

Day 2: Reykjavik Laugardalur area (page 146): Reykjavik Family Park and Zoo, Ásmundur Sveinsson Sculpture Museum, Laugardalslaug thermal pool. Consider the ferry to Viðey Island, especially in the summer. See page 151. (The Ferry port here is not walkable from the other attractions. Without a car, you can take the ferry from Harpa instead.)

Day 3: Golden Circle (page 61). Chose a minibus tour or drive on your own if you have a car. Minibus options include: Geo Iceland (GeoIceland.com) or Back to Iceland (btitravel.is)

Day 4: Explore the Reykjavik Old Harbor area (page 132). Take a whale watching (page 132) or sea angling boat tour (also page 132) if it's not winter. See the Whales of Iceland Museum (page 131), or take a tour of Omnom chocolate (page 128). If the weather is decent, head over to Harpa (page 139), checking out what you can find on Tryggvagata Road (page 135)

Day 5: Head south to Tjörnin pond (page 143) and enjoy the sculptures that surround it. Walk into City Hall and see the 3D relief map of Iceland. Head to the National Museum of Iceland (page 145) .

Day 6: On your way back to the airport, explore the town of Keflavik, including Viking World (page 164) or the Icelandic Museum of Rock 'n' Roll (page 165), as well as the harbor area: the Giantess in the Mountain (page 166) and the nearby Ásmundur Sveinsson sculpture the kids can climb on (page 165).

Guided Walking Tours

You can also try a guided walking tour of Reykjavik. I Heart Reykjavik (IHeartReykjavik.net) offers a well-regarded tour, but book ahead! We chose the Citywalk tour (CityWalk.is), which is "free", but a donation is expected at the end. Citywalk still wants you to register for a tour ahead of time, but they shouldn't be sold out.

You'll get a good cultural and historical overview of Reykjavik, with 5-15 minute stops along the way. The kids would have rather kept walking for some of the stops, but overall they mostly stayed interested. And at the end, we got to sample some Icelandic licorice.

How much to tip if you choose CityWalk? I feel like 2000 krona for adults and 1000 for older kids seems reasonable? That's about a third of the price of the I Heart Reykjavik Tour, but you may be with 3 times as many people. But you can decide based on how much you enjoyed the tour!

Reykjavik City Card

If you plan to visit a few museums in Reykjavik, the Reykjavik City card can save you some money. First and foremost, you should realize that you may NOT need to buy a card for your children. All of the museums are free for kids under 18, and so the card does your kids no good for museums. It will still save you money for kid's admission to the zoo and the Viðey Island ferry. And bus fare-- city buses are included too!

Prices for adults are: 3800 krona for a 24 hour card, 5400 for 48 hours, and 6500 for 72 hours. Suppose you did the Day 2 itinerary for Reykjavik (left column) including the Viðey ferry. Then on another day you went to the Settlement Center (page 123) and The National Museum of Iceland (page 145). Total cost for an adult: 7730.

So the 2 day ticket can make sense. But unless you're really going to work to visit many museums and swimming pools, it seems hard to get a lot of value out of the City Card.

See VisitReykjavik.is and click on City Card at the top.

Touring planning

On the next pages, we'll start our detailed touring information with the Golden Circle, perhaps the most famous part of the country for tourists. We consider this a shortcut to the beauty of Iceland: A geothermal area, a beautiful national park with a ton of history, and a world class waterfall—and all within a day trip from Reykjavik.

The Golden Circle can be a little out of the way if you're seeing the rest of the country, so it takes a little planning to figure out how and when to cover this area. We'll show you how to do it, and a dozen or more lesser-known places nearby that you may want to consider seeing.

See our map on the next pages, followed by descriptions of the points of interest. Remember, not every single point is covered here. If you find something else you like, add it in!

Borgarnes

Ljósafoss Power Station
Lesser known but worthwhile museum--
and it's free!

Thingvellir
Famous national park with hiking trails
and stunning views.

47

Akranes

1

48

Thingvellir

36

36

Mosfellsbær

Hveragerði
A small town with geothermal bakeries
and a tiny earthquake museum.

Reykjavik

Kópavogur

Garðabær

Hafnarfjörður

1

Hveragerði

Gardur

42

38

38

Sandgerði

Keflavík

Raufarholshellir Lava Cave

425

43

42

427

427

38

425

Grindavik

Strandakirkja

Raufarholshellir Cave
Explore the first part of this cave on your
own, or join a tour to see more.

Blue
Lagoon

Geiser
Famous geothermal area, with a geysir that erupts every dew minutes.

Gullfoss
Famous and beautiful double level waterfall

Laugarvatn Fontana
A fancy geothermal spa with multiple pools and hot tubs

Faxi Waterfall
Lesser known waterfall that still impresses, especially since you can get so close to it

Friðheimar
Famous and beautiful double level waterfall

Secret Lagoon
Famous and beautiful double level waterfall

Slakki
Unpretentios petting zoo where the locals take their families.

Keriδ Crater
The most famous crater in Iceland. Walk around the rim or head down to the bottom

O **Gullfoss**

Geiser O

30

37

Laugarvatn Fontana O

36

365

37

Faxi Waterfall O

Friðheimar O
Reykholt

Skálholt •

Secret Lagoon O
• Flúðir

Slakki O

O **Ljósafoss Power Station**

36

• Sólheimar Ecovillage

31

30

O **Keriδ Crater**

30

32

26

Selfoss •

26

• Hella

Eyarbakki •

• Stokkseyri

Þykkvibær •

1

• Hvolsvöllur

N

0 miles   8   16

The Big 3: A Golden Circle Day Tour from Reykjavik

Let's start with an easy day that covers the 3 main attractions of the Golden Circle. Just see the Big 3 if you want a relaxing day, and time to enjoy each attraction.

Þingvellir National Park

That Þ at the start of Þingvellir is pronounced like a "Th"; you may find it spelled "Thingvellier". See page 9.

I recommend you don't park at the Visitor's Center, though it doesn't matter all that much. To see parking options, go to thingvellir.is/plan-your-visit and click on "Parking - Assembly Site." I like parking in P5. From there, you can hike up the hill to the Visitor's Center, or walk to what I think are the two best attractions in the park:

Law Rock. Þingvellir is famous for two reasons. First is that the Parliament met here for over 800 years, starting in 930 AD. The government officials would stand here and read the laws to the citizens. Stand by the Law Rock and imagine reciting the laws to thousands of people standing here:

Your kids might love actually shouting some laws! GPS: 64.259444, -21.122500

Silfra Continental Rift. This is the other thing Þingvellir is famous for-- the continental divide. You're more or less looking at it in the picture above, and you can also find it in other places in Iceland. For example, see the Bridge Between Continents on page 164. (Or inside a mall in nearby Hvergarði! Find it by the Quake 2008 museum and a Bonus grocery store. See page 67.) But the famous spot is where people go to scuba dive or snorkel; see the picture at the top of the next column.

This area may be crowded with divers during the day, but our evening visit was peaceful. (Perhaps that's an excuse to reverse the order of your tour?) Go ahead and take a drink of the water! GPS: 64.255278, -21.116667

From this area, you also may be able to see the waterfall Öxarárfoss off in the distance.

Silfra continental rift

Geysir

The names of this geothermal park get confusing. Geysir is the name of a geothermal area with lots of bubbling cauldrons of super hot water. Pay attention to areas that are roped off-- this is seriously hot water, and Iceland expects you to pay attention to warning signs.

Geysir is also the name of one specific active geothermal area in the park. It used to erupt, and the English word comes from this spot. But today, Geysir rarely erupts; once a year or less. Wander past it and other active areas of the park.

But the main attraction today is Strokkur, which erupts reliable every 4-10 minutes. Stay to watch a few; each one is different.

Strokkur erupting

Across the street from the geothermal area, you have a lot of food choices. There are three restaurants in the visitor's center, and you can also opt for the very fancy restaurant in Hotel Geysir. (My first choice for lunch is the Friðheimar tomato greenhouse if you have time; see page 63.)

Gullfoss

Gullfoss is a famous double waterfall, about 10 minutes from Geysir. It's fine to these two in either order.

There are two parking lots at Gullfoss. If you park at the visitor's center, you'll need to walk down a moderately long flight of stairs (down a hillside) to get to the falls. If you don't need food or bathrooms, ignore the sign that steers you left, and head right to the lower lot. On Google Maps, search for "Gullfoss car park" for the main lot with steps, or search for "Gullfoss parking" for the lower lot.

In the picture (below left) you can see the walkway on the left; if it's not muddy or icy, you can walk down this path to a platform right next to the falls. At the end you'll get an up-close view of the falls. But be careful-- this path is wet every minute of every day. Even if it's a perfectly dry day, water droplets from the falls make this slippery.

Here's the view from the end of the walkway. Yes, you'll get a little wet!

A longer Golden Circle Tour

There are enough attractions in the Golden Circle area to last you a week. But here is a list of add-on sites that would result in an extremely full day, or perhaps a two day tour of the Golden Circle. Use the map to see them in a sensible order, and you'll still only have about 4 hours of driving time, starting and ending in Reykjavik. But you should probably skip a couple of the places listed below if you only have one day!

Let's call these our tier 2 choices. See the big 3 above, and then add in what seems interesting from the next section.

Faxi waterfall

We just covered the three major attractions. Faxi is probably the easiest 4th stop to add in. It's 10 minutes from Geysir, and just a minute off of the road, so you can make a quick detour if you want to see another waterfall.

I really like the waterfall (which translates to "horse's mane"), as well as the fish ladder next to it. Your family may enjoy it as much as Gullfoss.

Faxi is tough to find-- you need to turn when you see a sign for a small cafe (Við Faxa) next to the waterfall. GPS is 64.225698, -20.337192.

Raufarholshellir lava cave

If you're going to explore most lava caves, we recommend you go with a guide. ExtremeIceland.is does offer a tour of this cave. (Also consider a tour of Gjábakki Cave; see page 67.) But, as long as you are extremely careful, you can explore the first part of Raufarholshellir on your own. There are some openings in the ceiling of the cave past the entrance, which let in enough light to let you walk through the first 50 meters or so. But be extremely careful-- it's very easy to twist an ankle or hit your head.

Kerið Crater

The landowners recently started charging 400 krona for adults (13+) visiting the crater. That's a little frustrating since it was free until recently, but it's a stunning place to see. You can hike around the top of the crater, or the bottom around the lake, or both.

Snacks at Þrastalundur

I don't always mention everywhere we stop for food. But you'll be passing right by here; it's a restaurant and mini market. We bought a long baguette and a package of sliced cheese for a total of around $5. An excellent deal. Watch out for it on your left; it's tough to see until you're almost past it.

Ljósafoss Power Station Visitor's Center

You can make your first stop of the day at another power plant museum-- Hellisheiði Power Plant. But it's not free, and we don't like it as much as Ljósafoss. You are going about 20 minutes out of your way (roundtrip) to get to this one, though.

Ljósafoss is free, and they have free hot chocolate, coffee, and orange juice. This is a hydropower station, not geothermal. It's right on a river, and you can see some of the original equipment, still running since the day it was installed in 1934.

GPS coordinates are: 64.094309, -21.004797.

Slakki, the petting zoo.

Slakki is only open in the summer, and I only recommend it if the weather is nice. But kids under 10 or so should love it. My kids ranked it as one of their favorite things in Iceland! It's a petting zoo, plus miniature golf, plus digging machines, plus more.

It took me a little while to figure out what made Slakki feel different from most other places we had been around the Golden Circle. And then I realized: Other kids were coming up to my kids and asking them questions. In Icelandic! The owner told me that 80% of visitors come from Iceland; many come from Reykjavik to visit a more rural area. It's a very different crowd than you will find at Geysir or Gullfoss.

Check facebook.com/slakki to see opening hours.

Friðheimar- the tomato greenhouse

You'd better like tomatoes if you stop here-- everything on the menu has them as an ingredient. Even the ice cream. Even the water pitcher has a cherry tomato in it! The unlimited

Slakki has lots of animals to see, hold, or even feed. My kids even got to hold puppies and rabbits, though every day, or at least every week, is different.

tomato soup with bread and butter is a good deal for kids, if they like the soup.

This is a fun experience; there are basil plants on each table; scissors are provided so you can cut your own to add to your soup! And the desserts are served in terra cotta flower pots.

Opening times are only 12-4. If you are confident in your arrival time, you can make a reservation avoid a potential wait- - just e-mail fridheimar@fridheimar.is. They say to include: "Date and time, how many, what service you wish for (book a table, greenhouse visit with introduction, horse show), Name, and Nationality." They will hold a table for 15 minutes past your reservation window.

Golden Circle swimming

On the map on page 59 you'll notice two swimming facilities we haven't covered yet.

Laugarvatn Fontana

Fontana is a fancy thermal pool facility, with 4 separate pools / hot tubs. There's a long skinny one you get to as soon as you walk outside; a hot pot up the stairs in the upper right; a smaller pool on the near left; and a natural (unchlorinated) pool area in the back left. Apparently, each pool has a name? The web site (fontana.is) says: "Lauga, Sæla, and Viska are connected outdoor mineral baths that vary in depth, size and temperature." Each pool varies in temperatures, so your kids can find one that they are comfortable in.

Prices are 3800 krona for adults, 2000 for kids 13-16, and free for kids under 13. This is less expensive than the Blue Lagoon, and also slightly less than Mývatn Nature Baths. But it's still pricey, though not terrible if your kids are under 13.

I liked that the temperature of each pool was clearly marked; from 32 and 34 (Celsius, of course!) for each of the two treated pools, to 38-40 for the other 2. Overall, I thought that Fontana was ... nice? It was pretty, and the setting right by Lake Laugarvatn was lovely. But it's also kind of small- there's no sense that you can spend a lot of time exploring like we could at Mývatn Nature Baths or the Blue Lagoon.

One interesting note is that there is a door you can go through that leads to the lake. You are exiting the pool facility, and heading to a public area. If you walk down the shore, the water gets warmer and warmer; eventually, the water will be hot enough to burn you.. Fontana uses this heat with their Rye Bread experience, where they bury bread in the hot black sand to cook it. You will need to book ahead if you are interested in this. The Rye Bread experience happens every day at 11:30 and 2:30.

The rocks in the water are slippery, and remember that this is not a part of the Fontana facility; you're on your own. But you should be able to find a nice warm spot in the lake to bathe in. And presumably you could do this without visiting Fontana at all!

Fontana offers a lunch and a dinner buffet. Lunch is 2900 krona for adults, and possibly half price for kids. (We were told 2 different things.) If there is a discount for kids, this can be a nice option, consistent with our belief that buffets in Iceland are a very good deal for families. The dinner buffet for adults is a pricey 3900 krona.

The day we were there, the main course options for lunch were a white fish, vegan lasagna, chicken (which the kids loved), and they also had plokkfiskur (fish mash) along with smoked fish, various salads, and soup options.

Secret Lagoon

This is the other "fancy" spa in the Golden Circle area. The Secret Lagoon just opened in 2014 as a spa, although 125 years ago, this was actually Iceland's first swimming pool.

The Secret Lagoon is cheaper than Laugarvatn Fontana, at 2800 krona per adult; kids under 15 are free, and Seniors 67 and older are half price.

This is a much more natural experience than any of the other spas. Fontana has one untreated pool, but it's still a concrete shell with geothermally heated water pumped in. Secret Lagoon has a rocky floor, with an occasional huge slimy rock that can easily scrape an ankle. The water is also a warm 38 or 39 degrees Celsius; Fontana offers options at 32 and 34 that my kids seem to prefer.

In keeping with the natural theme, Secret Lagoon is in an active geothermal area-- there is actually a little geysir. It erupts every 5 or 7 minutes or so. This is no Strokkur: sometimes, the water spurts out a few (or occasionally 6) feet high. Still, it's a nice diversion for the kids, and it shows a lot of natural Icelandic features in one place.

The water is about 4 feet deep throughout most of the lagoon. Some of the edges offer shallower areas, but you'll have to get through the deeper areas first to get to them. Like every pool and spa in Iceland, they have water wings available for children to use.

The Secret Lagoon is an interesting option, especially if you have older kids. Younger kids may find the lagoon too deep, too hot, and/or too rocky to enjoy for more than 15 minutes. Also note that there is no substantial food available. They only offer drinks and a handful of candy bars.

Golden Circle- Even more options and Guided Tours

Let's call these the Tier 3 options. If you have more than one day, or something here catches your eye, got for it!

Skálholt

Technically, this church isn't historic, as it was built about 55 years ago. But the country's first bishop settled on this site in the 11th century.

You can go inside the church for free, as long as there isn't a service going on. But for 500 krona for adults (and free for kids), you can visit 2 small museums. One is in the visitor's center just down the hill from the church. This covers the history of the church and the site. Kids may enjoy ringing a 17th century bell, though it is ear-ringingly loud!

The second museum, covered under the same admission price, is in the basement (crypt?) of the church itself. Here you will find the sarcophagus of a bishop from around the year 1200. The best part for kids may be the "secret" tunnel that leads back outside.

Ultimately, Skálholt may not be worth the stop for many families, though it is only 4 minutes from Slakki (page 63). And we think Slakki is definitely worth the stop!

Engi Greenhouse

Engi is a farm stand that also offers a fun hedge maze. But it's only open on summer weekends, 12-6 PM.

You can shop for fruits, vegetables, and plants in the greenhouse, and/or head over to their hedge maze. The maze costs 500 krona per person, though younger kids might be free if you are lucky. This is a serious maze, with dead ends, twists and turns, and row after row of identical looking lanes.

Your goal is to get to the platform in the middle. Once you get there you can climb up and look out on the area while savoring your victory. There is also a guest book you can sign. This was a great family activity, but you may not want to let younger kids wander by themselves.

Engi also has a "barefoot garden" where you can walk over

different materials. Some are wonderful (wool) and some are downright painful (rocks and pine needles.) It was seriously painful ... and my kids did it twice!

The hedge maze at Engi

Efstidalur II Ice Cream Bar

Yes, that's a 2 at the end of their name; without that, in your GPS search you may end up next door. You will likely pass by on your way from Þingvellir to Geysir.

You'll have your choice of over a dozen flavors of ice cream, homemade on site. And, you can sit in the dining area and look at the cows that made the milk that went into your ice cream!

Iceland Riverjet

Iceland Riverjet (icelandriverjet.com) claims that their trip offers "breathtaking excitement." The boat was smaller than I expected; I think it can only hold 10 people plus the driver.

The name of the game is speed here. The boat goes up to 55 mph, which is really fast for a boat. The driver does hard turns, 360 degree spins, and heads right toward rocks before veering at the last second. There's no history, no education– it's all about going fast and having fun.

My boys both enjoyed it, though the younger one (and I!) felt a little shaken up afterwards. If you're looking for adventure, this is the place to go. They only allow ages 8 and up, though you can take younger kids if you ask. But they won't tailor the ride for younger kids, unless you pay for a private trip. So make sure your little one is a thrill junkie before booking!

The price is 14,900 krona for adults, and 8,900 for kids 8-15 (or younger.) That gets you 40 minutes on the river, plus all of your safety equipment. Their office is right next to Cafe Mika, just down the road from Friðheimar, the tomato greenhouse restaurant (page 63).

Gjábakki Cave with Laugarvatn Adventure

Laugarvatn Adventure (caving.is) offers tours of several different caves, but Gjábakki is supposedly a little bit easier for children. All of the company's tours are led by Smári Stefánsson. He teaches outdoor studies at the University of Iceland, so you're in good hands.

The cave opening is tough to find without a guide. As with all of these lava caves, at first you can see by the light coming in from the entrance. But as you move further back, you rely more and more on your headlamp. Eventually, it's completely dark; as long as there are no other people around, you can turn off your headlamps and experience total darkness- it's the same whether your eyes are open or closed!

Lava caves are formed by flowing lava; the top part that is exposed to the air cools first, leaving a rushing river of hot lava below. This lava carves a cave. As you look around, you can see remnants of this lava as it cooled and hardened into various rock formations:

Walking through the cave, you come to what looks like a dead end. Smári pretended that he didn't know where the exit was, and he made the kids search for it. The youngest in the group climbed around and found it, and we all followed him

toward the exit. We'd gone about 1,200 feet underground.

The footing is uneven throughout the cave, and you are relying on your headlamp to light the path in front of you. All of our kids did just fine (and had fun!), though it might be a challenge for a child younger than, say 6 or so.

The cost of the tour is 9,900 krona, or a little under $100 for adults; kids under 16 are half price. You're in the cave for around an hour, plus the 15 minute van ride each way, plus some time getting your helmets on and for safety training. Figure about 2 hours total.

That puts this in the category of expensive tours, but I do think you get a premium experience. The guide is an accomplished outdoorsman taking small groups.. And you're is right in the heart of the Golden Circle (less than half an hour from both the Þingvellir Visitor's Center and Geysir) you can add it to your Golden Circle day.

Finally, let's take a look at two towns labeled on the map. Both are easy stops on your Golden Circle trip.

Hveragerði

Hveragerði calls itself the hot springs capital of the world. They use geothermal energy to keep many many greenhouses warm.

Lots of people love Hveragerði, but I think it's skippable. One fun diversion is the free Earthquake Museum. It's in a shopping mall with a Bonus grocery store, if you're looking for lunch or snacks. An earthquake of magnitude 6.3 struck Hveragerði in 2008, and this small museum tells that story.

Back on page 61, we covered Þingvellir National Park, which is famous for being on the border between two continental plates. But this fault line runs up and down most of the country; apparently, it also splits this shopping mall:

You also have the option to pay 300 krona per person to try out their earthquake simulator. You go inside a house thing, and someone turns on the shaking for maybe 10 seconds. It's not much fun, and I doubt the violent shaking back and forth is really what an earthquake feels like.

We were excited to head to Kjöt og Kúnst for a snack. It is a bakery that uses geothermal heat in their cooking. The kids opted for cake. And I hate to say it, but we were very disappointed. I rarely mention mediocre food; you'll only see the memorable meals. But my son got a tiny piece of cake for over $10. The other pieces of cake did vary in size, and so this might just be bad luck. But the other kids didn't really like their cakes, which is also extremely rare. We all left disappointed, which is almost unprecedented for a bakery.

We skipped perhaps the most popular tourist attraction in Hveragerði: the hike to Reykjadalur Hot Springs. This could be a great activity for your family, but our kids weren't up for the hike-- 2 miles each way. (Reykjadalur closed for part of 2018 due to environmental strain, but it's back open as of May 2018. But the same thing could happen next spring!)

So we didn't love Hveragerði, but that doesn't mean you won't enjoy it!

Flúðir

We enjoyed the attractions around Flúðir more. If you're in this area to visit the Secret Lagoon, here are a couple of additional places to consider.

First is the very unusual Footgolf in Markavöllur, just a few minutes south of Flúðir. I wasn't expecting much, to be honest, and my expectations were well surpassed.

This is an 18 hole "golf" course, that is played with a soccer ball. You take your soccer ball to the tee box, and try to get it in the hole in as few kicks as possible.

The course is well manicured and well maintained. There are 2 cuts of rough. There are some doglegs. There are some shorter par 3s, just like you would find on a regular golf course. Many of the par 4s are 100 yards or longer.

We played in the rain, and the kids still enjoyed all 18 holes. The little ones didn't keep score, and just had fun kicking the ball ever closer to the hole. It was nice how adaptable the game was to any skill level. The price was also nice for younger kids: 2000 krona for anyone over 16; 1500 for 12-16, and free for 11 and under. They also charge 500 krona to borrow one of their soccer balls.

Supposedly, the hours are only from 1-4. So call before you go (or e-mail well before you go). Or, if nothing else, call when you get there, as the owners live just a couple of minutes away. GPS is 64.099233, -20.326950.

Minilik Ethiopian Restaurant

Minilik is in the small downtown area of Flúðir, less than 5 minutes from both the Secret Lagoon and Footgolf. (How's that for three diverse activities in one afternoon?) The restaurant is run by an Ethiopian woman who moved to Iceland about 10 years ago.

Note that, even though the ads we saw said the restaurant was only open for dinner, it seems they are also open for lunch in the summer, but it might be worth calling ahead.

The menu offers unique options, and the prices seem very reasonable. Here is number 22, the vegetarian combination:

That costs 2200 krona; you can end up paying that much for fish and chips at a gas station.

Note that the food is made fresh, and service is slow; our food took 35 minutes to arrive after we ordered, and there was nothing on the table except for water until then. Also, most dishes do not come with utensils; you are expected to use pieces of bread (called injera) to lift up bites of food. This could be fun for littler kids, if they are willing to wait.

South Coast

The South coast of Iceland is filled with things to see and do, and many of them are very close to the main road (Ring Road). You'll find Seljalandsfoss, a waterfall you can hike behind. You'll find Reynisfjara (page 73), a beautiful black sand beach. (Don't go there before you understand the unpredictable ocean waves!)

And you'll also find the Westman Islands (page 79), perhaps our pick for the most underrated place in Iceland. A 35 minute ferry ride (summer only-- it's much longer in the winter) gets you to an island that was very nearly destroyed by a volcano in 1973. Memories of the eruption are still fresh, as is the lava—hike up a hill that still has family houses buried beneath your feet.

Here is a sample itinerary for your visit to South Iceland. You can cover this in a day, or 2 or 3 days, depending on how much you want to see. In the list below you'll see a couple of potential points where it can make sense to turn around. (And we don't cover everything– there's always more to see if you want to explore!)

South Coast touring tips

• If you are making a day trip from Reykjavik, think about how much driving you will do. People often ask me, "Can I get to Jökulsárlón Glacier Lagoon and back in a day?" And the answer is ... yes? But I think it's a bad idea. It's a 4 1/2 hour drive each way. That's a whole lot of driving. Turn around sooner and have more time to enjoy the closer attractions. I'll give two options for places to turn around.

• If you want to find lodging on the South Coast, book it as soon as possible. There is a severe shortage of places to stay. The first things you should do when you plan your vacation are book airfare and reserve a place to stay on the South Coast. And maybe not even in that order!

• I'll say this again on page 73. But be very careful at Reynisfjara, the beautiful black sand beach. Imagine your favorite ocean spot. Now imagine the waves coming in and out, as waves do. Then imagine that, after 15 or so waves, the 16th wave goes 50 feet past where any of the previous waves went. Not 5 or 10 feet, but a full 50 feet.

I've never seen that happen at a beach, but that's what can happen at Reynisfjara, and without warning (though usually only in the winter.) Stay well back from the water, and leave yourself an exit plan. That is, if you have to run 50 feet away from the water, make sure there isn't a rock mountain behind you.

People die here every year. You should not get anywhere close to the water. Don't let this scare you away, though– it's a fun and interesting stop.

Urriðafoss waterfall

Let's pick an arbitrary starting point on the west for what's considered South Iceland: The lesser known waterfall called Urriðafoss. (The suffix foss means waterfall– you'll see it a couple more times in this post!) One of the benefits of the south coast is that many attractions are very close to the road, and Urriðafoss is no exception. But the road to Urriðafoss is easy to miss; look for Urridafoss on Google Maps to make sure you don't miss it. After a couple of minutes on a slightly bumpy gravel road, you'll come to the waterfall, which is at least partially visible from the parking lot.

But get out of the car and head down the walking path— watch out for the high winds! You'll be rewarded with a shallow but complicated, multi-layered waterfall. By the end of your journey, you may be tired of seeing waterfalls, no matter how incredible. But as our first waterfall, Urriðafoss was a great start, and one that was just a few minutes out of the way.

The Lava Centre

The Lava Centre is a brand new museum that opened in 2017. Reviews seem to be very positive– it's a great museum for the whole family. There are lots of interactive exhibits that cover different kinds of volcanoes.

This newest and perhaps most interactive museum in Iceland is also one of the most expensive, at least for admission for one adult. Adult admission tickets including the cinema are 2900 ISK, and kids 12-18 are 1450. (Kids 11 and under are free.) You can save 10% by booking online. However, don't miss the family pack: 2 adults and all of your kids can see the museum for 4950 ISK– less than the price of 2 adults, even with the online discount. (I don't think the 10% discount applies to the family pack.) That 4950 is a very good deal, especially if you have a lot of children!

There is also a full restaurant on site, called Katla Mathús. You can order off of the menu, or choose from a few different buffet options (including the full buffet, or soup and salad only) for 2260 to 3400 ISK. But kids (12 and under?) can eat from the buffet for just 1250 ISK.

Westman Islands

Here's your first big decision. If it's summertime, and you have extra time, I highly recommend a detour to the Westman Islands. If the weather is good, it's a 35 minute ferry ride each way. If the weather isn't good, or if the close port is closed, that ferry ride turns into a 2 hour 45 minute trip. Or you could get stuck for a night! See all of the details on page 79.

Seljalandsfoss waterfall

Seljalandsfoss is one of the most famous waterfalls in Iceland, and it's right by the road (Ring Road, or Route 1.)

Note that the landowners recently (July 2017) began charging a parking / entrance fee of 700 ISK. I feel very comfortable paying this– a rockslide closed the walking path behind the falls in September of 2017, and it seems reasonable to pay the landowners to maintain the area. (The walking path re-opened a few days later.)

You'll get a little wet walking behind the waterfall, but it's not a long hike. Just watch out for little feet (or any feet, really) on the slippery path.

If you're up for a hike to another waterfall, follow the sign that points to the left to Gljúfrabúi. It's about a third of a mile to this "hidden" waterfall. You'll have to wade through a shallow river to get to it, though. So come prepared, and maybe skip this one with younger kids-- stick with Seljalandsfoss.

Skógafoss waterfall

Seljalandsfoss and Skógafoss are often mentioned together– they are two wonder waterfalls less than half an hour from each other. You can't walk behind Skógafoss, but you can choose to admire it from the base, or take the (370!) steps up to the top for a view of the south coast. We chose to just admire this one from the bottom.

Arcanum Tours

Less than 15 minutes east of Skógafoss you'll find the tour company Arcanum, which offers glacier hikes, snowmobile rides on a glacier, or ATV quad bike tours. All of the tours are excellent, though if all of your kids are over 10 and willing to hike, we recommend the glacier hike. See our detailed write-ups of our experiences with Arcanum on page 82..

Sólheimasandur plane crash site

I generally recommend skipping Sólheimasandur, now that the landowner has closed the site to car traffic. It's now nearly a 2 mile hike each way over flat, but boring terrain. It is fun to see the US Navy plane that crashed in 1973 (everyone was fine!) but the walk takes a long time. If you do decide to hike, make sure you have sun protection and water with you– there's nothing on the way but black sand!

We happened to see the plane on a day they were filming a movie. It's not on fire!

The Arcanum ATV tour or new bus ride will get you to the plane crash site without walking; see page 82.

LANGJÖKULL

Urriðafoss
This lesser-known waterfall makes for a good starting point on the South Coast

•Mosfellsbær

—REYKJAVIK

—Kópavogur

Seljalandsfoss
Famous skinny waterfall right next to the main road. You can walk behind it!

Hveragerði• **Urriðafoss**O

1

Skógafoss
Famous wide waterfall, also right next to the main road

Stokkseyri•

Arcanum Tours
Fantastic glacier walks, snowmobile rides, or black sand ATV tours

LAVA CentreO
Hvolsvöllur

LAVA Centre
A brand new interactive volcano museum

1

SeljalandsfossO

MÝRDALSJÖKULL

SkógafossO O**Arcanum Tours**

O**Solheimasandur Plane Wreck**

Westman IslandsO

O**Vik**
DyrhólaeyO O
Reynisfjara

Westman Islands
A small inhabited island accessible by a 35 minute ferry ride

Sólheimasandur Plane
Famous crashed US Navy plane. But it's a very long boring walk from the road.

Dyrhólaey
A top South Coast attraction-- rock arches jutting out of the ocean

VATNAJÖKULL

Fjallsárlón
The less famous Glacier Lagoon. Less clear water, but stunning icebergs

Jökulsárlón
The more famous Glacier Lagoon. Multiple boat tour options.

Þórbergur Center
A museum that looks like a line of books. A good stopping point for the South Coast.

Kirkjugólf
Natural hexagonal stone "tile" floor

Stjórnarfoss
Lesser-known waterfall right by Kirkjugólf

Foss á Síðu
Famous black sand beach. But be aware of the unpredictable waves.

Skaftafell Visitor Center

Kálfafell●

1

O**Foss á Síðu**

KirkjugólfO O**Stjórnarfoss**
O**Fjaðrárgljúfur**

Kirkjubæjarklaustur●

1

Þórbergur Center

O **Jökulsárlón**

O **Fjallsárlón**

Skaftafell Visitor Center
Free National Park Visitor's Center; a small museum and hiking information to Skaftafell waterfall

Fjaðrárgljúfur
A canyon with stunning views

Vik
A small town close to the South Coast attractions. Convenient stopping point.

Reynisfjara
Famous black sand beach. But be aware of the unpredictable waves.

N

0 miles   20   40

Dyrhólaey

Dyrhólaey is another top attraction of the south coast–walk around and play on all of the crazy natural structures around there. My kids could have spent an afternoon here just exploring. (Picture on page 75.)

Loftsalahellir cave

You'll pass this cave on the way to Dyrhólaey, but if you have trouble, the GPS coordinates are: 63.421944, -19.151389. It takes a couple of minutes to walk up the steep pathway, and it gets a little slippery right at the top. But you are rewarded with a fantastic view from a cozy spot.

Reynisfjara

Let's start with the safety warning. Sometimes, an occasional wave will go 50 feet past any recent wave. Not 5 or 10 feet, but a full 50 feet. I've never seen that happen at a beach, but that's what can happen at Reynisfjara, and without warning (though usually only in the winter.) Stay well back from the water, and leave yourself an exit plan. That is, if you have to run 50 feet away from the water, make sure there isn't a rock mountain behind you.

People die here every year. You should not get anywhere close to the water. Don't let this scare you away, though– it's a fun and interesting stop. The expansive black sand and the hexagonal basalt columns are a must see on the South Coast.(Picture on page 75.)

Vik

Just a few minutes past Dyrhólaey and Reynisfjara you will come to the town of Vik. That makes Vik a convenient stopping point for a meal or an overnight stay. But there isn't so much here that is noteworthy—it's simply convenient.

You will find a black sand beach that is much quieter than Reynisfjara. I assume it's also safer, though you should still probably be careful with the waves.

I was a fan of the unique sculpture on the beach, but my kids just thought it was weird. It's called Voyage, and the cool part is that it is facing an identical looking sculpture … across

the ocean in England! England and Iceland fought in a series of open water skirmishes called the Cod Wars. The conflict was over how much of the ocean Iceland could control around its borders. Could England fish within 200 miles of Iceland's borders? 50? 2? The conflicts were resolved, and these sculptures memorialize the peace.

In town, you'll find a couple of restaurants and the Víkurprjón wool store; you may find some information that there is a factory tour here. But the "tour" consists of looking over a railing at some workers sewing sweaters. I don't think there are any bargains here, but you will find a nice selection of winter clothing.

Vik is a good opportunity to talk about a couple of things you may run across on your trip:

Curvy and steep roads.

Yes, Ring Road is the primary highway around Iceland. But before you get into Vik, the speed limit goes down to 50 kmph as you wind your way up and around some mountains. Take it slow!

Grocery store hours.

We arrived in Vik just after 6:00 PM on a Saturday. The grocery store had just closed at 6:00, and wouldn't reopen again until … Monday morning! So bring some food with you, or plan to eat out. We ended up walking up the hill across Ring Road to Sudur Vik Restaurant. It was a nice place, though service was slow. Perhaps there were a lot of us who arrived after the grocery store closed …

Turn around here?

If you only have 1 day budgeted to the south coast, and especially if you did a tour with Arcanum (page 82), this can make a good time to turn around. The next attraction I'm listing is about a 50 minute drive east.

Fjaðrárgljúfur

The next stop on our journey east was around the village of Kirkjubæjarklaustur , which boasts several natural attractions. First was a stop at Fjaðrárgljúfur canyon. The drive to get here ended up being about 10 minutes each way off of Ring Road. Near the end the road was like a washboard, which was not much fun for the baby!

You park in a parking lot toward the bottom of the canyon, and you need to hike up the hill to get the view. Besides the hill, it's an easy hike- it's a nice path, and you won't have any trouble with slipping. You can get pretty high up, and see for miles. But there are lookout points on the way that provide you good stopping points if you want to turn around.

You can also head directly into the canyon and play around in the water. But, you'll need to wade through parts of it, and be careful walking on the rocky shoreline.

Note: Fjaðrárgljúfur was closed due to mud, but reopened in mid-2018. Check SafeTravel.is-- click "Conditions".

Kirkjugólf

After a stop for lunch and gas (and stocking up on prepaid gas cards) we headed to Kirkjugólf, a natural "floor" of hexagonal basalt rock.

Back at Reynisfjara we saw tall basalt columns that varied in height. Here you are more or less standing on top of a bunch of hexagonal basalt columns that are all about the same height (see photo above.)

And you end up with a tiled stone floor made by nature. It's very cool, and also very strange that it's just out in a field behind the gas station. But I guess that's what you get when nature is in charge.

In the picture below, the N1 gas station is behind us. There

are two options for getting to this spot. You can park at the N1 and walk to here; you need to head northwest and cross the street (NOT Route 1, but the smaller 205.) By the information signs, there is a ladder you can climb up and down to cross the fence line.

The other option is to park in the parking lot at the back of this picture—there's actually a tiny car parked in the lot. Then there is a walking path to the stone floor.

Stjórnarfoss

We missed this. But if you park at the parking lot (the second options above) you're also very close to an adorable little waterfall called Stjórnarfoss. You may also see this area called Systrastapi. From that parking lot, walk away from Kirkjugólf until you see water, then turn left. Hopefully, you'll find it in a few minutes. If you're in the area and have some extra energy, you might want to try to find Stjórnarfoss!

Foss á Síðu

The main draws of the South Coast: Dyrhólaey (this image), Loftsalahellir cave (middle left) and Reynisfjara beach (bottom left)

(Foss á Síðu, continued from previous page)

Back on Ring Road and heading east, on your left you'll pass by another waterfall. You're going to see that sentence a lot, and we decided not to stop. This one is called Foss á Síðu. You'll have to find parking on the right and walk across if you want to get a closer look.

Fossálarfoss

Back on Ring Road and heading east, on your left you'll pass by another waterfall. Okay, I won't use that sentence any more! But these falls are literally right next to the road, though again you'll need to watch for the parking area on the right and walk across the street. GPS coordinates are: 63.852500, -17.839167. They are more like large rapids, or a small waterfall. But it's a nice area for a quick stop, though you can also just drive by and (safely) take a peek.

Or maybe turn around here?

We've already covered a lot– likely more than you can see in one day. This is a good point to turn around if you don't plan to cover the entire Ring Road; Skaftafell is going to be another 40 minute drive, and you'll need to hike 30-45 minutes to see the waterfall.

Skaftafell

Next we stopped at Skaftafell Visitor's Center, or Vatnajökulsþjóðgarður if you want something easier to pronounce. It's open from 9 AM to 7 PM.

The names get a little confusing here, even beyond pronunciation. There used to be a Skaftafell National Park, but in 2008 it became part of the much much larger Vatnajökull National Park. So this is technically the Skaftafell Visitor's Center inside of Vatnajökull National Park.

This national park is huge. Iceland is just under 40,000 square miles in total land mass. Vatnajökull National Park is 5,250 square miles of that—13% of the total land mass of Iceland! Imagine if there was a state park that took up 13% of the United States. It would cover the entire state of Texas. Plus California. Plus Missouri.

The glaciers that we'll get to east of here are also in the park (see Fjallsárlón and Jökulsárlón, next.) But the main draw in this area of the park is the waterfall Svartifoss . Head left to begin the hike to Svartifoss. Now, if you ask people how long the hike to Svartifoss takes, you'll get answers that range from 15 minutes to 45 minutes. It turns out that the hike is just over a mile long, but it's very uphill.

If you can maintain a brisk walking pace, it won't take long at all. But we were tired, and the 2 mile roundtrip required to get to the top wasn't going to happen. Here's what our reward would have been:

"Svartifoss" by Norton Ip is licensed under CC BY 2.0

Inside the visitor's center, you'll find a lot of information about the park (including a movie) and the various hiking trails, bathrooms, and a gift shop. You can buy a trail map of the park for 300 krona, or about $3. There are also some small exhibits to peruse.

Your food options are a little limited. The gift shop has a cooler with drinks, some Skyr, and some other snack food. And as you start to walk to the left toward Svartifoss, you'll pass a food truck called Glacier Goodies (June - September). They had baby back ribs, fish and chips, lobster soup, and a giant chocolate bar with a picture of a glacier on it. The food was pricey, but it's your only option here for hot food.

The Skaftafell Visitor Centre is free, not too far off the road, and worth a stop. Just leave plenty of time and energy if you want to hike to Svartifoss! Bring water with you for the hike, or buy it in the gift shop.

Fjallsárlón

Ring Road continues along just south of Vatnajökull National Park. Our next stop will be Fjallsárlón glacier lagoon, a lake left behind by melting pieces of glacier ice. This is the much less popular glacier lagoon, and we'll get to the more famous Jökulsárlón soon. They are only about 10 minutes apart; it's worth seeing both if you're out here.

Fjallsárlón doesn't look like much from the road, or even the parking lot; I assume that's one reason why it's less popular. We had signed up for a Zodiac boat tour, and the first step (after a bathroom break) was to put on the coveralls and life jackets.

You have to be at least 6 to do the tour. But my son, who at the time was a week or so away from turning 7, had some issues with his coveralls. The smallest size they had was an 8-10, which is really a 10. We made do. The company that runs the boat tours told me that 8-10 is the smallest size coveralls they have found.

The issue came with the next step, which was the roughly 10 minute walk down to the glacier. For me, this was incredible, because you finally reach a point where you can actually see the reason we're here.

But for my son, it was a really long walk in a very heavy outfit. The walk back up was especially hard; he rested a couple of times. He still had fun, but keep this in mind for your younger kids.

Down at the boats, the guide talked about the glacier for a couple of minutes, as well as boat safety. You sit on the outside inflated part of the boat. This seemed scary, but it wasn't really; it's a nice smooth ride, and the sides are quite large.

You may have noticed the water color in the pictures; the sky is blue, the ice in the middle has that classic "glacier blue" tinge to it, but the water, is, well, brown. There's just more sediment in it. It's not as picture perfect as Jökulsárlón is, but I don't think it's a huge deal. Though maybe that's another reason why Fjallsárlón is less popular?

The boat cruises around the lagoon at a fairly gentle speed. This made a huge difference to my kids, compared to the Westman Islands ferry (page 80) they had been on a few days earlier. I think my girls would rank fairly high on the "prone to seasickness" scale; they almost didn't go. But they did go, and were glad they did. If you're looking for a "starter" boat ride to see how it goes, this would be a good choice.

You'll get to enjoy the beautiful scenery. And then the guide will go hunting for what he called 500-year-old Popsicles. It turns out that pieces of ice that have been exposed to the air and wind take on the bright white color. But when smaller pieces of ice have just broken off, they are much clearer. The guide went hunting for a small piece that was clearer for us to taste. He worked to smash pieces off of it, for us to hold and eat. The kids really enjoyed this. They also learned a fair bit about glaciers.

You are actually on the boat for about 45 minutes, though with getting the coveralls on and hiking to and from the lagoon, you're closer to 80 minutes. The cost is 6,800 krona for adults and 3,500 for kids 6-15. That's not cheap- $200 for a family of 4. But I think it makes sense to pay a premium for the more intimate tours- the boats only hold up to 11 passengers. It's a memorable experience, it's not very stressful, and it's even educational. If your kids are old enough, I recommend this as something the whole family can do together.

The web site for the boat tours is fjallsarlon.is. New in 2017 is a restaurant with sandwiches and a buffet.

Jökulsárlón

My hope was to head to Jökulsárlón, take their boat tour of a glacier lagoon, and compare. Unfortunately, it was incredibly windy. I don't know if it was the wind by itself that canceled the boat rides for the day, or the fact that the wind had blown tons of ice right into the harbor, blocking the boats. But it was windy. It was so windy that I just hopped out of the car, took a few pictures, and we continued on our way. It's odd that Fjallsárlón, only a few miles away, was very calm. Maybe the hill down to that lagoon protects it from the weather?

Jökulsárlón. No boats are getting past that ice today!

Wind in Iceland

Jökulsárlón was the first time I worried about my car doors. The winds can be very strong in Iceland. Imagine you park your car with a strong wind coming from behind you. You open your door just a little, and the wind starts pushing into that door, pushing it forward. If you're not thinking about it (and normally I don't!) you can lose your grip on the door. This can push your door right into the car next to you. Or, if it's a strong enough wind, it can push your door to its stopping point, and actually bend the hinges. Both are really sad, and both really happen! Just be aware. And maybe consider that minivan, so the kids have doors that slide!

The company at Jökulsárlón, whose web site is icelagoon. is, offers a zodiac boat tour, just like the ones offered Fjallsárlón. But they also have an amphibian boat tour, which you may call a duck boat.

The zodiac tours run on a fixed schedule, June through September. Tours cost 9,500 krona for adults, and 5,000 for kids 10-12; they don't recommend kids under 10 go on the zodiacs. Fjallsárlón is less expensive, and allows kids as young as 6.

The amphibian boat tour allows kids of all ages—0 and up! The cost is 5,000 ISK for adults, 2,000 for kids 6-12, and free for kids under 6. (Actually, the web site says 0-6 is free, so your 6-year-old may not have to pay.)

Jökulsárlón also has a building with a café, which is open year-round, 7 AM to 7 PM. They have sandwiches and hot and cold drinks.

One lane bridges

South Iceland might be your first introduction to one lane bridges. Most of them are just platforms over rivers, but there is a more memorable one right before Jökulsárlón. (and I mean right before ... the left turn to get to Jökulsárlón is maybe 200 feet past the bridge.) There is always a sign warning you about an upcoming one-lane bridge and a place to pull over. In almost all cases, traffic from both directions is treated equally—whoever looks to be getting to the bridge first has the right of way. Still, go slow, and make sure the other car / cars are planning to pull over.

Diamond Beach

Across Route 1 from Jökulsárlón is Diamond Beach. Literally across the street-- when you see the sign for Jökulsárlón, turn right instead of left. You'll find a beach possibly littered with pieces of ice. Some will be small (think tennis ball) sized and some will be huge (think person sized.)

Þórbergur Center

Here's a name that's a little easier to remember if you know that the Þ is a letter called a thorn, and it makes a th sound as in, well, thorn. So this is a name that is pronounced "Thorbergur." The Icelandic for Þórbergur Center is Þórbergssetur.

This is a museum about Þórbergur Þórðarson. But there's a good chance your family will call it the book museum.

The building is about 10 minutes east of Jökulsárlón, and you can see it from Ring Road. In the picture above, you can see the restaurant at the far left corner. Our lunch there was pricey but good. The kids mostly chose either lamb soup or smoked trout sandwiches; there was no kid's menu.

Þórbergur Þórðarson was an Icelandic author, poet, and lover of Esperanto. The museum has a nice atmosphere— it's a dark space with nice lighting. But ultimately, it's not that exciting unless you know something about Þórbergur. Adults pay 1,000 krona, and kids are free. But your best bet might be to enjoy looking at the outside and maybe buying some cake.

The end of the road?

Jökulsárlón is a very common stopping point for people not doing all of Ring Road. With no stops, it's about 4 1/2 or 5 hours of driving from Reykjavik to Jökulsárlón. If you have less than a week in Iceland, stopping here and turning around makes some sense. The downside is that there's not much of an alternate route back—you're just backtracking back to Reykjavik. Well, it's about 4 hours of backtracking to Selfoss; after that, you can head north and cover the Golden Circle.

There's plenty to see on the South Coast, and I think turning around here (or even sooner) can make a lot of sense. Doing all of Ring Road means more driving-- if you keep heading east, it's 11 1/2 more hours of driving back to Reykjavik!

The Westman Islands

Very few tourists make it to the Westman Islands, a small inhabited island a few miles off of Iceland's south coast. (The island is actually called Heimaey, and it's just one of the islands that makes up the Westman Islands archipelago. But people use "Heimaey" and "Westman Islands" interchangeably.) About 4,000 people live on Heimaey.

One very good reason why few people visit is because they simply can't. The only ways on and off the island are a 35-minute ferry ride, which runs up to 5 times a day, and a couple of airlines that fly very short flights in very small airplanes. Almost everyone travels by ferry, and many of those spots are taken by locals.

This is a significant diversion from an Iceland adventure, and one you need to plan for. So why bother? Well, if you only have a few days in Iceland, you may not. This will take most of a day, or an overnight trip. But in exchange, you get a walkable and much less crowded part of Iceland with some amazing recent history involving a dramatic volcanic eruption. On January 23, 1973, a volcano called Eldfell erupted on Heimaey. Eldfell was considered a dormant volcano until the moment that it wasn't. At the beginning of the eruption, 3,500 cubic feet of lava and ash came out of Eldfell every SECOND. The island was quickly evacuated; by a stroke of luck, poor weather had caused the entire fishing fleet to stay in port, and these boats were used to evacuate residents to the mainland of Iceland. No one was killed.

But the eruption lasted for 5 more months. During that time, a third of the houses on the island were destroyed. Another third were damaged. Stop and think about that– two thirds of all of the houses on the island were damaged or destroyed. High capacity water pumps were brought in to cool the encroaching lava and save the town's harbor.

Hiking

Today, the lava has (mostly) cooled, and there are beautiful

hiking trails carved atop this volcanic rock. But you'll feel the power of that volcano when a signpost tells you there is a house buried 35 feet below your feet.

The Eldheimar Volcano Museum

You can (and should) also head to the Volcano Museum. The creators of the museum dug out one of the buried houses, and put a museum structure around it. Remember that this house was buried in 1973– some of the people in town were friends with the people who used to live in this house.

The museum just opened in 2014, and the technology is stellar. Wait a few seconds, and the audio guide (included with admission) will figure out your exact location in the museum as you walk; you will automatically hear an audio segment for

whatever you're standing in front of.

2,300 krona ($21) for adults, 1,200 ($11) for kids 10-18, and free for kids under 10. Families can pay a fixed 5500.

Just outside of the museum you can also see a house still partially buried in lava.

The Sæheimar Aquarium

But life marches on, and not everything on the Island is about the Eldfell eruption. You'll also find a quaint aquarium, whose undisputed highlight is the puffin who wanders around like he owns the place. (Sadly, this puffin, Tóti, passed away in August 2018. But there should be others here to see.)

You'll also find a room with a small live aquarium, and a room full of stuffed birds and other wildlife. 1,200 krona ($11) for adults, 500 ($4) for kids 10-17, and free under 10 years.

Sagnheimar Folk Museum

Most Icelandic towns seem to have their own folk museum, and Heimaey is no exception. One highlight of the Sagnheimar Folk Museum is information about rescuing baby puffins, or pufflings. Once the pufflings are big enough to fly from the nest, they have an instinct to head toward light (the moon, I think?) to get to the ocean. But the lights of civilization confuse them, and they end up lost and lonely on land.

This happens every year. The children of Heimaey get to stay up late during this season, typically in September. They find the lost baby birds, keep them in boxes overnight, and then release them near the ocean the next morning. The aquarium weighs and counts all of the pufflings. In fact, the puffin who lives in the aquarium was brought there as an injured puffling! See facebook.com/SaeheimarAquarium/.

You'll also find an exhibit about that volcano eruption. 1,000 krona for adults, and free for kids 17 and under.

Boat tours

A couple of boat tour companies can take you to see some of the fascinating rock formations on the island. My favorite: elephant rock. (See picture on the next page.)

I ended up in a more raucous, almost party-like atmosphere of the RIB boat with the company RIBsafari. These are small maneuverable boats that go fast just for the fun of it.

A RIB boat in the lovely Heimaey harbor

If that isn't your speed (hah), you can opt for a more traditional boat tour with Viking Tours (vikingtours.is).

A one hour RIBsafari trip is 11,900 krona ($107); 6,500 ($58) for kids 12 and under. ribsafari.is

Bus tours

You can cover a lot of the island during a 2 hour bus tour with Eyja tours (eyjatours.com). This is a family-run company that only operates a small bus, which I think provides a much better experience than a tour on a full-sized bus.

You'll see that elephant rock from the shore. You'll visit the aquarium and meet the puffin. You'll also head to the center of the Eldfell volcano. And you'll see a bird cliff, where the owner will give a live demonstration of cliff swinging from a rope, a skill that is sometimes still used to gather bird eggs.

7,000 krona for adults, half price for kids 12 and under.

Dining

With our kids, we opted for the less flashy but still delicious Fiskibarinn, which prepares fresh fish just brought in to the port a couple of blocks away.

But there also are some fine dining options that soar well beyond the size of this little island. You'll find some top tier dining experiences at restaurants such as Gott or Slippurinn.

Slippurinn in particular is developing a reputation as one of the best restaurants in Iceland, and certainly one of the most interesting. It's only open from May through August, and the owner goes out every day to forage for wild herbs and seaweeds.

If you are looking to save money and/or time, Heimaey also has locations of two of the best supermarket chains in Iceland: Bonus and Kronan.

Westman Islands Planning: The Ferry

I think the Westman Islands is worth the effort and time out of your schedule, but there are some things to keep in mind:

The map on the next page shows the ferry port called Landeyjahöfn. Note its close proximity to Heimaey. But this port is only in operation when the weather cooperates. It's a near certainty that you'll get to use this port all summer, but it's generally closed in the winter. In the fall and spring, you'll usually get to use Landeyjahöfn but it's a bit riskier.

When Landeyjahöfn is closed, the ferry company will use the port called Þorlákshöfn instead. What does this mean? It turns a 35 minute ferry ride into a 2 hour and 45 minute ferry ride. Given that some of our kids were feeling slightly unwell after the 35 minute ride, I would absolutely avoid the trip to/from Þorlákshöfn unless you're looking forward to the adventure of a much longer ride.

Over the winter of 2015-2016, the port at Landeyjahöfn closed on December 8th and reopened on April 15th. But don't assume that you can just use the closer port any other time; temporary closures will still be common outside of the summer months. The issue: If the waves are too high, the ships won't sail.

The company that runs the ferry is called Herjólfur. They do a nice job updating their Facebook page with the ferry schedule and information about which port is operational. Be sure to monitor facebook.com/ms.herjolfur .

You can also do your own wave forecasting. Check out the forecast at this web site:

www.vegagerdin.is/vs/WaveEpsogram.aspx?la=en

Make sure your latitude and longitude are set to 63.5 and -20 respectively. You'll get a graph that shows the wave forecast. If you see a spike up to 3 or 4 meters, you're at risk of ending up on the longer ferry ride.

Assuming that everything looks to be running smoothly from Landeyjahöfn, you have the option to take your car on the ferry or not. We did not; this saves money, and we were able to leave our car parked overnight (for free) at the port without issue. This did limit our ability to explore the outskirts of the island, but I don't think it matters. Nearly everything is within walking distance of the port on the island. Almost every single museum, restaurant, and tour described above is less than a 10 minute walk from the ferry port. (The Volcano Museum is the exception; it's about a 15 minute walk.)

You should book your ferry tickets ahead of time, since some trips occasionally sell out. Prices are reasonable: about $12 each way for adults, half price for kids 12-15, and completely free for kids under 12.

Most people on the ferry seemed just fine, so you can probably ignore this paragraph unless you are prone to seasickness. But we found it much better to stay outside during the journey; bundle up with lots of layers and lots of wool. Inside the boat, you will find a cafeteria with sandwiches, hamburgers, drinks, chips, etc. (You'll pay about $10 for a hamburger). But it's hot inside, and the cold sea air helped us avoid any potential seasickness.

The Westman Islands are a fantastic experience. Remember the main downside: You're at the mercy of the ferry. Even if it's running from Landeyjahöfn, the ferry is very occasionally canceled. If that happens, you may find yourself stuck on Heimaey for another day. But that's the price you pay to experience a place freshly re-formed by a volcano, and an island ready to show you a unique slice of Icelandic life.

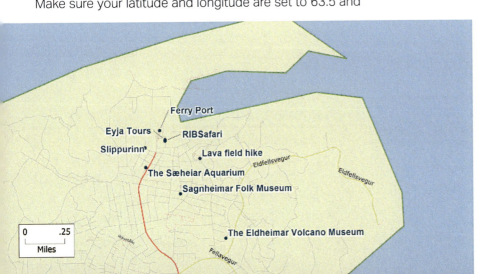

Elephant rock!

Arcanum Tours (arcanum.is)

The South Coast of Iceland is one of the most popular areas for tourist to visit when they venture out of Reykjavik. There's a lot to see and do: waterfalls, glaciers, black sand beaches, and more.

Arcanum is a tour company that operates in south Iceland, and can take you beyond what you are able to see and do on your own. They offer 3 different tours; we were lucky enough to try all 3 with various subsets of kids. Any of these tours could be a highlight of your vacation.

Glacier Walk on Sólheimajökull Glacier

Our first trip was a glacier walk. Right away, you should know that this was by far the most physically demanding of the tours. I guess that's obvious, since the other tours involve machines you get to ride on. But this was hard work; children have to be 10 years or older to do the glacier walk. (Note that all of these tours have a different minimum age.)

We started at the Arcanum glacier walk office (GPS 63.530590, -19.370345; you go to a different location, which is about 10 minutes away, for the snowmobile or ATV tours.) At the office they will fit you for your ice walking gear. You walk to the edge of the glacier in your regular shoes, and then put the crampons on once you reach the edge of the ice. Make sure you wear sturdy shoes or hiking boots.

Interestingly, the walk to the edge of the glacier is getting longer every year, as the ice is receding at a rate of 150 feet per year! But it was a lovely hike past a glacial lagoon housing some of that melting ice.

Holding the ice pick and the crampons proved difficult for my kids, especially the youngest of this group, who was 10. I ended up carrying her equipment and mine. Given the hike was also hard work, I would consider this only for adventurous 10-year-olds! At the foot of the glacier we stopped to put on our crampons. It's a little tricky to strap them on properly, but the patient guide went around and took care of everyone.

Then, after a brief lesson about how to walk on the ice (step down to make sure those spikes on the crampons are going to dig into the ice!) we started climbing. I think it's hard to appreciate just how much the crampons make a difference; after a few steps, you more or less forget that you are walking on a literal sheet of ice.

Up and up we went. You may stop in little crevasses in the ice, depending on conditions and the time of year. We marched higher and higher up the glacier, stopping once in a while to catch our breath and learn something about the area. We saw a device scientists are using to measure how much the glacier is receding, and we were also able to fill our water bottles with fresh (and ice cold!) glacier water. It's windy at the top, so make sure you wear layers; see page 10.

Then it was time to start the journey back down. The kids were happy to start walking downhill rather than trudging ever higher. At the bottom, we reversed the process, removed our crampons, and walked back.

We opted for the 3 hour tour, and the kids were definitely worn out by the end. You may want to consider the 2 hour tour. Note, however, that you spend an hour walking to and from the glacier and getting your crampons on; so that means the 3 hour tour gives you 2 hours on the glacier, while the 2 hour tour only gives you one.

Prices are: 11,990 / 14,990 (2 hour walk / 3 hour walk) for adults, 8,393 / 10,493 for kids ages 10 or 11. I think these are reasonable prices; it's not cheap, and there is no transportation provided, but you're getting a good value by Icelandic standards.

The building you start and end at also has bathrooms and a small restaurant, the Arcanum Glacier Café. I wasn't overly impressed by the food, or rather the value; the kids very much enjoyed their hot chocolate to warm up after our tour, but I thought the food was somewhat overpriced. I guess that's to be expected when you are hungry next to a glacier?

I think there are a few picnic tables, so you could pack a lunch to eat after you visited the glacier.

If you have kids under 10, or the glacier walk just isn't right for you, you can also park out here and walk by yourself to the glacier's edge. You should NOT walk on the ice without a guide, but you can hike to see it, and then buy some hot chocolate when you return.

Snowmobiling up Mýrdalsjökull glacier

My 7-year-old couldn't go on the glacier walk, so I took him snowmobiling in the afternoon. Yes, snowmobiling up a glacier; it's certainly much easier to let the snowmobile handle the climb up (a different part of) the glacier!

Note that you start from a different building for the snowmobile and ATV tours; you want to head up Road 222 for these tours; the glacier walk is off of Road 221. GPS is 63.494459, -19.328233 for snowmobiling and ATV tours.

We arrived, and they suited us up before we got into a vehicle to find the snow and ice. In the winter time, you may be able to hop on your snowmobile right from the office. But as the snow melts in the summer, they move the snowmobiles higher and higher up the mountain. So in the winter, your 2 hour tour can involve nearly 2 hours on the snowmobile; in the height of summer, you may only get an hour.

The rest of the time is spent on a very bumpy ride in a truck. You drive on a road that was closed after the Eyjafjallajökull volcano erupted in 2010. The road is no longer maintained by the government, and it sure is bumpy. It's off limits to other vehicles. (While we were riding in the truck, we saw a tow truck pulling a tourist's car off of the road; my guess is their small sedan was ruined by the road. Don't do this!)

We drove maybe 15 minutes each way; the road gets bumpier and bumpier as you go. Then, we saw the array of snowmobiles ready to go.

I've never been on a snowmobile before, but after a 2 minute training session, I was ready to go. We started slowly while I got the hang of it; you need to adjust to the fact that the snowmobile will slide a little bit on the snow. My son said it was a little too bumpy at first, but by the end he was having a great time; he sat behind me on the snowmobile.

After a long climb, we arrived at the top, or at least what seemed like a good stopping point. The guide used the snow to draw a diagram of the glacial system, and which parts are connected and where the melting snow goes. I enjoyed this, but my son just wanted to play in the snow. I guess you can't blame him, since being surrounded by snow at the end of May is quite the novelty.

There was plenty of time to ask questions and relax and enjoy the magnificent views. You can see the mountains, other glaciers, and even the Westman Islands. The quiet is striking, especially after the roar of the snowmobiles.

Then we headed back down. This is a long, continuous ride. Heading up, I felt like we kept going and going and going, with the top of the glacier seemingly never getting any closer. But the trip back down seemed faster, and before we knew it we were back with the rest of the snowmobiles.

This trip is significantly more expensive than the glacier walk. Adults cost 26,990; kids 5-11 are 18,893. (If you're wondering about the strange price for kids, it's a 30% discount from the adult price.)

Snowmobile drivers need to have a valid drivers license.

But if two parents are both up for driving, this could be a nice activity for the whole family. And a family of 2 adults and 3 children can also work; the third child can ride with the guide.

Unlike the glacier tour, you don't need to bring warm layers, since Arcanum provides warm overalls. A warm baselayer would be good for the summer, though you may want another layer or two in the winter.

My son really liked the trip; it was new and different for him. I enjoyed it as well, and I recommend it. It's expensive, though I think it's a fair price given that they have to maintain the snowmobiles and pay for insurance. Oh, and be careful–something like 5% of people manage to tip their snowmobiles over! But if you're careful enough to land in the other 95%, and this sounds interesting to your family, you'll have a great time.

ATV / Quad bike tour

Finally, I took an ATV tour with my older son. This is similar to the snowmobile, where you can drive as long as you are a licensed driver, and your kids can ride behind you. But unlike the snowmobile trip, where kids as young as 5 can ride along, children need to be at least 12 for the ATVs.

We cruised across the black sand beaches of South Iceland. It hadn't rained in several weeks, which is extremely unusual, and so we kicked up a lot of dust. But other than getting my camera dusty, this didn't impact the trip at all; we still had the opportunity to do some hills, flats, water crossings and see some amazing things. You ride from the office (the same office as the snowmobile rides start from) but immediately head downhill, away from the glacier, toward the ocean. And the plane crash site.

Over 40 years ago, a US Navy plane crash landed on the beach in South Iceland; the site is now called Sólheimasandur. (Note the similarity to the same of the glacier Sólheimajökull: "Sólheim glacier" vs. "Sólheim sand".) Until a couple of years ago, you could drive your car down a path on the beach to see it. But because people were driving off of the path, the landowner closed the area to car traffic. There is a small parking area down the road, which this sign is pointing you toward. You'd need to park and walk almost 4 miles roundtrip to see the plane. And this is a boring flat walk!

But Arcanum has permission to take you onto the land and ride right up to the plane on their ATVs. As of 2019, Arcanum

Thanks to Alex Geerts (Unsplash) for the picture of the plane not on fire!

will be offering bus transportation to see the plane crash site. This is cheaper than the ATV tour, but also less exciting!

(See page 70 to see the plane how we saw it. No, the plane is not still on fire today. This was some sort of movie shoot, and more than likely won't look like this when you see it! (Supposedly they were shooting a web series; let me know if you know what the series is!) I think the site was even closed to foot traffic this day, and so we were some of the only people to see the plane like this.)

But the plane isn't the only thing you'll see. I really liked this orca (killer whale) skeleton; this is about half a mile from the plane.

You'll also catch a glimpse of the Dyrhólaey rock arch off in the distance.

Of course, I'm leaving out all of the fun. You get to drive fast, leaving tire tracks in the sand as you go. Toward the end, once you're more comfortable driving the ATV, you get to try some hills and water crossings.

You have the choice of a 1 hour tour or a 2 hour tour; I think the longer tour gets you much closer to Dyrhólaey.

Prices are: 18,990 / 26,990 (1 hour tour / 2 hour tour); that's the price for anyone 12 and up; you have to be 12 to do the tour. If you have an odd number of riders, you'll need to pay an additional 10,000 for the single rider.

Which tour to choose?

I recommend the glacier walk, though I'm probably biased by the prices here. My kids each loved the snowmobile and ATV tours. They were great experiences, and if they sound exciting to you, I recommend them. Here are the prices for a family of 4, assuming all of the kids are 12 or older:

2 hour glacier walk	$435
3 hour glacier walk	$544

Snowmobile	$979
1 hour ATV	$689
2 hour ATV	$979

At today's exchange rate of 110 krona per US dollar.

(Both the glacier walk and the snowmobile tours have discounted pricing for younger kids.)

I'm partial to the glacier walks; the walk was challenging, and I think that made it more exciting to me. But you can't go wrong with any of the tours with Arcanum.

Thanks to Arcanum for sponsoring our tours! Check out the options at arcanum.is.

Other tour companies

During our trips to Iceland, we took tours with many different tour companies. And each and every one was excellent. (I'm sitting here trying to think of a poor experience, and I can't think of a single one.) Organized tours in Iceland seem to be universally excellent.

If you've booked a tour with a company I haven't mentioned in the book, should you still go? Of course! Check some reviews online, and unless the company you chose is a rare outlier, the reviews will be stellar. And so will your experience.

For example, Icelandic Mountain Guides (mountainguides.is) also offers glacier walks. We went with Arcanum and loved them, but Icelandic Mountain Guides also looks great. The exception here is car rental companies: I recommend Blue Car rental (see page 22) as there is a small chance you'll have a poor experience with some other companies. But not for organized tours. Sure, if you choose a big bus company for the Golden Circle or South Coast, you may feel rushed, or part of too large a group. Choose a small tour company with some good reviews and you simply cannot go wrong.

Another group doing the glacier walk

East Iceland

East Iceland can often be a decision point for your vacation: Do you visit the south coast and turn around, or cover the entire Ring Road and head east? The stunning glacier lagoons Fjallsárlón and Jökulsárlón make a good stopping point. Or, you can keep going and explore some of our favorite small towns in Iceland, including Djúpivogur and Seyðisfjörður. In exchange for fewer tourists, you'll spend more time diving on windy roads that hug the coast or soar through mountain passes.

Keep an eye out for reindeer as you go—in Iceland, you'll only find them in the east. (Reindeer were imported from Norway in the 1780s, and only survived in the east! If you want to learn more, check out: east.is/en/inspiration/nature/reindeers. Or visit the East Iceland Heritage Museum; see page 91.)

Reindeer outside of Egilsstaðir

Höfn

Vik and Höfn are the two largest towns on the south coast. Below we'll cover some of the things we found in Höfn. But looking back on our trip, neither of these towns was especially memorable. Yes, they both offer grocery stores, restaurants, swimming pools, lodging and things to do. We were happy to explore, but don't feel obligated to take a lot of time—use them as places to rest and eat, but spend your time in nature between them!

Note that there is a town west of Höfn called ... Hof. Hof is much smaller; you'll see it mentioned mostly because of an old turf church, built in 1883. The whole sides of the church are turf, which is kind of fun. And there's actually another Hof in northeast Iceland, just to add to the confusion. Anyway, remember that we're talking about Höfn here, and not Hof.

There are multiple towns with the same names in Iceland; see "Should We Go to Reykholt, or Reykholt?" on page 39. There are a couple of museums in the main town area in Höfn. There's the Gamlabúð Folk Museum, which is attached to the Visitor's Center by the harbor. It's a small 2 story museum, but it's free!

Next door is the Maritime Museum, which is also free.

Swimming in Iceland

We also tried the Höfn swimming pool, which features pools of varying temperatures and several waterslides. This is a good time to stop and talk about swimming; we'll cover even more later (See page 171.) The pool at Höfn was very nice. But every town has a very nice pool. I think this is literally true—every town with more than, say, 500 people is going to have a pool. And maybe even towns with fewer than 500 people. You'll always find one or more geothermally heated lap pools, and one or more hot tubs (called hot pots). And many also have waterslides, a children's pool, and an ice bath(!) People swim year-round, no matter the weather. Watch for temperature signs by the hot pots. Adults might enjoy temperatures of 40 or 42 Celsius (104-108 degrees Fahrenheit), but most kids seem to top out at 36 or 38. Most children's pools seem to be around 36. The city pools are very inexpensive. At Höfn we paid 800 krona for adults ($7 or so) and 200 krona for kids (under $2). Whether you make it outside of Reykjavik or not, be sure to try a local thermal pool! Just make sure your kids are ready to be cold for a few seconds before they sink into the warm water. You may want to send an adult out to map the exact path your kids should take to get to a lower temperature hot pot, or the children's pool. At Höfn, we highly recommend the red slide, but you'll probably get stuck on the blue one and have to push your way down.

Finally, for dinner we opted for the somewhat fancy Pakkhús Restaurant. (Open for lunch and dinner, 12-10.) Service was very efficient-- some people may find it rushed, but with kids we were pleased. And the food was very good. There's lots of langoustine on the menu (a type of lobster that Höfn is famous for), but we opted for some very good lamb at Pakkhús.

Actually only a couple of us opted for Pakkhús; the rest headed to a tiny fish and chips restaurant called Hafnarbúðin down by the harbor. There are only a handful of tables, and so the kids ended up getting takeout. But while you wait, you can do the 1 or 2 minute walk over to the harbor and the kids can play on an old boat that is now on land

Again, I don't have much bad to say about Höfn. You'll find several more restaurants that we didn't cover, many of them known for their langoustine lobster dishes. There's a rock and gem museum called Huldusteinn, which was closed when we visited in late May. The museum shows a family's collection, so I don't know if it's closed or only open in the summer. And all of this is walkable from the downtown harbor area.

But there are towns we liked a little more as we headed further east and then turned north. Maybe it's because we had adjusted better to life in Iceland? But the next town we'll get to is Djúpivogur, which was one of my favorites.

The boat to climb on. From pxhere.com (297179) licensed under CC by 2.0

Djúpivogur

On the previous page, I noted that, in my opinion, neither Vik nor Höfn, was especially memorable. But I really liked Djúpivogur, the next major town past Höfn; it's about an hour and a half drive, most of it hugging the curving coastline.

There were lots of unique things to do in Djúpivogur, the museum was a good value, and it's home to some of our favorite stores. It's also beautiful. Not that the other towns weren't, but the view from the hillside was stunning, especially in the sun.

In the picture above, that's our big white van on the right hand side (center left); we stayed in an Airbnb rental apartment, which took up half of the top floor of that building on the right.

Here are some of the things that made Djúpivogur unique:

The Eggs

I have to start with the eggs. If you could see further to the left in the picture of town above and there wasn't a hill in the way you'd see Eggin í Gleðivík, an art installation unveiled in 2009.

These are sculptures of eggs, lined up along the harbor. They are all the same size,

except for one. (That part is a little … artsy, since in real life all of these eggs would be different sizes.) But the shapes are different, and accurate. You can see in the picture how the second egg from the front is pointier than the other ones.

It's hard to convey how the eggs just wrap right around the harbor; you can see the small eggs in the background of the picture above. It's fun. I can't say you'll learn very much, though you can fund the puffin (Lundi) egg and see how pointed it is. Puffins lay their eggs on cliffs, and the shape helps the eggs to roll in a tight circle, instead of off of the cliff!

JFS- Icelandic Handicraft

This was one of my favorite stores in Iceland. It's in a guy's house. The guy is JFS, aka Jon.

Jon makes jewelry and crafts out of whatever materials he can find: reindeer bones, antlers, wood, you name it. He's very welcoming, and this place feels uniquely Icelandic. I bought a wool cap knitted by his daughter. The kids also bought a few things, including a toothpick holder carved out of reindeer bone.

Bones, Sticks, and Stones.

This may be the "competing" business to JFS Handcraft? It's much more striking from the outside:

I think everyone calls if Free Willy. The view from the store out to the water is stunning (above right.) The owner has a dog who will do some tricks if you ask the owner. (The dog scared us a little around the kids, but we're probably just paranoid. Still, this was a very high energy dog.)

Inside you'll find a lot of small rocks and other items. We liked JFS better, but there were some fun and less expensive options at Free Willy as well. Free Willy is right next to the eggs by the harbor, which also makes it more popular with tour buses.

Eggin í Gleðivík (The Eggs)

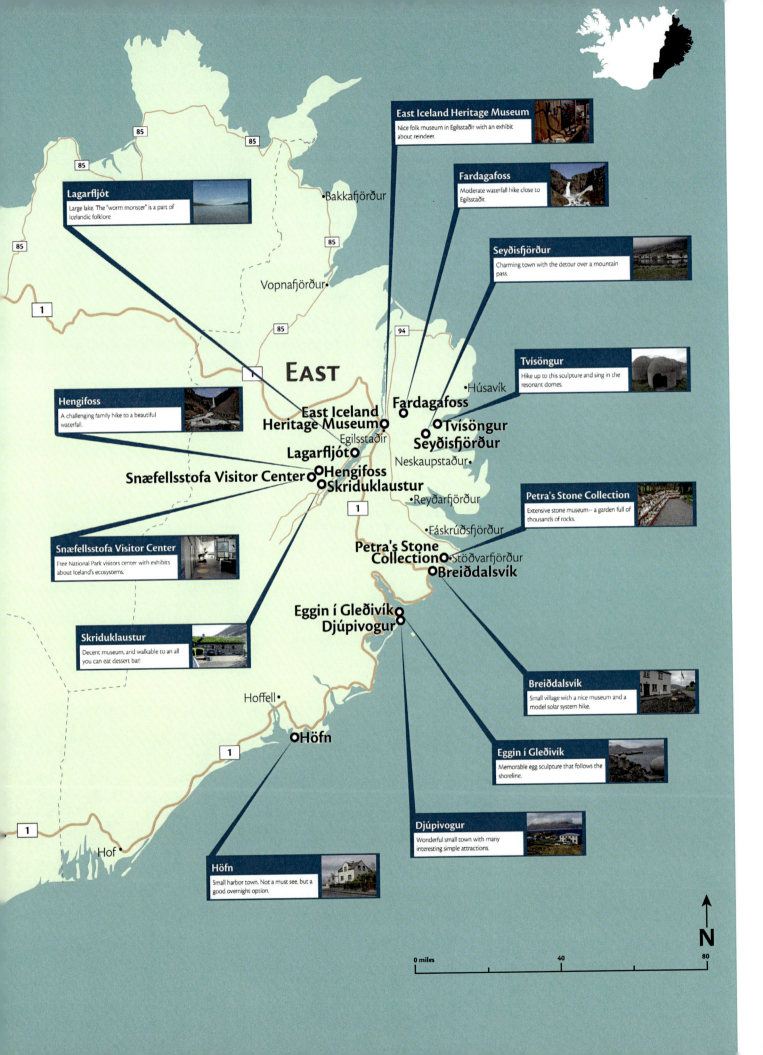

East Iceland Heritage Museum

Nice folk museum in Egilsstaðir with an exhibit about reindeer.

Fardagafoss

Moderate waterfall hike close to Egilsstaðir.

Seyðisfjörður

Charming town with the detour over a mountain pass.

Tvísöngur

Hike up to this sculpture and sing in the resonant domes.

Lagarfljót

Large lake. The "worm monster" is a part of Icelandic folklore

Hengifoss

A challenging family hike to a beautiful waterfall.

Petra's Stone Collection

Extensive stone museum-- a garden full of thousands of rocks.

Snæfellsstofa Visitor Center

Free National Park visitors center with exhibits about Iceland's ecosystems.

Breiðdalsvík

Small village with a nice museum and a model solar system hike.

Skriduklaustur

Decent museum, and walkable to an all you can eat dessert bar!

Eggin í Gleðivík

Memorable egg sculpture that follows the shoreline.

Djúpivogur

Wonderful small town with many interesting simple attractions.

Höfn

Small harbor town. Not a must see, but a good overnight option.

85
85
85
85
1
1
85
85
94
1
1
1
1

•Bakkafjörður

Vopnafjörður•

EAST

•Húsavík

East Iceland
Heritage Museum○

Fardagafoss
○

Egilsstaðir

Tvísöngur
○

Lagarfljót○

Seyðisfjörður
○

Neskaupstaður•

Snæfellsstofa Visitor Center○
○**Hengifoss**
○**Skriduklaustur**

•Reyðarfjörður

•Fáskrúðsfjörður

Petra's Stone
Collection○ •Stöðvarfjörður
○**Breiðdalsvík**

Eggin í Gleðivík○
Djúpivogur○

Hoffell•

○**Höfn**

Hof •

N

0 miles   40   80

Jon of JFS Handcraft

The vew from "Free WIlly"

Arfleifd leather store

This is another unique store; you'll find it in the same building as the gas station and grocery store. They sell leather clothing and leather purses and leather pieces. You'll find "leather" from fish and all sorts of animals. This seems like the kind of place most people just browse and never buy anything, but if you want a shirt made of fish skin, here's your chance. Hours are limited; stop by and see if they're open.

The boat to Papey Island

We were in Djúpivogur at the very end of May, and unfortunately, the 1 hour boat ride to Papey Island didn't start running for the season until a few days later. Actually, maybe this is for the best, since online reviews claim it's a rough ride and you may get seasick. But if you're up for it, you'll get to explore the uninhabited Papey Island. There are walking trails, and thousands of birds. It's about a 2 mile hike, plus the rough boat ride, so this may only be best for adventurous and/or older children.

It's a 4 hour trip: 1 hour each way on the boat, plus 2 hours on the island. The tour usually leaves at 1 PM. E-mail papey@djupivogur.is to see if they are running the tour that day.

The Heritage Museum

There are dozens of Heritage or Folk Museums around Iceland, and you don't have to see them all. But the one in Djúpivogur seemed better than most. It costs 500 krona for adults, and 300 for kids 6-12, and free for kids under 6. They ended up not charging us for any of the kids

The top floor was a good example of a Folk Museum, with

lots of old stuff to see. If you've seen several of these already, this might get old, but our kids enjoyed looking around. Downstairs, you more or less get a second museum, though it's still included in your admission. This one celebrates the work of Ríkarður Jónsson, a sculptor who lived in Djúpivogur.

Teigarhorn

A few minutes' drive outside of town, you'll find this is protected "National Monument" area. This means you absolutely should not take any rocks or anything from the site! In many places you might grab a rock or a shell as a souvenir, but you absolutely should not here.

That's because this area is home to a rock formation called Zeolites. This may be the most famous spot for zeolites in the world. As you walk around, look carefully for crystal-like structures in the rocks.

There's a visitor's center there, which was inexplicably closed when we visited. But the hiking trails were still a hit.

Djúpivogur is by no means a big town-- roughly 375 to 500 residents. But the amount of interesting things to see seems to dwarf that modest population. Also, you don't have that many other options for places to stop in this area. Our next stop, Breiðdalsvík, has a population of about 150! If you have time, spend some of it in Djúpivogur.

The heritage museum

Teigarhorn, and an interesting rock we spotted there (above)

Breiðdalsvík

Breiðdalsvík is probably the smallest town we're going to talk about in any detail. I'm sure we stopped at other smaller towns to find bathrooms and/or food, but Breiðdalsvík stands out for one reason: The Breiðdalsetur Research and Heritage Centre. Or, maybe more specifically, the husband and wife who run the Breiðdalsetur Research and Heritage Centre.

This is the museum above. See the funky orange ball? We'll get back to that. Admission to the museum is 500 krona; younger kids should get in free. (Note: In 2018 the museum was open by reservation only. Message them at facebook.com/100006119943506 (Breiðdalssetur Vísindasetur))

Most of the museum covers geology in Iceland, and some specific to East Iceland. There's a display of Icelandic spar, which has unique refraction properties.

You'll also find zeolites, which just saw on the previous page and are prevalent in East Iceland.

Many of the specimens have been gathered by the owners themselves. One of the best parts of the museum were the many rock samples from different volcanoes. The unique factors present for each eruption make wildly different types of rock. You can touch them all—some are dense, and some are surprisingly light. And some look like hair!

There is also an exhibit about an Icelandic linguist.

Back to that orange ball outside the museum. That's a scale model of the sun, and it's part of a scale model of all of the planets in the solar system; it goes through part of the town. We all loved this, and I think most kids would have fun. The first few planets are tiny and pretty close together.

But then they start getting much further apart, and this science exercise turns into a serious hike. Supposedly, Pluto is up the hill outside of town. Be careful walking down the street! It's a fantastic learning experience.

For lunch, we ate in the restaurant in the hotel, which we were told was the only restaurant in town. But it turns out I asked the wrong question—I asked for a restaurant, not a place to eat. Had I done the latter, I think we would have ended up at Kaupfélagið, a café / grocery store / gift shop. We could have made a decent meal from the grocery store, or they had some simple sandwiches and cakes too.

That's about all there is in Breiðdalsvík, though there are a couple of hotels. But the museum plus the planet walk makes for a great stop in a cute little Icelandic town.

The drive to Egilsstaðir

In late 2017, Iceland changed where Route 1 (Ring Road) is. What used to be Roads 96 and 92 became Route 1. You probably won't need to worry about it-- just follow the new Route 1 and you'll be good.

Petra's Stone Collection

Petra was a woman who was born in 1922 in East Iceland; she took hikes around her home and collected rocks and minerals. Eventually, her collection became too large to fit inside of her house, and so she started arranging and storing them outside.

Petra passed away in 2012, but the collection lives on; when you visit Petra's stone collection, you're really visiting Petra's house.

Admission is 1,000 krona for anyone 14 and over, and free for kids under 14. I think this is hit or miss for families with kids; you walk around the paths looking at the huge collection of stones. It's not very big, and just walking through will only take you a few minutes. If you take it at a slow, almost meditative pace, it can be a relaxing opportunity on a possibly rushed trip. But if you think your kids will be bored after 5 minutes, you might want to skip it. I don't think anyone will say this outright, but this isn't the place for the kids to run around.

Petra also collected pens, and you'll see that collection inside a small building.

Inside the main house, you'll find the quite impressive gift shop; there are some smaller stones available for purchase outside, but the good stuff is all inside.

Finally, there is a café inside the main building. There's only one non-snack item, which is the soup of the day with bread. It sounds like it's the same soup every day: A slightly spicy vegetable soup, with or without chicken. We didn't try it, but

1,200 krona isn't a bad deal for a meal if your family likes the option. If you just want something sweet, there are donuts for 300 krona, or smaller kleina (a fried, twisted pastry) for 200.

Off topic: Exploring Iceland

Let's talk about the picture below for a minute. First, note the snow on top of the mountains. This was taken at the end of May, but we're getting up into the mountains of East Iceland. The roads were fine when we were there, and they will be for the rest of the summer. But even though Iceland is a small country, the weather can be very different in different regions. Don't assume the sunny skies you're experiencing in one area will carry over to the area you plan to drive to the next day. Always check the weather (en.vedur.is) and the travel warnings (safetravel.is). See more on page 26.

Second, there's a cute meandering waterfall that's tough to spot at first. You can see it starting from the middle right, disappearing into a canyon, and then reemerging at the lower left.

This waterfall is called ... well, actually, I have no idea. We just decided to take a break while driving, and there was a sign for a pull off area. The kids got out and hiked for a few minutes, and discovered the waterfall.

There's no need to go find this particular spot, but if you care, the GPS coordinates are 65.038056, -14.347500. It's on the way between Breiðdalsvík and Egilsstaðir

The point is that we missed a lot of "must see" things in Iceland, and thoroughly enjoyed discovering a lot of "unknown" things. I think you need to have a rough plan. But things will change: The weather won't cooperate, or a museum will be closed. Make sure you leave some time to alter your plans, and maybe discover something you didn't plan for at all!

Egilsstaðir

Egilsstaðir is the largest town in east Iceland. Since it's right along Route 1, it makes for a good stop for food, rest, hiking, and exploring. We ended up using it as a resting place, spending several days in the area relaxing and writing.

But, while it's a nice place to get what you need in an otherwise sparsely populated part of Iceland, this is no Reykjavik. The population of Egilsstaðir is about 2,200 people. You'll only find one museum and a handful of restaurants in the main town area, and we didn't find it very walkable. But extend your radius a bit, and you'll find fantastic hikes, a giant lake (complete with a lake monster, as is the norm for Iceland) a national park visitor's center, and more. Let's dive in.

East Iceland Heritage Museum

One of the few attractions you'll find in the main town area of Egilsstaðir is the East Iceland Heritage Museum. There are two exhibit areas: One is about reindeer, and the other is a more of a typical heritage / folk museum, though it includes an old historical house you can go inside of.

The reindeer section included a lot of information about reindeer, and there were English translations throughout. Some things I didn't know about reindeer: 75% of the baby calves born in Iceland are born during the third week of May. And, the reindeer grow new antlers every year! The antlers are felted at first, then they grow into traditional, bone-like antlers, and then they fall off! The only exception to this are pregnant females- their antlers stay on throughout the winter. I guess they are better able to compete for food against the antler-less males.

One thing to keep in mind is that this section isn't overly child friendly; maybe we should just say that it's child confusing. There is a small area where kids can touch the antlers. But on the wall right next to that section, and everywhere else, you're not supposed to touch. Not a huge deal, but something to keep in mind.

On the other side, you can check out the inside of a historical house. There are displays of items used in rural houses like this one in east Iceland. I'll say it again: There are a lot of heritage / folk museums in Iceland. This was a nice example of one, though I don't think it will hold your kid's attention for too long.

But the museum's price is reasonable. You'll pay 1000 krona for adults, and kids under 18 are free. So for under $20, your family with 2 adults and any number of children can see both exhibits.

Café Nielsen

Just around the corner from the museum you'll find one of the restaurants in town, Café Nielsen. We chose to eat here because it was a buffet; note that the buffet is only an option for lunch, and not for dinner. The all you can eat price was 2,100 krona for adults 14 and over, 1,050 krona for kids 7-13, and FREE for kids 6 and under. We've paid 2,100 for a meal of fish and chips from quick service restaurants. But here, we had a salad bar, vegetable soup, and 3 entrées to choose from: pasta with salmon in a cream sauce, Indian chick pea balls, and chicken legs in a slightly spicy barbecue sauce, plus bread and butter.

The kids enjoyed this. As my son says, "[This was] very different than all of the buffets I've been to in the US, because they only had four entrées and a salad bar, and it was six feet long up against a wall ... but even though the restaurant was small, it was very good." Buffets can be a great option if you have some kids who can benefit from the discounted prices.

The Post Office in town shares a parking lot with Café Nielsen. If you're out in this part of the country, you're probably spending a while in Iceland. We walked over here and bought some stamps to send letters to family and friends.

Other Places Downtown

You'll find two well-stocked grocery stores in Egilsstaðir, which is a welcome change from the one small grocery store towns you've been passing through recently. Both Netto and Bonus are great options. The Bonus here is the only place in Iceland where the checkout clerk pro-actively offered me advice on what to see in the area. That's a sign that not a ton of tourists make it out here! On the other hand, the Netto has a giant wyrm mural on the side. See the picture below. We'll explain this wyrm thing on the next page.

Outside of town: Lagarfljót

To really experience this area, you need to drive out of town. The most popular area is to head toward and around Lagarfljót (a lake). See picture above. Supposedly, there is a sea monster, or worm (wyrm) named Lagarfljótsormur that supposedly lives in the lake. Supposedly.

Even with all of the kids looking, we didn't see the wyrm. Like all good sea monsters, this one has its share of legends, and even a video. Many people claim to have seen the wyrm. In 1983, a company was measuring how much telephone cable they would need. Here is a quote from them: "This cable that was specially engineered so it wouldn't kink was wound in several places and badly torn and damaged in 22 different places . . I believe we dragged the cable directly over the belly of the beast. Unless it was through its mouth." (Wikipedia)

Check out the video online and decide for yourself. Look for "the iceland worm monster" on YouTube. Maybe you'll spot it and become a part of Icelandic history!

Snæfellsstofa

At the far end of the lake, we went to Snæfellsstofa, which is a visitor center for the Vatnajökull national park. You may be thinking, "Oh, another national park!" Well, no. This is part of the same national park we visited in south Iceland (page 76)! Remember that this national park covers 13% of the land mass of Iceland.

We didn't actually visit the national park from this direction, though. Most of it is only accessible by F roads (see "F Roads" on page 30). So the visitor's center is the closest we'll get today.

This visitor's center focuses on wildlife; you'll find reindeer, of course, as well as information about other animals that live in the park area. There's an interactive display that the kids enjoyed.

Skriðuklaustur

Snæfellsstofa by itself may not be a must-see, but we enjoyed it, and it's free. Maybe more importantly, it's right next to the museum Skriðuklaustur. And, there's a great walk between them. Together, these two places make for a great stop, and a great destination as you drive around the lake.

On the path between them you'll see a wooden fort on the left; as well as a couple of other things to do and see along the way. And down the hill you'll find the ruins of a monastery from the 1500s. The kids had a great time exploring and turning this into a pretend world. You can pay 500 krona for a guided tour, but I think it's fine to go down and explore on your own.

Skriðuklaustur museum and restaurant are in a house built for the Icelandic author Gunnar Gunnarsson, who lived there for 9 years and then donated the house Iceland. The museum held the kid's attention for a little while, though I'll admit that learning about the life of Gunnar wasn't that exciting for them. My son did enjoy using the microscopes, though.

The restaurant in the building is called Klausturkaffi. In the summer, there is a very expensive lunch buffet that we really enjoyed. The prices went up quite a bit in 2017; you'll now pay 3,490 krona for adults and 1,745 for kids 6-12. (Of course, that means kids under 6 are free.) We're nearing a $100 meal for 2 adults and 2 kids. But this can be a memorable meal, even though it's a buffet. Some of the entrées are reindeer stew and lamb stew, and there were two soups: a mushroom, and an angelica. Angelica? Yup- it's a wild celery. There were dessert options, fruit, breads, and more. There's a lot of effort put into this for the price.

You can also order off of the menu, though once the kids saw the buffet they were hooked. But a kid's pizzabread for 650 krona might be a much less expensive option.

Okay. Let's stop talking about lunch

Go left to see Snæfellsstofa ...

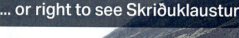

... or right to see Skriðuklaustur

and move on to the truly memorable option, again only in the summer. From 2:30 PM until 5:00, they offer a cake buffet. Yes, a cake buffet. 2,290 krona for adults and 1,145 for kids 6-12 gets you all you can eat dessert. Again, kids under 6 are free.

Remember that both the national park visitor's center and the Skriðuklaustur museum / restaurant are just a 5 minute walking path away from each other. Each building does have its own parking lot, so you can drive between them if the weather is bad or you're not up for the walk. But having all of this in the same area gives you some nice choices. For example, you could:

• Pack a lunch, and eat it outside of the Snæfellsstofa visitor's center

• Visit Snæfellsstofa

• Meander down the pathway between the buildings, stopping at the sites along the way

• Visit the ruins of the monastery

• Splurge for the cake buffet

All of that is free, except for the cake buffet.

The Wilderness Center

If you're up for more adventure past Snæfellsstofa and Skriðuklaustur, you can head to The Wilderness Center. My entire family was convinced that I was lost when we were heading to this place. I think the sheep thought so too. Past the sheep, the road gets worse, turns to gravel, and the sheep start acting as if they weren't expecting any visitors today.

Once you finally arrive (GPS is 64.964444, -15.154167) you'll find, well, a house. The family is very nice; they will happily feed you snack or a meal, most of which will be made from scratch in their kitchen. Oh, and you'll be eating with the family in that kitchen, and possibly even helping to prepare the meal. Check out the menu and prices at www.wilderness. is. (Given the limited seating, it's probably best to call or e-mail ahead.)

There's an interesting lodging option, which is built as a meticulous recreation of old-style communal Icelandic living conditions. These aren't ideal for families, though they do have one private family room.

There is a museum that the owner just finished at the start of the summer; the craftsmanship is very impressive.

You'll have to venture a good 20 minutes past Snæfellsstofa to get here, and it may not be worth it. But it's a beautiful area—it will give you a little taste of the highlands without needing to drive on F roads. And there's a good chance you'll get to interact with the owners, see their very impressive little museum, and maybe even do some cooking. You can also arrange for tours of the area.

Hengifoss

Heading back toward the lake, and just a few minutes past Snæfellsstofa and Skriðuklaustur, you'll find Hengifoss. Well, you'll find the parking lot for Hengifoss. (Foss ... waterfall!) TripAdvisor reviews say things like "Beautiful but hard" and "no pain, no gain."

Maybe a third of the way up, you get to Litlanesfoss, which is nice enough to be a good stopping point if the little legs (or any of the legs) in your group have had enough walking uphill.

But we trekked on. Given how warm it has been, there has been lots of melting snow and ice, and the water was actually starting to lap up over a short bridge. On we walked, taking breaks once in a while, and adding a rock or two to some of the many cairns along the way. (I think this is acceptable?)

After one river crossing that was deep enough to get our socks wet above our hiking boots, we arrived at Hengifoss.

There were some interesting chunks of ice in or near the river below the falls. And a pipe with a guestbook and a stamp (and even some food left by a generous hiker ... I wonder if anyone will actually take it?) Note that it's probably 10-15 degrees cooler by the falls vs. in the surrounding area. It was downright cold up close to the water!

This hike was hard, but I think it was a lot easier because we knew to expect a hard hike. Oh, and Google Maps doesn't know where the parking lot is. If you cross a bridge over the lake, and you're 1 minute away, turn left, not right. GPS for the parking lot is 65.073383, -14.880533.

It took us about an hour to hike up to the falls, and about

45 minutes to head back down. Our feet got wet at the river crossing near the falls. Remember that many of these rivers and streams are fed by melting snow or glaciers; that means that as the day gets warmer, the water flow will get stronger!

This was the hardest hike we tried, and my 6-year-old (almost 7) had a great sense of satisfaction when he got to sign the guest book. I should also note that we got a little lost. At some point, to your right you'll see a tourist sign with information about the falls. I thought this was just a lookout point, and we walked the other way. This turned into a much more difficult path up to the upper level; you don't want to do this. Go to the right, past the sign, and keep on going.

Fardagafoss

For a slightly easier hike, you can try Fardagafoss. If you learn nothing else from this book, you'll know that foss means

Litlanesfoss. on the way to Hengifoss.

waterfall, so of course this is yet another hike to a waterfall.

This wasn't on our list of things to do, but there are so many incredible waterfalls in Iceland that you simply can't get to them all. We've already skipped a couple of "must do" waterfalls, which I think is just fine. You truly can't see them all!

Another thing we learned is to not trust breezy Icelandic signs. The sign for Fardagafoss says it's a "relatively short hike" but "the slope can be a bit steep in places." And that "at the top of the path the hike becomes a bit more adventurous."

The first part is accurate enough, though the trail does go very close to the cliff's edge in places. Still, it took us about 25 minutes. But the part that is "a bit more adventurous" should be changed to "there's a chain that's anchored to the rock cliff, though one of the anchors is broken. Oh, and if you let go of the chain, you'll probably die." We quickly turned around at the edge of the waterfall; no chains for us. Even without using the chains, we got to write our names in the guestbook, and have a nice hike overall. I think this waterfall compares well to other better-known waterfalls in Iceland.

Google Maps again gets the location of Fardagafoss totally wrong. The GPS coordinates are 65.267778, -14.332500. You need to head a minute or so up 93, toward Seyðisfjörður, and the parking lot will be on your right. During the hike we had to cross some water and step through some mud, so be ready for that and bring hiking boots.

Superjeep Tours

There are several companies that offer Superjeep tours from Egilsstaðir. These are extremely expensive: You can pay

Hengifoss

Fardagafoss

It was a fun adventure that you can customize based on what you'd like to see. I can recommend the experience, but remember that it doesn't come cheap!

Miscellany: Swimming pool

Of course, Egilsstaðir has a thermal pool. Admission for one adult and 2 children cost just under $10- a great deal for 2 hours of entertainment. I didn't take any pictures, because sometimes that seems weird, but look for pictures at visitegilsstadir.is; click on "Things to Do."

Towns take great pride in their pools, and there are always lots of different pool options at lots of different temperatures. Does 36 Celsius sound good? Head to the children's pool (which anyone can use). 38? Try the cooler hot pot. 40? The warmer hot pot is for you. 4? Try the ice bath. Or maybe not!

Seyðisfjörður

Seyðisfjörður is a small town about half an hour each way off of Ring Road. It's not really on the way to anything else, so this adds an extra hour of driving to your trip.

And what a half hour that drive is, or at least can be. We're heading over a mountain pass. It's paved the whole way. But you're up high enough that, unless you're here in the middle of the summer, you need to watch the temperature signs. When you're driving, you'll see road signs with an LCD display.

$1,000 or more for a full day tour. But a full day can get you into the highlands in the summertime, which is difficult to do on your own.

We opted for a half day reindeer safari with jeeptours.is. Our guide Agnar had posted on Facebook for his friends in the area to notify him if they spotted any reindeer. A call came in when we were on our way. We drove to the general area, and Agnar spotted some with his binoculars. We spent a fair bit of time walking quietly to sneak closer and closer to a group of 4 male reindeer, though we ended up getting closer to them down the road in the jeep.

Their antlers fall off every year; right now, they have "felt" on the outside, which means they are both still growing, and also would feel soft and fuzzy!

We could have kept going around the lake and out to Snæfellsstofa, but we'd already been there. Instead, we opted to head up a steep dirt path just to try something different.

Weather warning signs

The sign pictured is not on the road to Seyðisfjörður, but all of the signs have the same general look. There are several pieces of information on the sign. But note that this is **not** the weather information for where you are right now; rather, it's the weather for a known dangerous spot up ahead. Generally this will be the highest point on the road within the next 10-20 miles. They provide the information before you get to that spot, in case you want to change your mind. The sign shows the wind speed and direction (from the North at 4 km/h) and the temperature (11 degrees Celsius.) There's also a spot for maximum wind gusts; in the picture, there are no significant gusts.

This is of course fine weather, though one can argue it's a little cold for June! But if the temperature is below freezing, you need to worry about snow or ice. And if there is a wind gust speed listed, and ESPECIALLY if it is in red, you need to think twice about continuing on. Talk to someone in the area

before you go any further.

Even at the end of May, there was a significant amount of snow on the sides of the roads. There were serious climbs, and then serious hills down where you need to use engine braking if at all possible. I loved the drive, but I'm not sure my family did. There are some tricky curves with speed limits of 30km/h, so take it slow!

But then you start winding around, heading down hill. And all of the sudden, Seyðisfjörður just appears before your eyes. It's like a mirage after the mountain pass, but it's real. You can be forgiven for thinking a place that looks like this doesn't really exist.

Seyðisfjörður was my favorite town in Iceland, though I really liked some other little towns in East and North Iceland. It could be because the tourist boom in Iceland hasn't really hit here yet, as most tourists don't make it out here. But Seyðisfjörður was welcoming, walkable, and just big enough to offer plenty of options for a stay of a day or two.

(Maybe it's not fair to say the tourist boom hasn't hit here, since as soon as one cruise ship left, another took its place.)

Pictured to the right is a huge white cruise ship behind the blue ferry terminal building. The ferry terminal doubles as the tourist Information Center. If you're on this side of town, walk or drive over and

pick up some brochures, or ask about activities.

If you're facing the ferry terminal, you can walk to your left to head toward the adorable main part of town. There's a walking path along the water.

On your left as you walk, you'll find a business that rents kayaks and bicycles. (The business is just called "Kayak Tours and Bicycle Rentals.") You can schedule a kayak trip for 1 hour all the way up to a full day, but for kids, the owner will also just do a short trip around the lagoon.

You'll pass a wool store that sells felted items, and then a hotel. Once you reach the other side of the lagoon, you'll be near several restaurants, and the grocery store too.

We opted for the very pricey Norð-austur Sushi and Bar, which is run by a chef from New York who now spends his summers in Seyðisfjörður. The food was very good—my kids really liked the salmon belly, which is raw fish served over a hot rock. The rock cooks the outside of the fish. It's fun, delicious, and incredibly expensive. I was surprised how much sushi cost, even given the price of food in Iceland. This was a fun splurge, but if I had it to do again, I would try a simpler option.

Technical Museum of East Iceland

We did have to drive to the Technical Museum of East Iceland, but it only took

2 minutes. They are officially opening for the season 2 days just after our visit (June 1st) but we got a sneak peek of this amazing museum. Note that they are now open year-round. I guess you can describe this as "several buildings with actual working machines from either a fairly long time ago or a really long time ago." Printing presses from the 1950s, a machine shop from the 1900s, Iceland's first telegraph from 1906, and more.

Not everything is working right now, but a lot of it does work, and the museum is very ambitious and very impressive.

The museum is (now) open year-round, though only on weekdays unless you make arrangements ahead of time. And the non-summer hours are only 1-4, so plan ahead if this is something you want to see. It costs 1,000 krona for adults, and free for kids under 18. That's a very fair price for a somewhat sprawling museum.

Tvísöngur

One of the main reasons I dragged my family out to Seyðisfjörður is to see Tvísöngur, a stone sculpture made of concrete domes that resonate in interesting ways. It's another minute or two down the road past the Technical Museum, though it's easy to miss. And once you're there you may not really trust that you're there. You'll see a small sign pointing to the parking lot. (GPS: 65.266853, -13.990268.)

You'll embark on a steep hike uphill, including a couple of water crossings. The water is shallow, but still slightly treacherous for little feet. And you can't really see your goal until you're almost on top of it.

So what is it? It's a sculpture of 5 domes that you can walk through. Supposedly, each of the 5 domes resonates at a different frequency, and those frequencies match up with notes from traditional Icelandic folk music.

The kids had a great time talking and singing inside of the domes; we had them to ourselves for much of the time. To me, this is a perfect activity for kids who are old enough to handle the walk; my 6-year-old had no trouble. You hike, you get to your destination, you sing(!) for a while and you head

back down. And the hike down was of course much easier than the trek up.

Note that there are a couple of the water crossings you will have to navigate. They aren't rivers, but really just melting snow running down the hill; during a different time of year, there may be very little water. Just be aware; I imagine little kids without high top hiking boots might end up with cold wet socks if they aren't careful.

One last Seyðisfjörður building bears a mention, which is the Skaftfell Gallery. This is over across the field from the ferry terminal, behind the gas station. The building houses a gallery space, which was hosting a somewhat "experimental" art installation while we were there. The kids liked wandering around for a few minutes, and you can't really go wrong since it's free. You'll also find a small gift shop upstairs. Downstairs is the restaurant Skaftfell Bistro, with an interesting selection of pizzas. You can get anything from a plain cheese pizza to one with reindeer meat as a topping!

Seyðisfjörður is out of the way, in a part of the country that's already somewhat remote. I liken it a little bit to the Westman Islands. If you have time to add it to your itinerary, I think it's a worthwhile and memorable detour.

Two more tips

These aren't necessarily specific to East Iceland, so read even if you aren't heading out east!

One lane bridges

We've mentioned one-lane bridges before (page 32), but are a LOT of one lane bridges in the south and the east. Watch out for this sign, slow down, and make sure you yield if a car coming the other way gets there first!

Using a GPS

First, for the first time, we had some GPS issues with Google Maps. The GPS tracking spent a fair bit of time thinking we were just to the left of the actual road. It made it so we missed a couple of turns, but it really just meant we had to pay a little more attention.

Northeast

Continuing counterclockwise, you'll leave the East province and head to the Northeast. I find this a little complicated, as I really consider this to be North Iceland. But there is no province called North-- just Northeast and Northwest. Still, let's consider this to be the North. Two tips:

Heading west toward Mývatn, there aren't many places to stop on the way. Bring some snacks!

One option between Egilsstaðir and Mývatn if you do need a stop is Möðrudalur farm, south on 901. This is about halfway through the drive, though you'll have to go about 5 miles each way on a gravel road. But you'll find a cozy restaurant here where you can get some soup and hot chocolate. It's supposedly a little pricey, but it might be worth it if you need a bathroom. Plus, you may get to see goats or even an arctic fox outside.

As usual, you'll have to decide with detours to take off of Ring Rd. Dettifoss is incredible, but it also adds substantial time to your tour. Mývatn and Akureyri are right on the main road, though.

Dettifoss

The one major site on the way to Mývatn is Dettifoss. This is not just another waterfall; it's the largest and most powerful waterfall in Europe. And ... we skipped it.

I'll give two excuses. First, just a few days before we were there, you simply couldn't get to the falls. Second, it's a major commitment to get to Dettifoss; this one isn't just planted by the side of the road. You actually have a choice of 2 different roads you can take. There is road 862, a newly paved road, or 864, an older gravel road that many people think provides a better view. (864 gives you the view you see in the movie Prometheus, if that's something you'd like to see.) Even the paved road will be an hour roundtrip from Ring Road, plus time to enjoy the views. Not to mention a hike to the other 2 nearby waterfalls.

That picture (below left) makes me think this might not be a

great place for kids anyway ...

So your options are the better view, but the bumpy gravel road, or the not as good view, but a paved road. We just skipped it; you too might be tired of amazing waterfalls by the time you get here!

Mývatn

If you're going to be in the north, you'll pass right through Mývatn. There's enough here to last you for a day or more: geothermal areas, hikes, and a natural spa. And everything is close to Ring Road.

Hverir

Our first stop was the geothermal area called Hverir; you may also hear this referred to as the Námafjall geothermal area.

Let's start right away with the most important thing: This place smells. I could tell you that it smells like sulfur, and you'd nod your head and move on. But this was more than sulfur; it was sulfur that permeates your nose, your lungs, and your clothes. The kids loved the area but hated the smell; we had to force them to walk around for more than a few minutes.

If your family can get past the smell, it's a wondrous place. Some of the steam shooting out of the ground makes a loud and powerful hissing noise; some are just bubbling cauldrons of hot mud.

The area is free, and it's right by the side of the road; you'll see it as you approach. It's not a big commitment, so try for a couple of minutes and see if you can handle the smell.

Krafla Power Plant

While we're in the area, you can head north for about 5 minutes and get to the Krafla power plant. There is a small visitor's center here; it's open in the summer only, from 10-5.

Drive straight past the power plant and you'll come to a parking area with hiking trails. We didn't do the hike, but it's not too bad of a journey to get to Viti, a volcanic crater:

Mývatn Nature Baths

My first reaction to the photo (above) is, "Hey, that water is a crazy blue color- just like the Blue Lagoon!" (page 169) My second reaction is, "Wait, does that mean it's also water from a power plant?"

And the answer is yes. I like that Mývatn is more open about this on their web site: "The water supplies for the lagoon run straight from the National Power Company´s bore hole in Bjarnarflag. The water has a temperature of about 130°C when it arrives to the huge basin beside the lagoon itself forming an impressive, man-made hot spring."

Based on the price of an adult ticket alone, I think the Mývatn Nature Baths are the second most expensive spa option in Iceland, behind only the Blue Lagoon. Prices vary based on the season:

	Adults	13-15	12 and under
October - April:	4200 ISK	1600 ISK	free
May -June:	4700	2000	free
July - September:	5000	2000	free

(Prices change every year; check myvatnnaturebaths.is for prices past 2018.)

Compare that to the Blue Lagoon summer prices: 54 Euros (minimum) for adults 14+ and free for kids 13 and under. As you can tell ... oh, right, the currencies are different. In dollars as of mid 2018, the Blue Lagoon is $63 for adults, and Mývatn is about $46 at the highest price. Also note that it's really hard to get those prices at the Blue Lagoon—you may have to book weeks in advance, or else you'll end up tacking on an extra 5 or 10 Euros as the cheapest tickets begin to sell out. (See page 169.)

You can also rent towels, but they cost extra. So what do you get for the money? Mostly, two large lagoons. The one you first enter (on the left) is warmer than the one on the right. This is a nice advantage over some other natural thermal spas like the Secret Lagoon (page 65), which we found to be too hot.

The kids spent most of their time in the cooler lagoon. Like most of the other spas, there's not a lot to do—the goal is to slowly wade around and just relax. There are also some steam baths, but they were too hot for us. The ground is natural, and is full of pebbles and rocks. Around the sides in some places, though, there are no rocks, and the ground is slippery.

We enjoyed Mývatn Nature Baths, though the kids wanted to make sure I noted the sulfur smell. This is nowhere near as bad as the smell at Hverir (page 98), but you'll notice it. We didn't really notice the smell at the Blue Lagoon; I think it's just a question of the sulfur content of the ground in that part of the country.

Inside, you'll find a small café. There are some healthy options, but they don't come cheap. There's a salad bar, which cost 2100 krona. You'll also find a couple of soup options, as well as a freezer with ice cream choices, chocolate bars, and other snacks.

If you're already doing the Blue Lagoon, I think you can skip Mývatn Nature Baths. You could stop for a snack (and bathrooms!) and look out over the water. If you do decide to do it, I think everyone will enjoy it. And if you're crazy like us and have a child under 2 with you, you may want to swim at Mývatn; The Blue Lagoon doesn't allow children under 2!

Sigurgeirs Bird Museum

This is a private collection of stuffed birds—the largest such collection in Iceland. The museum is in memory of a man names Sigurgeir; he started the collection, but tragically drowned in 1999. His family continued expanding the collection in his memory.

The setting for the museum is beautiful—it's right on the waters of Lake Mývatn. Outside of the buildings you may find some ducks hanging out. Inside the lobby of the main building, there's a telescope you can use to look out over the water.

The museum has two separate buildings. The first and main section is right off of the lobby. It's a circular room absolutely full of stuffed birds and eggs. Push a button and a light by the corresponding bird lights up to identify the bird. The second building, just a few seconds walk away, houses a boat that was once used to use to transport people across the water.

Back in the lobby you'll also find a couple of food options; ice cream for snacks, but some more filling food as well, including smoked char on rye bread. The museum costs 1,200 krona adults, 600 for kids 7-14, and free for 6 and under. Hours vary, but it is open year-round.

The bird collection offers an initial "wow" factor when you walk into the room, but it only kept our kids' interests for 10 minutes or so. This can be a good stop if someone in your family is very interested in birds, but it's not that great as a general interest museum. The setting is beautiful, though.

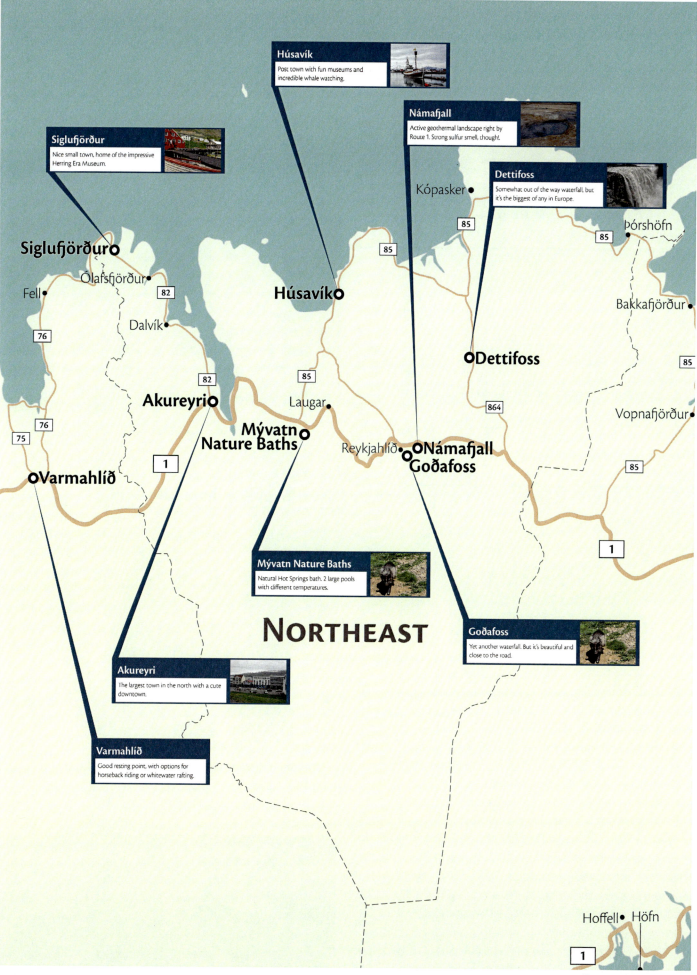

Húsavík

Post town with fun museums and incredible whale watching.

Siglufjörður

Nice small town, home of the impressive Herring Era Museum.

Námafjall

Active geothermal landscape right by Route 1. Strong sulfur smell, though!.

Dettifoss

Somewhat out of the way waterfall, but it's the biggest of any in Europe.

Kópasker •

ᵒSiglufjörður

Ólafsfjörður •

Fell •

`82`

`76`

Dalvík •

`82`

Akureyriᵒ

Laugar •

`85`

Mývatn Nature Baths

Natural Hot Springs bath. 2 large pools with different temperatures.

Húsavíkᵒ

`85`

`85`

`85`

Þórshöfn •

Bakkafjörður •

ᵒDettifoss

`85`

`864`

Vopnafjörður •

Mývatnᵒ
Nature Baths

Reykjahlíð•ᵒNámafjall
 Goðafoss

`85`

`1`

`1`

`76`

`75`

ᵒVarmahlíð

NORTHEAST

Goðafoss

Yet another waterfall. But it's beautiful and close to the road.

Akureyri

The largest town in the north with a cute downtown.

Varmahlíð

Good resting point, with options for horseback riding or whitewater rafting.

Hoffell • Höfn

`1`

Goðafoss

Goðafoss is another waterfall that happily falls into the category of "right by the side of the road." It's west of Mývatn, as you head on Ring Road toward Akureyri. This "Waterfall of the Gods" is a really nice waterfall. It's not going to be the biggest or the tallest or the loudest, but it's a nice example of an impressive Icelandic waterfall. But if you're heading counterclockwise around Iceland, you might be kind of tired of waterfalls at this point. I don't mean to diminish how nice Goðafoss is, but just know your kids might say "another waterfall?" There are some short paths you can walk on to get a better view; hold on to the hands of your little kids!

There's a lot we didn't cover in Mývatn; you could spend a couple of days here if the weather cooperates and you want to see more of the varied landscapes that Iceland offers. One thing we missed is Lofthellir Lava Cave, which is full of ice sculptures; you'll need to book a tour and allow a half day.

So you'll have to decide how much time this area warrants. If you're going to the Blue Lagoon, I think it's fine to skip Mývatn Nature Baths and explore the unique things you'll find in this area of Iceland.

Húsavík

I wish we'd spent more time in Akureyri, because I would have liked to visit all of the museums to write about them in more detail. I also wish we'd spent more time in Húsavík, but for a very different reason: I liked Húsavík. Not only was the whale watching the best we experienced, but there are some nice museum options, and it's all walkable.

But Húsavík is definitely out of the way. You'll have to make some decisions in this part of the country. Ring Road heads straight through the northern part of Iceland, and misses all of the fishing villages further north along the coast. We enjoyed Húsavík and Siglufjörður (page 107), but it's a non-trivial time commitment to get to either of them.

Húsavík is about a half hour north on Route 1, so it's an hour of extra driving. Or less if you take Road 87 up and Road 85 back down, since you end up skipping part of Ring Road.

Ystafell Transportation Museum

(Open summers only. Facebook: ystafellautomuseum)

On the way to Húsavík (or on the way back) you'll pass the Ystafell Transportation Museum on Road 85. You'll see a big truck on road advertising the museum. The museum houses a large collection of old cars and tractors. There are two buildings filled with vehicles—make sure you find the second one! And there are more old cars sitting outside in the parking lot. The kids didn't really appreciate this, and they only spent a few minutes walking around.

Ystafell costs 800 krona for anyone 12 and older; kids younger than that are fee. Most of the signs on the cars are in Icelandic, which makes it tough to spend a lot of time here. And the cars are really packed in, which seemed a bit overwhelming to me. But it's a cheap stop if you have young kids, and the owner seemed happy to share some stories.

The Húsavík Whale Museum

On to Húsavík. Our main reason for going was for a whale watching trip, but we squeezed in a couple of museums beforehand. But the whale watching trip can take up a good part of the day; we did a 4 hour tour, and you want to check in a half hour or so before that.

Our first stop in Húsavík proper was The Whale Museum. This seems like a good stop before a whale watching boat ride. I wish there was a package that gave you free admission to this museum with whale watching. Admission to The Húsavík Whale Museum is 1800 krona for adults, 500 for kids 10-18, and free under 10. There's also a family option that admits up to 2 adults and 5 kids for 4000 krona. That's pricey for what it is, but that doesn't mean your family won't enjoy it.

One main draw is a blue whale skeleton. It's over 75 FEET long, and seems to take up half the museum. But just seeing this may set your kids up to appreciate what they're hopefully about to see on the boat. Well, it's unlikely that they will see

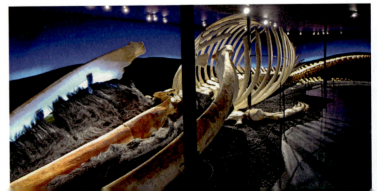

a blue whale, but the whales you can see are still huge: Humpback whales are common, and can be 40 feet long.

You can also see exhibits about smaller whales; some are skeletons and some are more lifelike representations. One potential downside is that the museum smells, well, fishy. I don't know if this is because of the bones, or because we're close to the water, but be aware.

In the back, there is a kid's play room, decorated as a yellow submarine.

The Exploration Museum

(Open June - September only. ExplorationMuseum.com)

Down the street and across from the N1 gas station is the Exploration Museum. The main focus of this museum was a surprise to us- apparently, Neil Armstrong and other Apollo astronauts came to Iceland in 1967 as part of their training for the moon landings?

Inside, there are three exploration themed rooms. One about the Vikings, one about ship navigation, and one about space exploration. The space room has memorabilia from the early days of the space program, including actual newspaper and magazine covers from the week when Neil Armstrong and his crew first landed on the moon.

This museum is pay what you want at the end of your visit. Open 10-3 M-F. Yes, they are closed on weekends!

Whale watching trip with North Sailing

Húsavík calls itself the whale watching capital of Iceland. Others who want to expand the title say it's the whale watching capital of the North, or of Europe, or even of the world. I can't advise you beyond Iceland, but I will grant it the title of whale watching capital of Iceland.

Be sure to see our section called "Whale Watching Tips and Tricks" on page 173 before you go whale watching!

We took a 4 hour whale watching trip with North Sailing (NorthSailing.is). Several other companies run whale watching out of Húsavík, including Gentle Giants, Salka, and Húsavík Adventures. Gentle Giants uses both traditional boats as well as smaller and faster RIB boats, and Húsavík Adventures only uses RIB boats. I recommend against the RIB boats; they are

A Húsavík humpback whale

less safe and less appropriate for smaller children. (See more in "Think About the Type of Boat" on page 174.)

You won't have a hugely different experience based on which company you choose. All of the boats from the different companies work together; if one sees a whale or a group of whales, they will share that information so as many visitors as possible can have a positive experience. With that said, we recommend North Sailing. The communication before our trip was great, the guides on board the ship were excellent, and the boat was quiet. If noise is a concern, you can e-mail North (info@northsailing.is) and ask when the new quiet electric boat Andvari is sailing.

We took a 4 hour Whales, Sails, and Puffins tour. It looks like this tour isn't offered right now, so you'll have to pick just one of the options, or none. (Whale watching only, Whales and Sails, or Whales and Puffins.) Most of the regular trips are 3 hours, though tours on the faster RIB boats can be shorter. A lot of that time is spent getting out to where the whales are. You may see some whales on the way out, or you may not. But plan for an hour of sailing out, an hour of whale watching, and an hour getting back. The companies do try to fill in some of the time, with education on the way out and some snacks (hot chocolate and some sort of pastry) on the way back. Still, there's a fair bit of down time.

"Puffin Island", as you might expect, is an island surrounded by thousands of birds. This helps to break up the trip out by making a stop on the way. If you're up for the longer ride, and you're here during the right time of year (May through mid

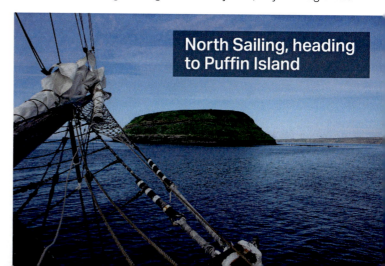

North Sailing, heading to Puffin Island

My son working the sails

August) this is a good option. And the addition of sailing is another option to help break up the trip back by getting out the sails on the way home.

I had two concerns about the trip. First, would one or more of the kids get seasick, and we'd have a miserable 4 hours? Second, what if there was only one brief whale sighting, and the kids missed it? That would also make for a miserable 4 hours, though definitely less miserable.

I think I have a pretty good handle on the seasickness issue. See page 173 to learn how to pick a day and time with low winds, and therefore low waves. Also check out our tips about Sea Bands and medicine to help with sea sickness. (Most companies will provide you with some sort of motion sickness pills, but I wouldn't trust that they have the correct dosage for your kids. Plan ahead and bring your own!)

As for my second concern, at first this is exactly what happened-- there was just a whale on the other side of the boat, and my kids missed it! But a while later, we were able to laugh those fears away, as our boat was surrounded by 3 or 4 different kinds of whales (several of each) and one would surface every few seconds! There must have been 20 or more whales to see. Apparently, whale watching in Húsavík has been particularly good the last few years.

I don't think this is common, and I don't want to oversell whale watching in Húsavík. In particular, if you're not circumnavigating Iceland on the Ring Road, I don't think a stop in Húsavík makes sense. But if you're passing by, the half hour detour to check out this cute town, and its impressive whale watching might be worth it.

North Sailing sponsored our tour. We only agreed to work with top-rated companies as sponsors, and all opinions are our own. (Check out North's excellent ratings on TripAdvisor!)

Akureyri

Akureyri, the largest town in Iceland that isn't either named Reykjavik or is close to Reykjavik. That makes this unofficial capital of the North a great place to stop on your journey and find lots of options for museums and restaurants and things to do. On the other hand, with a population of 17,000, Akureyri is a much smaller town than Reykjavik; while you will find some unique museums here, I don't think you'll find the overall "feel" of Akureyri memorably different than Reykjavik. But let's look around, and highlight some of the unique things you'll find here.

Downtown Akureyri

There is a nice little downtown area by the harbor. Our rental house was just a couple of blocks from the harbor, but everything slopes down toward the water. On a map, your 3 block walk to the main shopping area might look short, but it's going to be a downhill walk on the way, and a fairly steep hike back up home. This isn't a huge deal, but it can be a burden after a long day out.

You'll find a typical assortment of restaurants and shops on a couple of blocks in the main downtown area. The kid's liked the troll statues outside of one of the larger gift shops in town; the locals will identify you as a tourist when you take selfies here, but this seems like a fair trade. There's an impressive concert hall, called the Hof Cultural and Conference Center, a block or so away from the shopping area. There's a nice tourist information center in Hof, along with small displays from a few of the museums in town. Up the hill (and up a whole lot of steps) is an impressive church called Akureyrarkirkja. (Kirka means church—another useful Icelandic word!) If it's open, you can walk in and take a look at the beautiful stained glass windows, and see if anyone is playing the pipe organ up above.

Museums in Akureyri

Akureyri calls itself "A town of museums," and there are a lot of them given the size of the town. If you plan to visit several of them, there is an Akureyri Museum pass that covers 5 of the museums in town. There are more museums in town, and we'll cover those in a minute, but let's start with the ones that are operated by the city of Akureyri and covered by the pass. The museums are only open in the summer, so only consider these if you'll be in town between June 1 and mid-September. Check the web site minjasafnid.is for the exact dates and times; click on the British Flag at the top left to switch to English. I wouldn't be surprised if they begin to offer limited but regular hours outside of summer.

You'll pay 2000 krona for adults for a pass to all 5 museums, and nothing for kids under 18. This is a day pass, so you'd need to visit all of the museums in one day. But each museum

Sights in Akureyri (Clockwise from the top:)
A view down the hill to the harborfront shopping area
The trolls in that same downtown area
The Akureyri Museum of Aviation
A view up the steps to the church
The impressive town swimming pool (one of two!)
Akureyri harbor, viewed from near Hof cultural center

by itself costs 1200 krona, so you're saving money with your second museum. You should be able to buy the pass in the first museum you visit. The 5 museums are:

The Akureyri Museum

(June 1 – September 16). A few minutes south of town, and close to several other non-city museums (The Industry Museum and the Motorcycle Museum are down this way, and the Aviation Museum is further down this road.) You'll find lots of typical themes here for an Icelandic Museum: Viking relics, and folk items from the Akureyri area.

But there's also a unique exhibit called "Are you ready, Madam President?" It's about Vigdís Finnbogadóttir, who served as Iceland's 4th president (from 1980 – 1996), and was the first democratically elected female president in the world. We didn't make it to this museum; reviews online say that it is small, but well thought out.

The Old Turfhouse Laufás

(June 1 – September 12)

I would say this barely qualifies as being in Akureyri; it's a 25 minute drive out of town. It's paved the whole way, and it's only about 10 minutes out of the way if you're heading up to Húsavík.

The turf house dates from the 1840s. This was a rectory built to house the priest who oversaw the nearby church. As you enter, you walk into a very long and narrow house that definitely feels old—dark and damp and full of dirt. I don't mean dirty, but rather dirt floors. You walk straight back from room to room; an English brochure will help you understand what room you are in. The rooms keep coming as you keep walking and walking. You don't need to visit every turf-roofed building in Iceland, but this one is a nice example.

You'll find a nice gift shop in the main building, with some hand knitted hats. The kids enjoyed a piece of rhubarb cake, a welcome snack before the drive back.

Nonni's House

(June 1 – September 1) 1200 krona for adults.

In my opinion, the next 3 museums on the list are less appealing, and only worth a visit if you bought the museum pass and want to get more value out of it. You've already saved some money by visiting the first 2 museums, so these could be worth a quick stop.

Nonni's house is a minute's drive from the Akureyri

Museum. A Jesuit priest named Jón Sveinsson grew up here; he was called Nonni. I'd put this in the category of folk museum—you'll see a typical example of an Icelandic house and its furnishings during the 19th century.

Davíðshús - Davíðs Stefánsson Museum

(June 1 – August 31) 900 krona for adults.

The home of a poet; he lived here until his death in 1964. You'll find an impressive library (impressive for a private home), along with an apartment where present-day artists can live.. The house is in a quieter part of town, which could be walkable based on where you are. The address is 6 Bjarkarstígur.

Sigurhæðir - Matthías Jochumsson Museum

(June 1 – August 31) 1200 krona for adults.

This museum is right in the heart of downtown Akureyri- it's just down the hill from the church Akureyrarkirkja. Matthías wrote the Icelandic National Anthem, and this house / museum rents out space to artists and writers.

Beyond the Akureyri City Museums, you'll find even more choices:

Icelandic Aviation Museum

(June 1 – September 30)

The Icelandic Aviation Museum, which proudly portrays the history of aviation in Iceland, and displays a lot of historical airplanes. The museum is housed in a hangar that is adjacent to the Akureyri airport. The admission fee is 1500 krona for anyone 12 and older. flugsafn.is (See picture on prior page.)

On the left hand side is an exhibit about a British airplane that crashed in a remote part of Iceland in 1941. The plane was lost to history, until the founder of this museum went out and recovered it almost 60 years later.

Let me warn you that this is not a happy rescue story. For more details, look online for a story titled "WW2 crew recovered from their ice tomb." But it is a story about a guy who likes aviation who decided to go try to find the plane, and he found it when no one else had. You'll see some actual pieces of the plane, as well as maps of the location of the crash. The exhibit is mostly in Icelandic, but if you're lucky the founder himself will walk you through the exhibit.

The rest of the museum is airplanes. You can walk into a couple of them, but most of them you just walk around and look at. I think this can be hit or miss for kids; if they're into it, you may spend hours here as you look at every plane. If not, they may be done after 10 minutes. There's a very small gift shop area up front.

Akureyri Art Museum

Back in the heart of the town, and easily walkable from the downtown area, is the Akureyri Art Museum, or the Listasafnið á Akureyri. It had an exhibit on architecture in Akureyri, including information about a few buildings which we saw later that day. But the exhibits rotate.

Admission is 1000 krona. I would probably skip this unless a current exhibit listed on their web site catches your interest: listak.is. Otherwise, there are several art galleries in town you can walk around in and browse for free, especially with older kids.

Botanical Gardens

(June 1 – September 30)

A roughly 10 minute walk out of town will take you to the Akureyri Botanical Gardens. While it's only "open" in the summer, you can walk through here year-round. There is a café that will only be open in the summer; here you'll find wonderful, though expensive, hot chocolate.

Industry Museum

(June 1 – September 14, plus Saturdays in the off season)

Back out on what I'll call museum row, you'll find the Industry Museum in Akureyri. You'll find this one between the Akureyri Museum and the Aviation Museum. I'll let my daughter describe this one: "They had a lot of cool machines, like a sock-knitter and a candy machine."

You wind through section after section of ... stuff. Old computers. Machine for making and repairing shoes. Old typewriters. Old cell phones. Lots of machines for packaging and producing food, complete with displays of containers of said foods. Old clocks.

The web site is idnadarsafnid.is, though it's only in Icelandic. Admission is 1000 krona for adults, and free for kids 17 and under. I think the museum is well priced for it size. Many Icelandic museums seem to feature collections of old stuff, and I think the Industry Museum is a good example of that. There's no cohesive theme, but some of the individual displays that show a particular machine are very well done.

Swimming in Akureyri

Every town in Iceland has a thermal swimming pool. And I don't think this is an exaggeration—swimming is popular, and the power to heat those pools is cheap. You should definitely visit a thermal pool while you're in Iceland. (See page 85.)

Akureyri has two thermal pools, and I highly recommend the main one, called simply Akureyri Thermal Pool. The address is Þingvallastræti 21; this was just a few minute walk from our rental house, and walkable from downtown. (The other pool is Glerárlaug Thermal Pool, which features an indoor pool. You'll have to drive about 10 minutes to get to it, but this could be a good option if you're not up for an outdoor pool.)

But the Akureyri Thermal Pool features something I only saw in one other place, and that's the most expensive place to swim in Iceland: The Blue Lagoon. (See page 169.) There is a very small indoor area; I guess you could call it an indoor pool. The sole purpose of this area is to allow you to get into the warm water before you go outside into the cold air. Then you go through a door that leads outside—you avoid the cold walk to and from the outdoor pool!

(The glass walled area in the middle of the picture is the indoor entrance to the outdoor pool.)

This is one of the bigger swimming complexes you will find in Iceland. My criteria for that is the number of lap pools. Akureyri has 2 lap pools—one warm and one not quite as warm. You'll also find waterslides, hot tubs, and steam rooms.

From the swimming area, you can walk to an area with miniature golf and a large chess board. You can also get to this area without going through the pool. There's a small booth at the entrance where you can pay for miniature golf, or buy some snacks.

The pool is open every day of the year, except for the two Icelandic national holidays: May 1st (May Day) and June 17th (Icelandic National Day). Yes, even in the middle of winter, you can (and should!) swim here.

There's more to see in Akureyri, including the famous ice cream store Brynja. If you decide to spend some time exploring Akureyri, I think it's time well spent. And if you decide to drive straight through, well, I think that's okay too!

Siglufjörður Fjord

Siglufjörður is the northernmost town in Iceland. Diversion alert: All of the towns mentioned in this section are on the Siglufjörður Fjord; covering them means about an extra hour and a half of driving, and then skipping some of Ring Road. On the journey, you'll pass through the towns of Dalvik and Ólafsfjörður (before Siglufjörður), and Hofsós (after Siglufjörður.)

By Ólafsfjörður, you'll come across some serious tunnels. The first is a one lane tunnel that is over 2 miles long. Let that sink in for a second. One side will have pull-off areas; if you see a car coming and those pull-off areas are on your side, pull over and let them pass. If those lanes are on the other side, you can assume that the other person will pull over, but beware of tourists who don't know what's going on.

If the light is red at the entrance to this tunnel, pull over until it turns green. Also, rarely you may come across a large truck that is too big to pull into the pull-over areas. In this case, you'll need to cross the to the pull-over areas on the other side. Happily, we crossed the tunnel several times and didn't have to worry about anything in this paragraph.

Past Ólafsfjörður you'll get to two tunnels that total 6.8 miles. Fortunately, these are 2 lane tunnels. These tunnels were just completed in 2011, and make the journey to Siglufjörður a much more viable option.

Let's take the towns in order as you come from Akureyri.

Dalvik

Dalvik is another small town along the coastline. Population: 1,400 or so. In a town that size, you can expect the usual: A folk museum, a handful of restaurants, a nice thermal swimming pool, and some outdoor guided tour options. Oh, and really nice views over the water. We visited the folk museum and tried another whale watching tour.

Hvoll Folk Museum

(A reasonable 700 krona for adults, and free for kids. Every day in summer; may only be open Saturdays in winter.)

The Dalvík Folk Museum is called Hvoll. Here you'll find a typical assortment of old artifacts from life in this area, throughout several rooms. There is also a room with a nice assortment of stuffed birds, and a room dedicated to an earthquake that struck this area in 1934.

One unique section is dedicated to Iceland's Tallest Man. By the entrance to the museum, there's a cutout that shows how tall Jóhann K. Pétursson really was; it's fun for everyone in the family to compare their height to his (7 feet, 8 inches!)

The section of the museum dedicated to him shows some of his actual clothing, which the kids enjoyed. Stand next to a pair of his shoes and again make the comparison between your feet and his.

Whale Watching with Arctic Sea Tours

Given how much we liked our whale watching trip in Húsavík, we decided to try again in Dalvik with Arctic Sea Tours (arcticseatours.is). In Húsavík (page 102), I talked about how the whale watching companies tried to fill in the travel time to and from the whale watching area of the day; you can add in puffin watching or sailing.

One the way out from Dalvik, we had a nice view of Hrísey island, the second largest island in Iceland, behind Heimaey on the Westman Islands.

And on the way back, we went fishing! Everyone gets a fishing pole. If your child is lucky enough to catch a fish they may need help reeling it in- you're sending your fishing line to the bottom of the water, and it's a fair bit of work to get it back up.

We didn't catch anything, but others did. The fish were processed on board, and the parts we weren't going to eat were thrown back in the ocean. This attracted a fair number of birds, and so we also had a few minutes of bird-watching.

And we got to try some freshly caught Icelandic cod once we got back to shore. My youngest son, who is not a big fan of fish, though it was excellent. And I agreed; it well well-grilled and well-seasoned. And we got to see the process from start

to finish, which was a treat.

I skipped the most important part- whale watching. This trip was also a success, as we saw several humpback whales. One tip we've learned is that you typically see the fluke (tail) when the whale is going down for a deep dive, which can last several minutes. So you most likely won't see that whale again for a little while.

We enjoyed this trip, but it made us appreciate the Húsavík one even more. I think some of this is luck. If you're going to or passing through Dalvik, this is a fine option. But Húsavík offers many more whale watching companies and many more options.

Siglufjörður : the Herring Era Museum

(May through September, sild.is)

Besides being a lovely Icelandic town, the main draw in Siglufjörður is the Herring Era Museum. This is an impressive place-- 3 huge buildings housing ships, tools, and information about herring fishing and processing in this area.

Apparently, herring migrate in a rather unpredictable fashion, and they left north Iceland in the 1960s, taking the herring industry with them. Some of the herring migrated to East Iceland, and so that part of the country now has a herring industry. This explains where the name of the museum comes from: The Herring Era was an era of expansion and prosperity in Siglufjörður, but that era ended in 1968 or so.

The museum costs 1500 krona for anyone 16 and older, and is free for younger kids. For that, you get a very cohesive museum. That's been one of my complaints about folk / heritage museums in Iceland: Some are just a collection of old stuff. Here you get three buildings, each with a theme: One covers the history of the herring era and herring migration. One has a large herring boat and shows some of the tools used. And the third is a now inactive processing plant you can walk through. It's a lot of information about herring, but it's also more than that, since you start to imagine the fortunes of a town rising and falling with the herring population.

If you're up this way, visit the Herring Era Museum.

Folk Music Museum

(June - August) Some of the kids walked over to the Folk Music Museum (folkmusik.is) in town. Admission is 800 krona for adults, but this almost doesn't matter- your ticket from the Herring Era Museum gets you free admission here.

The museum is fairly small—it looks like any other house in town. The best part for the kids was getting to play an Icelandic fiðla, a two stringed instrument.

Hofsós pool

(Year round.) We skipped this. But on your way out of Siglufjörður, you'll pass by Hofsós if you're heading west. If you've been following along, you'll know that a small town in Iceland means a thermal swimming pool. This one is special because the thermal outdoor pool is an almost infinity pool right on the ocean. So you get a beautiful view of the possibly-snow-covered mountains and the cold ocean from your warm pool. The pool was designed by the same architect who designed the Blue Lagoon. You won't find any waterslides, but the kids should still have a good time. And for 700 krona for adults, 300 for kids 7-18 and free for under 3, it's a cheap outing. Check it out if you have time and you're up for another thermal pool.

Siglufjörður. The buildings in front are part of the Herring Era Museum.

Varmahlíð

We're back down on Ring Road and heading west. Varmahlíð is the next "town" you will come to. This isn't really even a town—there's a gas station at the main intersection with a restaurant and a grocery store in it, but everything else is spread out. We spent the day here enjoying a couple of adventures: Horseback riding and whitewater rafting.

Hestasport horseback riding

(April – October for the short ride we did)

Our first stop was Hestasport, whose web address is quite fitting: riding.is. They have some rental cottages you can stay at, including some that would work for larger families. But for the most part, they do horseback riding. Hestasport offers tours as short as an hour, which is what we did, up to 8 day adventures. Even though we didn't come close to a longer trip like that, it was nice to know we were getting an authentic experience with a knowledgeable company.

The hour long ride was called "Pleasure in Every Hoofstep." After a short tutorial where the kids learned how to ride, we were on our way. The guides tried to match the kids' experience level to the horses. A beginning rider will get a horse that has no interest in going fast, and will usually just follow the horse in front of it; a more experienced rider will get a horse that responds better to feedback from the rider. It's a peaceful walk through the quiet Icelandic countryside, including a shallow water crossing. Toward the end, you will have the option to try a tölt. This is a gait that is unique to the Icelandic horse. It's a faster pace than a walk, but it's still smooth for the rider. (See more on page 175.)

Kids as young as 6 can do this ride; longer rides may require kids to be at least 10. Everyone enjoyed the ride, and we recommend it. You can find many places to ride Icelandic horses, and you don't need to make a special trip out here to ride. But Hestasport seems like a top-notch company. (See more horse riding options on page 175.)

Note that the building you first go to is not where the ride leaves from; you need to drive from the office to the stables. Be sure to arrive 15 minutes or more before your scheduled ride time.

Viking rafting

(May – mid-September)

I don't think most people associate Iceland with whitewater rafting. But this is unique whitewater rafting, fed from melting glacier water. Yes, the river you raft down is the runoff from a melting glacier! First and foremost, that means it's cold—just a few degrees above freezing.

Viking Rafting (vikingrafting.is) offers a few rafting trips. We opted to try out their "Family Rafting" trip; they also offer a more adventurous "Whitewater Action" trip, as well as a 3-day trip. The family rafting trip was more than enough for us, or at least right at our limit. But if you have kids, this is a moot point; kids as young as 6 can go on the Family Rafting trip, while the Whitewater Action trip is only for adults 18 and older.

Because of the cold water, there's a fair bit of work to get ready. We wore wool baselayers (that we came wearing) and to put on top of that we were given dry suits, gloves, and rubber shoes. The shoes are mostly to protect the dry suit from getting ruined by walking directly on the suit itself.

My 6-year-old had some minor issues with the dry suit. It needs to be tight around the neck to keep water out, but he had some gaps. The guide tried to tape it up, but ended up getting some of his long hair in it. Eventually, he agreed that he didn't want to swim (more on this in a minute) and so he was allowed to go without the tape.

After we suited up, a bus took us to the start of the trip. There we got a pretty intense safety lecture; one part of this was training us to paddle (the guide tells the right and left sides of the boat to paddle or not, or paddle backwards) and the other part was telling us what to do if we fell out of the boat (don't panic.) This was a little scary, though if you pay attention, there seems to be little risk of falling out. But the guide WILL tell you to dive into the middle of the boat if we are approaching a fierce section; you and your kids need to listen and react!

The journey starts off at a gentle pace, and then the short bursts of rapids begin. There are a few activities during the journey. First, you stop at a specific point and have hot chocolate. Even though you're paddling through freezing cold water, there is a hot spring off to the side; grab a cup full of naturally heated hot chocolate. (The water is a little sulfury, but the chocolate covers it up.)

Next, you have the option to jump off of a 15-foot-high cliff into the water below. My kids had no interest in this, but I'm a fan of the picture of me making the leap (at right).

Toward the end, you have the option to hop out of the boat and hold on to the side as it glides down a quiet portion of the river. This is much less scary than the leap, and some of my kids had fun with this one.

The trip was a lot of fun, and it's an exciting adventure, especially if everyone in your family can participate. There's a lot of preparation, though; getting dressed and undressed and taking the bus takes up a lot of time.

You can enjoy free hot chocolate back in the office. You can also prepay for a dinner after your afternoon trip. But you don't know what you're going to get, as the chef just makes one meal every day. It looked like a good value for a lot of food, but not if your kids won't eat it. Finally, you can pay for a USB drive with pictures of your trip. This option seems very expensive to me ($40.) But it is nice to have the digital pictures; this is a better value than buying a few prints at a ride at Disney World, and you get a USB drive. (Use it to back up pictures from your camera! And be sure to back up the pictures that came on the USB stick too.)

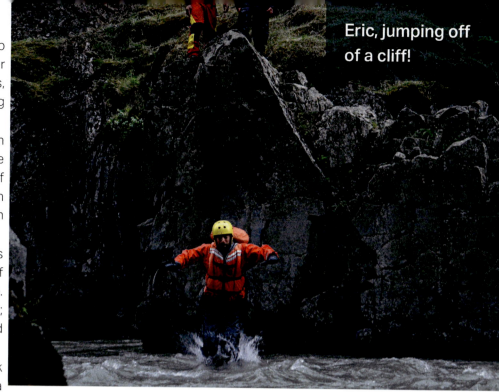

Eric, jumping off of a cliff!

Glaumbær

(April – mid-October)

After a day of horseback riding and whitewater rafting, Glaumbær (glaumbaer.is) was closed before we could go visit. This is a turfhouse farm; many of the buildings look similar to Laufas (page 101). But there are 13 structures to explore here.

Admission is 1600 krona for adults, and free for kids under 18. This lets you explore most of the area, except for the church. The church is open from June through August, and costs an additional 1000 krona for adults. There is also a café on the property, which is open from February through September.

Viking rafting

Hvammstangi

Heading west from Varmahlíð, we're starting to get into the area which doesn't have many things to see. We made a couple of stops along Ring Road, in and around the town of Hvammstangi.

Kolugljúfur

About 10 minutes out of your way, you can find Kolugljúfur waterfall. Unless you're on a mission to see as many waterfalls as possible, you'll have to pick and choose which ones to see. This one was very nice, but there are no food or bathroom options nearby.

Once you turn off of Ring Road, it's a slightly muddy ride down a gravel / dirt road; I got one of my favorite pictures of a gang of sheep blocking the bridge (see picture on page 41). But once you get to the waterfall and its small parking area, you're overlooking a beautiful lush green valley with a waterfall rushing through it.

There are some walking trails you can use to go along the side of the canyon. There's no fence here, though, so be careful with the kids. There wasn't anyone else here while we visited, which made this stop remote and exciting.

Icelandic Seal Center in Hvammstangi

(Open all year)

20 or so minutes past Kolugljúfur you'll come to the town of Hvammstangi. Actually, the town is north on Road 72 a few miles.

At the edge of the harbor, you'll find the Icelandic Seal Center (selasetur.is). This is a working research center that doubles as a museum. The highlight for us was a 30 minute movie in a small theater. The movie showed a seal pup being born, as well as lots of other adorable seal footage. You'll also find a display with some seals and birds, an old boat, and a small kid's section. Surprisingly, there is also a small area where you can peruse academic research papers the Center has written about seals and their environment.

Admission fees are 1100 krona for adults, 750 for kids 12-16, and free under 12. If you think your kids will like (and sit for) the movie, this can be worthwhile. If not, it's a pretty small museum and you may not spend much time here.

Seal Watching boat tours

(May 15 – September 30)

A separate (though maybe affiliated?) company runs seal watching boat tours. Note that these boat tours only run May through September, while the museum is open year round. You can book tickets for the boat tour in the museum. The day we were there, the boat tours were not running because the water was too rough.

The company is just called The Sealwatching company; sealwatching.is. The 1 hour and 45 minute trip costs 7000 krona for adults, 3500 for kids 7-15, and free for kids 6 and younger. This seems like a scaled down version of a whale watching trip—you'll go on an oak-paneled boat that looks smaller than the whale watching versions, have a shorter trip, but still get hot chocolate and pastries. Tours run at 10:00 AM, 1:00 PM, and 5:00 PM.

But unlike with seeing whales, you don't need to boat ride to see seals. Seals mostly hang out on rocks by the shore. We didn't take the time to look for them around Hvammstangi, but the people behind the desk at the museum can give you a map and information about the common spots where you might find some seals. The boat ride does make this more of an adventure, and I assume the guides will know exactly where to go for the best views that day.

Food in Hvammstangi

From the Icelandic Seal Center, you can walk to the upscale restaurant Sjavarborg. This can be a good option if you have some time to kill waiting for the seal watching boat.

We opted for the grocery store that was part of the same

building that housed the restaurant. So again, it's a quick walk from the Seal Center. The acronym name for the supermarket is KVH; like most grocery stores outside of Reykjavik, the hours are limited. It may close as early as 6 PM many nights.

Kidka Wool Store

(year round)

On the way back in or out of town, you'll find the Kidka Wool Factory Store (kidka.com.) It's actually on the street a block closer to the ocean; turn right at the Orkan station to find Kidka. Kidka's wool products are made in Iceland, and in fact are made in this building. But they are not hand-knit, and are instead made by sewing machines.

This isn't good or bad, though purists may argue these are not traditional Icelandic products. Kidka claims their fabric ends up "softer and fluffier" than those that are traditionally hand-knit. If you're in the area, check out the store and see what you think; you'll also find their products sold in several stores in Reykjavik.

Next up are two more attractions as you continue heading west. The first is right off Route 1, but the second is not; Eiríksstaðir makes more sense if you're heading to Snæfellsnes or the Westfjords.

Folk museum Byggðasafn Húnvetninga- og Strandamanna

(Summer only)

West of Hvammstangi and back on Ring road, you'll soon come to another folk museum, called Byggðasafn Húnvetninga og Strandamanna.

Byggðasafn is a word you'll see around. Safn is museum. I think the true definition of the word is "regional museum" but you can be pretty sure you'll be getting a folk museum. You don't need to visit all of these. Here you'll find a big boat, and old tractor, and lots of old farm equipment, including a wool making machine. As my kids said: "Cool artifacts, but small." Adults cost 1200 krona, and all kids should be free. There is a café there, so this makes a good stop for some food and/ or bathrooms.

Eiríksstaðir Museum

(June – August)

Eiríksstaðir (leif.is), is a museum housed on the site of the longhouse residence of Erik the Red and Leif the Lucky. This is about 15 minutes outside of the town of Búðardalur, which we'll cover as we head to the Westfjords (page 114). The road at the end is gravel, but it wasn't too bad going slowly.

I'm not sure it makes sense to call this a museum. It's more of a ... live performance? in a turf house. And the house is a replica of the house that used to be here a thousand years ago, or at least an educated guess of what it looked like.

A "Viking" tells stories and teaches you the history of this family around a fire inside the house. It was a slow day, and so we had the house to ourselves for about half an hour. Once the door is closed, it definitely feels like a different world.

At the end, there was time to try on some Viking helmets, and try out some swords and shields. This is a little more expensive than other museums in Iceland-- it's 1250 krona for anyone over 12, free for kids 12 and under. But it's also unique.

When we arrived, there was a group already in the longhouse. We were offered the opportunity to join them, or wait for our own private visit. We opted to wait, and hung out on the small but interesting gift shop building; there are also bathrooms nearby you can use if you are paying to see the longhouse. Had it been a busier day, we may not have been able to wait to have the house to ourselves.

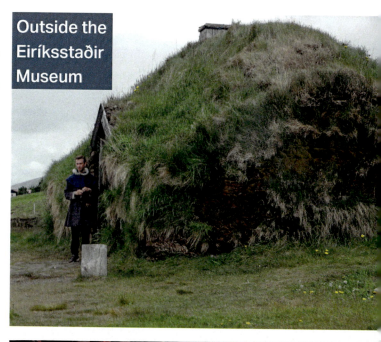

Outside the Eiríksstaðir Museum

And inside the Eiríksstaðir Museum

Westfjords

We're now only about 2 hours from Reykjavik if we follow Ring Road back down. But that cuts off two major parts of the country: the Westfjords and the Snæfellsnes peninsula. While the Westfjords was one of my favorite parts of the country, this is a major commitment. Ísafjörður, the largest town in the Westfjords, is over a 4 hour drive off of Ring Road. Each way. We'll be heading off of Ring Road here and heading up to the Westfjords; if you want to skip that part, catch up with us on page 121.

The Westfjords are left off of most tours of Iceland; data from the Icelandic Tourist Board shows that fewer than 1 in 5 visitors spend a night up here. It's easy to skip: if you follow Ring Road around Iceland, you'll end up missing the Westfjords. And, there's a lot of driving to get anywhere. Beautiful driving, but still driving.

But there are great stops along the way. Your kids may enjoy the Icelandic Museum of Witchcraft and Sorcery (page 116), or the Sheep Farming Museum (with a day camp!) And the town of Ísafjörður rewards you with a less touristy feel, beautiful walkable streets, and the best value in a restaurant for families we have ever seen. (If you make it up here, you may consider eating every lunch and dinner at Tjöruhúsið.)

The western portion of the Westfjords has some of the worst roads in the country. We skipped this area, though the Latrabjarg Bird Cliffs may be worth it if you're up for a bumpy ride.

A few things to think about. First, if you're going in winter, I think it's easiest to just skip the Westfjords. You could try it of course, but that 4 hour drive is likely to take longer than 4 hours; you'll spend a lot of time driving. And road conditions can be worse here than in the rest of the country; be sure to check road.is daily.

Second, there are sections of the Westfjords that are on some pretty bumpy roads. The Látrabjarg bird cliffs are a famous spot, and Google Maps will certainly show you a way to get there. This takes 4 and a half hours, and it's not on the way to Ísafjörður. If you want both Ísafjörður and the bird cliffs, it's 7 ½ hours. But the time to Látrabjarg is going to include some rough roads. You know it's bad when even the Icelanders say it's bad. From the organization Visit Westfjords:

"To visit attractions such as Látrabjarg, Rauðasandur and Norðurfjörður you will have to brave some gravel roads, but they are open for all types of cars throughout the summer."

We skipped this western portion of the Westfjords, sticking instead to the east side up to Ísafjörður. (I've joked that maybe this book should be called "Iceland on Paved Roads," as that was a major goal with a 4-month-old baby!)

If you're like us and have a strong preference for nice smooth pavement, you may want to invest in a printed map of Iceland. You can buy one in the airport (try the bookstore Penninn Eymundsson before you exit the secure area, or the 10/11 convenience store after), or just about any gas station or bookstore in the country. Or buy one before you leave: search Amazon.com for "Iceland Travel Reference Map."

I'll give you one hint about paved roads now: You can make it to Ísafjörður on only paved roads. You need to take Road 1 (Ring Road) to Road 60 to Road 61. Most mapping sites will not recommend this way—they will cut off some distance by cutting across Road 59 or going up Road 68. You might (or might not) save some time on the gravel roads, but it wasn't worth it to us.

A domestic flight?

One final thought before we move on. For something very different, you could fly one way to Ísafjörður and rent a car and drive back. Flights on Air Iceland Connect (airicelandconnect.com) to Ísafjörður are not as cheap as the used to be. But still, a family of 2 adults and 2 kids under 12 could fly one way for a TOTAL of about $350 if your dates are flexible. The car rental company Holdur / Europcar (holdur.is) offers one-way rentals from Ísafjörður back to Reykjavik. See a little bit more detail on page 57.

Búðardalur

We'll start in the town of Búðardalur. You can argue that this is at the very end of the Snæfellsnes Peninsula, but we're going to use it as our gateway into the Westfjords.

Services

This is a good place to get some gas and supplies; things will start to get a little sparser as we head north. There's an N1 gas station and a Samkaup Strax grocery store; the Strax brand is the smallest type of grocery store chain you'll find in Iceland. It's better than a convenience store, but it's not going to have a vast selection. Hours are also limited, though this location offers later hours; they are open until at least 8 PM every day of the week.

There are also a couple of restaurant options; we got takeout pizza and hamburgers from Guesthouse Dalakot. It's just a minute off of the main road; head down the side road right across from the grocery store and gas station. You should see signs. At the end of that road and off to the right is the Leifsbúð Café. It sounds like a good option, and it's attached to a tourist information center. But it was closed when we were there (late).

Finally, right next to the gas station there is also a restaurant called Veidistadurinn, which also receives positive reviews. These are all good options in a small town.

Note that the Eiríksstaðir Museum (page 112) is only about 20 minutes from Búðardalur.

Laugar in Saelingsdal

We spent a night in a small area called Laugar in Saelingsdal. There's a Hotel Edda here, a small folk museum, a swimming pool (of course!) and apparently a natural hot pot. We had a nice enough stay, but this isn't an area you need to necessarily come to; the closest grocery store is still back at Búðardalur!

Natural Hot Pots

The natural hot pot is a fun option, and you will find many more of them throughout the country. It's made from natural water. The most important thing to know about truly natural hot pots is that they are SLIPPERY. Every rock surface will have a layer of natural algae on it, whether you can see it or not. If you or one of your children gets in without thinking about it, it's very easy to slip. Remember this for any natural bathing area.

This hot pot (pictured below) is called Guðrúnarlaug, named after a Viking Guðrún who lived here a thousand years ago and bathed in these waters. There's a small changing shed you can use. You'll have to hike a couple of minutes up the hill from the parking area, but using the hot pot is free. Oh, and you may end up with small pieces of algae on your body.

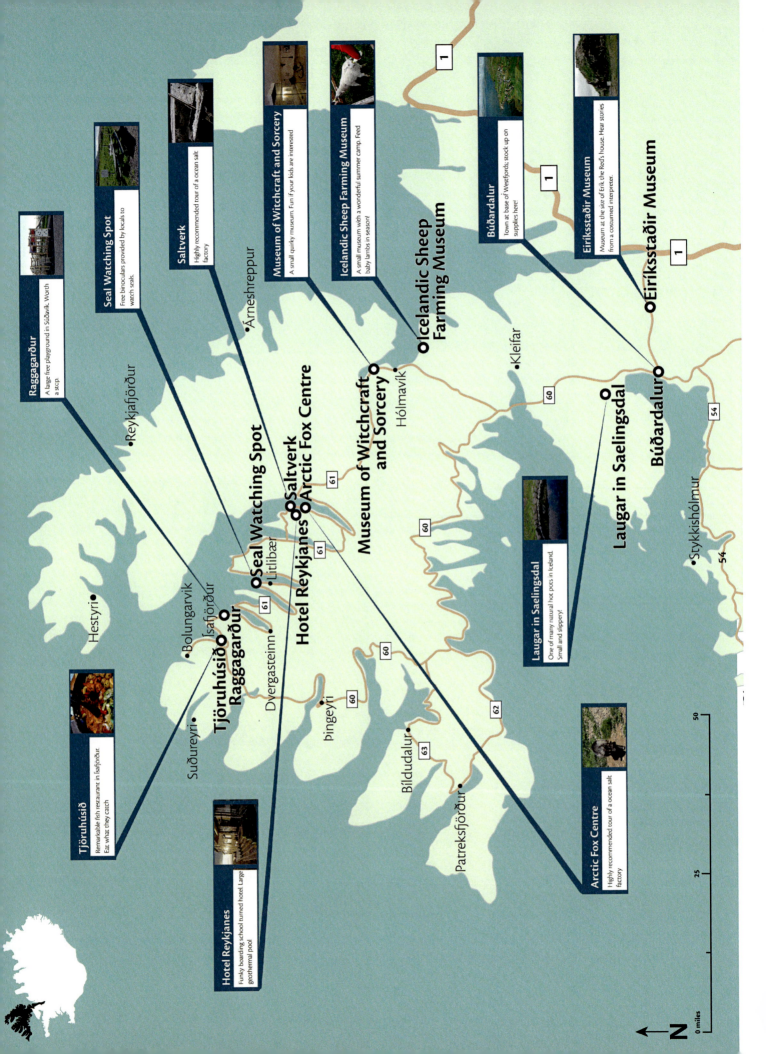

Hólmavík

The next town of any size you will come to is Hólmavík.

Icelandic Sheep Farming Museum

(Summer only)

Just south of Hólmavík is the Icelandic Sheep Farming Museum (search online for Saudfjarsetur.) It's tough to find—as you head north on Road 61, turn right on Road 68; drive a few miles and you'll see it on your left. GPS coordinates are: 65.640833, -21.583611.

They have a lot of nice information about the Icelandic sheep; the displays are all in Icelandic, but they have English versions in binders that you can carry around. The main draw may be the opportunity to bottle feed a little baby lamb; the lambs weren't at the museum yet when we were there, as it was a little early in the year; you may want to check with the museum before heading over.

The museum costs 800 krona for 13 and over. There is a nice café up a few stairs from the main museum. Without the lambs, this may not be worth it, though the museum does cram a lot of information into a small space.

The Icelandic Sheep Farming Museum does offer a rather unique opportunity, and that is a day camp. Now, I realize that this seems kind of crazy at first; sending your kids to a day camp while you're on vacation? But before you dismiss it, read my son's description of their afternoon:

"The day camp was four hours long. We first went down to the beach and found a lot of shells and bones. A little while down the beach, we walked to an island that we could only get to when the tide was low. On the island, there were a lot of Eider duck nests. Eider duck nests are made out of down that is really soft. After that, we walked to a line of bird nests, and most of them had eggs in them. A little while later, we found a baby duck that's mom had just left, so we got to see it up close without the baby's mom trying to get us away from the baby. After we left the baby duck, we went into an old building and the person who was leading us told us a ghost story. After she finished the ghost story, we walked

back and had hot dogs. After we finished eating, we started playing games outside. A little while later, it started raining so we had to go inside. We played a few more games, and then we went out and fed two lambs with bottles of warm milk."

(The camp was a few days later than our first visit, and the lambs had arrived!)

We sent all 4 of our kids (well, besides the baby), ages 7-14. So they got to spend the afternoon together. The Icelandic children who also attended the camp were very welcoming; my guess is they switched to speaking primarily in English without even really thinking about it. The museum says the camp is appropriate for children 6-14.

The cost for the afternoon (1 PM – 5 PM) was 3000 krona, and that includes a snack. The adults in your family could head up to Hólmavík for a late lunch without the kids. I think this is a unique and memorable opportunity if you're up this way in the summertime.

Contact the museum for more information about the camp or other events. I found them very responsive on Facebook: facebook.com/saudfjarsetur .

Icelandic Museum of Witchcraft and Sorcery

(Year round)

Up in Hólmavík proper you will find the Icelandic Museum of Witchcraft and Sorcery. This was a fairly small exhibit, detailing the history of magic and spells in Iceland. The kids very much enjoyed it; again, there was an English version of the exhibit information you could carry around.

I wasn't a huge fan of this museum. Its two medium-sized rooms house models of various items used in potions, or as part of magic spells. I guess you could see it as a folklore museum. One of the items is a recreated pair of "necropants."

Folklore claims that if you take the skin of a dead man from the waist down, put a coin in the skin (I won't tell you where) and wear the pants, you'll become rich. You can kind of see the pants in the background of the picture (bottom right of previous page). If you think your kids will follow along and think this is cool, it might be a good stop. It's not overly expensive: 950 krona for adults, and free for kids 15 and younger. There's a restaurant in the main lobby area as well.

Other services in Hólmavík

Don't let the population of Hólmavík fool you (maybe 400-500 people): you'll find plenty in the town. There are two gas stations, including an N1, a small grocery store, and several restaurants. Since the population is very sparse up here, Hólmavík serves as a hub for the area.

We ate lunch at Café Riis, which is right across the street from the Museum of Witchcraft and Sorcery. So right in this area you have the choice of the restaurant in the museum or Café Riis. The meal was expensive, but the food was good.

Hotel Reykjanes

The name of the Reykjanes Hotel (reykjaneswestfjords.is/) confuses me, since to me Reykjanes is the peninsula where Keflavik and the airport are (page 161). But this is a hotel in an area of the Westfjords where you will find few hotels. And they have 2 and 3 bedroom apartments, so this is a place that can hold your whole family comfortably.

If you're not staying here, this can still be a good stopping point. There's a restaurant, though you can also just buy ice cream and snacks at the check-in desk. There is also a stunning geothermally heated swimming pool. Apparently this is Iceland's longest swimming pool and also the country's largest hot pot. They meant to make is 50 meters long, but they made a mistake and made it a few inches longer.

The temperature in the pool varies depending where you are, and so most people can find a spot that is a temperature of their liking. It was very relaxing, and, unlike some other natural geothermal pools, not slimy at all!

Saltverk

Behind the Reykjanes hotel is the Saltverk factory. It's probably best to drive there, though we walked about 5 minutes from the hotel. Founded 5 years ago, Saltverk has revived a 17th century process to extract salt from the ocean using geothermal energy. This process results in a "flaky" salt. When we got there, we weren't sure we'd really found it, as all you see is a handmade wooden sign that says Saltverk.

We had asked them for a tour of the facility. You'll want to set this up ahead of time, to make sure someone will be there. Send them a message on Facebook (facebook.com/saltverk)

We started by looking at vats of ocean water that were being evaporated to higher and higher salt concentrations. Ocean water starts off around 2-3% salt. Once it gets to be around 10 times more concentrated than that, you can harvest the salt from it. The interesting part of the Saltverk

The pool at Hotel Reykjanes. See a picture of the hotel on page 18.

Seal Watching Spot

As you wind your way around the fjords, you'll see a sign with a picture of seals. This is a place where seals like to hang out, and you may be able to spot them. Look for the picnic table. There the locals have kindly left binoculars in a plastic container that you can borrow for some seal watching. GPS coordinates are 65.994167, -22.816944 .

operation is that they are using geothermal heat to help speed up the process of evaporating the water.

They don't boil the water, because they claim that hurts the taste of the salt. This is a seriously impressive operation. Once we got to the pools of highly concentrated salt, we got a demonstration of how the salt is harvested, by putting a rake like tool in and getting the salt out.

This salt is then dried on racks, and then it can be flavored (or not), packaged, and sold. At the end of the tour, you'll have an opportunity to purchase salt in their little shop room. You will also find Saltverk salt for sale throughout Iceland, but it's fun to buy it directly from the factory.

This was a true factory tour, where you are seeing the actual production process. It involves climbing ladders to see evaporation rooms that are something like 110 degrees Fahrenheit, and wearing shoe covers and hair nets once you get to the final product. It's a very cool experience, and free.

Recommended and memorable.

I didn't realize until later that I had captured the sheep walking down the road in the far background of the picture above; they passed us a couple of minutes later on their journey south. Be careful when driving! (See page 41.) For a better picture of those same sheep, see this book's front cover!

Inside the binocular container, you may also find jars of jelly for sale; it's an honor system, so leave some cash if you'd like to buy some jelly! Finally, as a sign above the table indicates, a little further south on the road there is a historic turf roof house where they serve coffee, waffles, and some other desserts.

When we were there at the seal watching spot, we were easily able to see a couple of seals. They are somewhat far away, and it took the kids a minute to spot their heads bobbing out of the water. But it's worth a quick stop since it's right next to the road.

Súðavík

About 20 minutes from our destination of Ísafjörður, you'll come to the smaller town of Súðavík. There's food and gas if you need it, though you'll have many more options once you get to Ísafjörður. But there are a couple of interesting places to check out here.

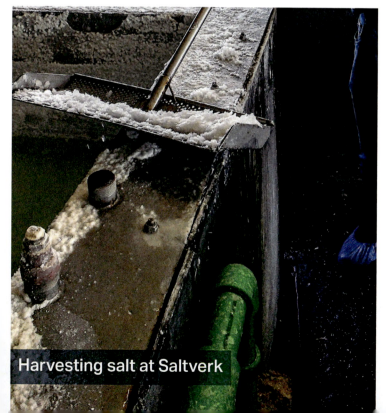

Harvesting salt at Saltverk

An Artcic Fox at the Súðavík Arctic Fox Center

Súðavík Arctic Fox Center

(open year round)

The only museum in Súðavík is a unique one: the Arctic Fox Center (melrakki.is). They have a couple of rooms with exhibits and a video about the arctic fox. You'll see several stuffed foxes, some hanging pelts, and information about the foxes in Iceland.

But the main draw is the 2 foxes they have in a cage out back, which were found by hunters as babies (and without a mother). Admission is 1200 krona for anyone 15 and older, and free for kids 14 and under. There is a small café as well, with drinks, cakes, a vegetable soup, and a fish stew.

Raggagarður

(Summer only)

This is an amazing playground. (See picture below.) There's a zipline, plus several different playgrounds. And it's all free, so it's a great stop on a road without all that many places to stop. You'll see a point of interest sign from the main road which says Raggagarður; turn left and you'll see the park.

While you're up here, you may see a memorial. There was an avalanche in 1995 from that steep mountain behind you. Today, the government only allows people to be in this part of the town from May through October.

Ísafjörður

Ísafjörður is the largest town in the Westfjords (population: 2,600). As you can tell by the population, the title "largest town in the Westfjords" doesn't mean it's a huge town. But Ísafjörður is full of shops, bakeries, and cafes. There's a walkable downtown area, beautiful views, and the best food we had in Iceland. Surprise!

See all of the pictures from Ísafjörður on the next page.

Gamla Bakaríð

We started our day with a nice breakfast of pastries from Gamla Bakaríð, a lovely little bakery. At the end of our day, we went back to get some rolls for snacks later on. The servers were very nice, there were dozens of different pastries to choose from, and they were all good (at least the ones we tried).

Westfjord Heritage Museum

(open year-round)

The Westfjord Heritage Museum seems to also be called the Westfjord Maritime Museum. The museum is on 3 floors, and had a nice selection of displays about fishing, and, strangely, accordions. They also had a very detailed movie about life as a fisherman, which our whole family found surprisingly riveting.

Admission is 1000 krona for adults. The sign in Icelandic says the museum is free for kids "in primary school", which I guess would be up to about age 12? Hopefully this is a little flexible, given that the sign doesn't list a specific age.

There's still a lot of the traditional Icelandic folk museum pattern here: Lots of random old stuff in a building. But this is one of the better examples of one, and the price to stuff ratio is very good.

Tjöruhúsið - My favorite restaurant in Iceland

Open (very) roughly April through October.

Next door to the museum is the restaurant Tjöruhúsið, where we went for lunch. This was both the best and the least expensive meal we had in Iceland. That's a pretty amazing combination-- best AND cheapest. Kids under 14 eat free!

We had to wait about 15 minutes before lunch service started, presumably because they are bringing in today's catch from just down the street. At lunch they bring you huge pans of fish, straight from the kitchen. It's tough to convey how large these pans are, but try to get a picture of your kids' eyes when they put the pan on the table.

The dinner buffet is 6000 krona for everyone over 14; that includes soup and several entrées. Lunch cost varies based on which fish they catch, and so you won't really know how much it will cost until you get there. But the range is 1500

Ísafjörður, by Gamla Bakaríð

The amazing food at Tjöruhúsið

Westfjord Heritage Museum

Westfjord Heritage Museum

to 3500 krona. We ended up paying 1500 krona per adult, and all of the kids ate for free. So that was 3000 krona total. Paying less than $30 for 6 people (plus a baby) for one of the best meals we've ever had-- it feels very close to stealing.

Various reviews claim that Gamla Bakaríð is the best bakery in Iceland, and that Tjöruhúsið is the best fish restaurant in Iceland. We thought both were excellent; Tjöruhúsið is a ridiculous value if you have kids. And both are in small but impressive Ísafjörður.

Beyond Ísafjörður

We turned around after Ísafjörður and headed back. There is more past here, if you have both the time and the interest. Be sure to read up on the three-way tunnel you'll need to handle. (Yes, a tunnel with a junction!) Head up to Bolungarvík to see the well-regarded swimming complex and the Ósvör museum, where the curator dresses as a traditional Icelandic fisherman. Bolungarvík is about 20 minutes past Ísafjörður.

West Iceland

In West Iceland, we'll focus mostly on the Snæfellsnes Peninsula. Once again, you'll have to venture off of Ring Road if you want to see it. We're also close to Reykjavik now—a 2½ hour drive from Reykjavik gets you close to the end of the peninsula.

Actually, that 2½ hours gets you to the coastal towns of Arnarstapi and Hellnar. There's a magnificent hike between them that was a highlight for us. Just past that is Snæfellsjökull National Park, with a lava cave hike, a black pebble beach, and much more. If you're looking to venture outside of Reykjavik but limit your driving time, either Snæfellsnes or the south coast (page 69) are good choices.

Although West Iceland is known for the Snaefellsnes Peninsula, let's start with a few other attractions before heading to the Peninsula.

Into the Glacier

Into the Glacier (IntoTheGlacier.is) lets you do exactly what's the name says: go into a glacier. This attraction just opened up a few years ago, in June of 2015. As far as I can tell, a bunch of smart and motivated people decided to drill / mine a tunnel into a glacier, and then take tourists there. But because the ice is always shifting, and more snow is always falling, eventually the caves will collapse. So in ... 10 years? ... Into the Glacier will no longer exist.

Into the Glacier isn't really close to anything. It's a 2 hour drive from Reykjavik, and it seems to be a 2 hour drive from just about anywhere. You have the option to drive all the way to their office, called Klaki Base Camp, or take a shuttle for the last 20 minutes of the ride (for an extra 2000 krona per adult). Take the shuttle. Why take the shuttle?

The drive to Klaki Base Camp is along road 550. The company says on their web site that 550 is a "rough gravel road ONLY suitable for 4X4 vehicles. Please use the shuttle from Húsafell if you do not have a 4X4 vehicle." More importantly, there was literally a sticker inside our rental car with this information on it; I think most car companies have a similar sticker. "This car is not allowed for highland driving (F Roads) Kaldidalur (550) or Kjölur (35)."

If you drive on 550, and have a problem, they will fine you 2000 Euros. Yikes. So we stopped at Hótel Húsafell and took the shuttle to Klaki base camp. That means we started on a large bus and then transferred to the glacier shuttles.

There were so many people on our tour that we ended up on the little brother of the main 8-wheeled glacier vehicles. The ride up to the tunnel opening is fairly rough, and we slid around quite a bit. Maybe this is because we were on the smaller truck? But eventually we made it to the tunnel.

They give you crampons to put over your shoes, and you spend about an hour walking around the various rooms that have been created in the glacier. Because you're inside a glacier, the temperature is at freezing, or slightly above. There's no wind, so it doesn't feel too bad. But make sure you dress warmly, even though you may be too hot on the ride to and from the glacier.

Then it was back down the hill (with sliding again) and back to the other shuttle to our car. Is it worth it? It was nice that everyone in the family could participate, since kids or babies of any age are allowed. But it was a lot of travel, and you're not really seeing "natural" glacier formations. I think I preferred the glacier walk we did with Arcanum better (page 70), though that's only for ages 10 and up.

Hótel Húsafell and the buildings around it offer bathrooms, a small convenience store, and a restaurant. It's a nice option to get some food before or after your glacier visit. Behind the building (past the restrooms) there is a little play area for the kids. There is an old tractor they can climb on and a tire swing, and some see saws. (See picture below.)

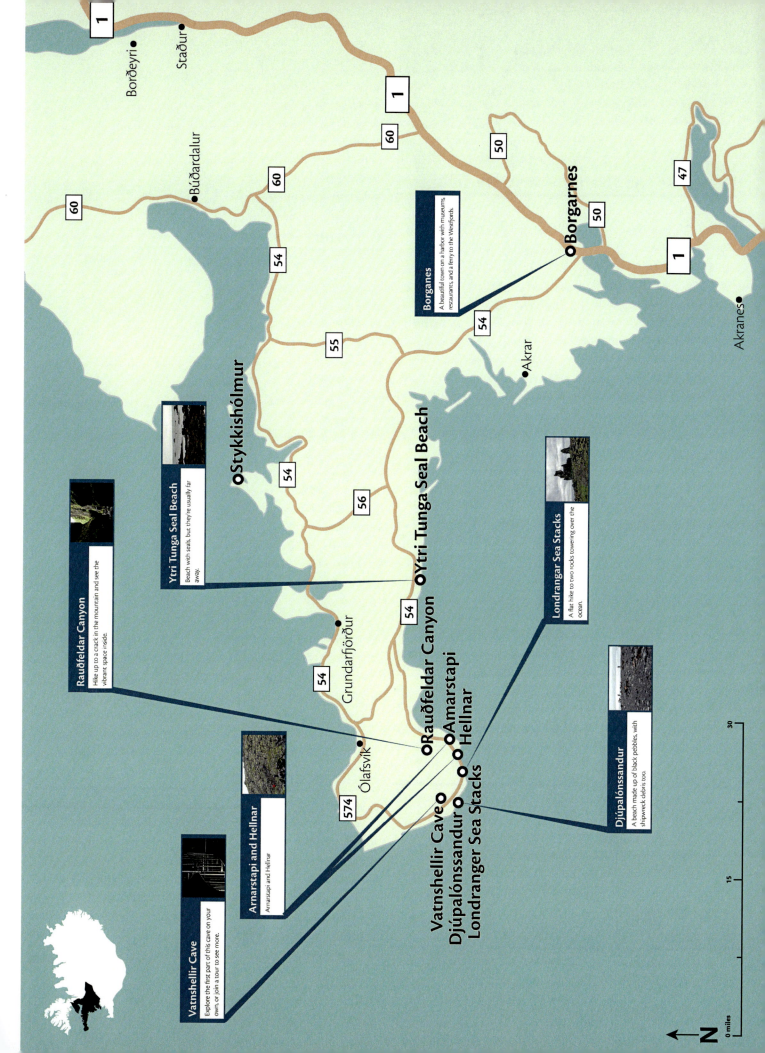

1

Borðeyri●

Staður●

1

60

50

Búðardalur●

60

47

60

54

Borgarnes

Borganes
A beautiful town on a harbor with museums, restaurants, and a ferry to the Westfjords.

50

1

55

54

Akrar●

Akranes●

Stykkishólmur

Ytri Tunga Seal Beach
Beach with seals, but they're usually far away.

54

Rauðfeldar Canyon
Hike up to a crack in the mountain and see the vibrant space inside.

56

○Ytri Tunga Seal Beach

Grundarfjörður●

54

54

○Rauðfeldar Canyon
○Arnarstapi
○Hellnar

Londranger Sea Stacks
A flat hike to two rocks towering over the ocean.

Ólafsvík●

574

Arnarstapi and Hellnar
Arnarstapi and Hellnar

Vatnshellir Cave○
Djúpalónssandur○
Londranger Sea Stacks

Djúpalónssandur
A beach made up of black pebbles, with shipwreck debris too.

Vatnshellir Cave
Explore the first part of this cave on your own, or join a tour to see more.

N

0 miles   15   30

Barnafoss and Hraunfossar Waterfalls

Close by Húsafell is the waterfall Barnafoss; you'll see a parking area on your right maybe 5 minutes after you leave Hotel Húsafell. There were nice flat gravel paths to walk on and explore. Before getting to the main falls, and right next to the parking lot, you get a beautiful view of a waterfall called Hraunfossar (above). This is different from most of the other waterfalls we have seen: water seems to gently cascade down the lava rocks in dozens of different places. It's a nice view, given that you barely have to get out of the car to see it.

Then just a minute or two down the path comes Barnafoss. I feel like I didn't capture it well in my pictures, but the water is falling through an arch in the middle. It was an easy walk to a nice waterfall, given that we were already in the area!

Reykholt

As you continue heading back from Barnafoss on Road 518, you'll come to the town of Reykholt. There are several pairs of towns in Iceland that share the same name (see page 39). But I think the two Reykholts is the most confusing one. Look on TripAdvisor for things to do in Reykholt and you'll get a mixture of things from both towns—two hours away from each other!

This Reykholt (GPS coordinates 64.664906, -21.292241) has a statue of Snorri Sturluson, a famous Icelandic politician and poet from the 1200s. There's also a small hot pot here, which supposedly has been there since Snorri's time; it's called Snorralaug.

The OTHER Reykholt, which is in the Golden Circle area, has Iceland Riverjet, a company that runs boat rides. See our experience there ("Iceland Riverjet" on page 66).

Deildartunguhver

We didn't stop here, but if you're heading this way, at the end of Road 518, you'll come to Deildartunguhver. This is a geothermal area where steam is erupting from the ground. Supposedly it has the highest flow of hot water / steam of any hot spring in Europe. This can be worth a quick stop if you're up for it. Note that you will most likely experience a strong sulfur smell!

Borgarnes

You may end up in Borgarnes coming or going from several different places. It's on Ring Road just an hour north of Reykjavik. It's also where Ring Road meets Road 54, which is a major road into the Snæfellsnes peninsula (and THE major road coming from Reykjavik.)

If you are heading to the Snæfellsnes Peninsula, Borgarnes is a good place to stop for gas and groceries. Maybe I should word that more strongly: stop here for gas and groceries before you head into Snæfellsnes. You'll find some grocery stores in towns on the north side of the peninsula, but there's very little on the southern side. The Bonus and Netto grocery stores in Borgarnes are going to seem like a wonderland of food once you get back on Road 54 heading west.

Borganes Museum

(Daily May - August; weekday afternoons otherwise)

If you have more time to spend in town, there are a couple of museums. First we came to the Borgarnes Museum in the library. The main exhibit is called "Children Throughout a Century", which tells the story of childhood in Iceland through photographs. (See picture at right.)

But, some of the photographs double as doors, revealing an item behind the wall. There are dozens of pictures that open, and it was fun for the kids to spot them and see what was hidden behind. The text is in Icelandic, but a guidebook you can borrow provides an English translation. You have the option of a few other languages as well.

In addition, after you walk through a dark hallway to symbolize the lack of electricity, you can see a recreation of an old cottage. And, if none of that interests you, you can check out the crazy mirrored room of birds. (It's not nearly as big as it looks, since the walls are mirrors!

This museum was much more unique than many other folk / heritage museums we have been to. At 1000 krona per adult and free for kids under 18, I think it's a worthwhile family stop.

Settlement Center

(year-round)

Half a block down the road is the much more famous Settlement Center. Here there are two exhibits-- one about the first settlers in Iceland, and one about the Sagas, the narratives based on historical events in Iceland. For each, you weave your way through a well-designed exhibit, paced by a digital audio guide. Numbers along the walls and rooms keep you looking at the right thing.

Each exhibit uses a different headset; in between you can take a break, or even have a snack in the café upstairs.

The start of Snæfellsjökull National Park on the Snæfellsnes Peninsula

There's no way to fast forward the audio guide, so you're there for half an hour at each exhibit. They are both very well done, but also very, very detailed. Are the kids bored when the audio guide starts talking about which person settled in which place, or what they named each of the rivers? Well, your options are limited.

The kids enjoyed the saga story more. This can be a great museum; just know what you are getting into. Admission is 2500 krona anyone 15 and older, and free otherwise. That covers both exhibits and the audio guides. Dare I say that for the price of one adult at the Settlement Center you can get the whole family into the Borgarnes Museum exhibit? That would be my choice, especially for younger kids.

Snæfellsnes Peninsula

We toured the southern part of the Snæfellsnes peninsula, which is where many people head for day or overnight trips from Reykjavik. It's a fair bit of effort to get there- you're driving about 2 hours from Reykjavik before you get to any of the points of interest we're going to list here. But once you get there, there's a lot to see within a half hour drive. Let's go in the order you'll come to things.

Ytri Tunga Seal Beach

First was Ytri Tunga, otherwise known as seal beach. And we did see seals, but they are really far away. I had to zoom in on the camera to make sure we were really seeing seals. Given that we had already seen seals that were a little bit closer in the Westfjords ("Seal Watching Spot" on page 118), we didn't stay for very long. But it's a lovely area.

Rauðfeldar Canyon

This is a good example of what the Snæfellsnes Peninsula is like. We weren't planning to stop here, but we saw a sign for an attraction, and a fair number of cars parked. It didn't look like much from the road-- just an interesting looking rock formation with a gap in the middle.

After a 10 minute or so hike (uphill!), it turns out this is more than a crack- it's an opening into a secluded area with an otherworldly feel. (See picture below.) It's open on top, and so the lighting is good. Note that you have to carefully step across the shallow river in order to get in.

Arnarstapi and Hellnar

This may be the most famous attraction on the peninsula, or at least on the south side. You'll first come to the town

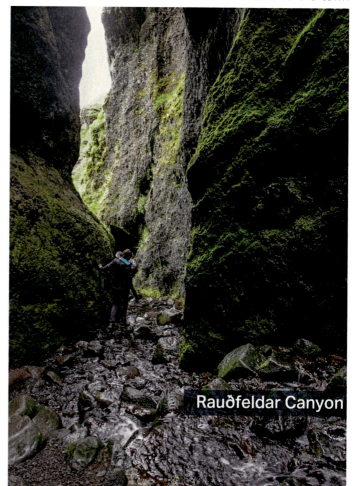

Rauðfeldar Canyon

of Arnarstapi, which has ... well, not much. There are some summer homes, and a hotel, and not much else. We stayed in Arnarstapi; fortunately, we had stocked up on food in Borgarnes! But this is the start of a great hike that is perfect for the slightly adventurous family. Arnarstapi also features a huge stone statue that marks the start of the trail- it's supposed to represent Bardur Snaefellsas (a man); it's tall enough to walk through. The trail is not too long, it's only slightly challenging, but it's beautiful. The hike takes about 35 minutes each way. You'll walk through lava fields, and get to gaze over rock formations jutting out of the ocean below.

You'll end up in the next town over: Hellnar. Hellnar has a little more to offer, including a restaurant that's right at the end of the walking path, Fjöruhúsið Café. Lots of people were sitting outside enjoying the view. Food was expensive, but you can always opt for desserts or smaller items, including hot chocolate and waffles.

Down the hill toward the water, there is a beach area with a cave. We let the kids play down there for a while, and we stayed up at the café. It made for a nice destination at the end of the hike before heading back.

Londrangar Sea Stacks

The last 3 attractions listed here are inside of Snæfellsjökull National Park. The picture at the top of page 124 is the start of the park, and you can see the Londrangar Sea Stacks off to the left. This is another place that we hadn't planned to see, but it turned into another nice hike. From a distance (and from the right angle), it looks like a natural castle. But it's two separate rocks towering up over the water.

Icelandic folklore says that elves live in this area, and that in fact these two rock formations are ancient trolls! The alternate story is that this was a large volcanic crater; this rock was inside it and much denser than the earth surrounding it. When that land eroded, we were left with these rocks.

It's about a 15-20 minute hike each way to the base of the rocks. It's flat more or less, except for right by the parking lot. Make sure you turn around to see where you came from— you won't be able to see your car until you're almost back.

Djúpalónssandur

You may have seen one or more black sand beaches in your travels. This is a slightly different take on that theme. It's not a black sand beach, but rather a black PEBBLE beach. Like Reynisfjara on the south coast (page 73), the waves here are unpredictable, and can be dangerous. Stay embarrassingly far away from the water. Perhaps as evidence of the power of the water, the beach has the scattered remains of a ship that crashed ashore here in 1948. 14 of the 19 people aboard didn't survive. Look, but don't touch the wreckage!

It's a hike down from the parking lot, about 300 meters with

a bunch of steps. There are also longer hiking trails marked, which we skipped.

Vatnshellir Cave

(year round)

Vatnshellir Cave is an 8,000 year-old lava cave; a few years ago Summit Adventure Guides started offering guided tours. If you stop without wanting to take a tour, there is a little area of the cave you can see. (Very little.) But access to the cave itself is through a spiral staircase that is locked at the top. (See picture below.)

The 45 minute tour is offered on the hour several times per day; hours vary with the season, so check their web site (SummitGuides.is). I think the price is a little expensive for adults, but extremely cheap for kids: 3,750 krona for adults 18 and older; 1,500 krona for ages 12-17, and free for 5-11. $10 or so for teenagers and free for younger kids is an excellent deal.

Kids under 5 are not allowed; the minimum age was raised from 3 to 5 in 2017. You'll have to decide if this tour works for your kids between 5 and 7 or so. Younger kids will be able to handle the walk just fine, though they need to be able to use the provided flashlight to guide their way. But one part of the tour might be an issue. I'll let my son explain:

"A while into the cave, our guide told us to turn off our flashlights. Once we did, it was so dark that you couldn't see anything, and no matter how long we stood there, our eyes didn't adjust, because there was no light in the cave."

Otherwise, a guide walks you through the cave to explore all sorts of colored rock formations. 45 minutes seems like a nice length. It's long enough to let you get pretty far into the cave, but short enough that your kids shouldn't have much time to be bored.

The hike from Arnarstapi to Hellnar. Fjöruhúsið Café is at the left, and the trail goes off in the distance from there.

Four smaller pictures, clockwise from middle left: Another shot of the hike from Arnarstapi and Hellnar; Djúpalónssandur black pebble beach; Djúpalónssandur again with part of the shipwreck visible; Londrangar Sea Stacks as seen partway through the hike.

Reykjavik: Downtown

Our Reykjavik coverage could almost be a book by itself. You won't run out of things to do here: You could spend weeks exploring the dozens of museums, boat and walking tours, the concert hall, thermal pools, and restaurants.

But you shouldn't: Make sure you get out and explore the country! Still, take a day or two to explore the options in the Capital of Iceland. Work in time for whale watching (page 132) if you won't be heading to North Iceland. Walk along the shopping streets of Laugavegur (page 140) or Skólavörðustígur (page 141). Head to the top of Hallgrímskirkja (page 141), the famous landmark church. Try an Icelandic hot dog (page 138), or maybe fish and chips(page 135). And leave time for a thermal pool ("Laugardalslaug" on page 150, though there are many other options; see page 85 and page 134.) The Blue Lagoon near Keflavik is remarkable (page 169), but a city pool is a much less expensive experience not to miss.

We'll cover everything you need for a multi-day stop in Reykjavik. For more, see our web site: IcelandWithKids.com. Or e-mail us for advice: Eric@IcelandWithKids.com. Let's start with the walkable downtown area, from west to east.

Grandi Harbor

Grandi Harbor is an area most people didn't talk about much up until a few years ago. It's seen a resurgence in the last few years, and most of the attractions we're listing here haven't been here long. For example, the Saga Museum moved here a couple of years ago, and Omnom Chocolate just moved here in 2016!

Saga Museum

The Saga Museum used to be in the Perlan (page 153), but it's now in its new home by the harbor. All of the sculptures and backgrounds were moved and are set up in the same configuration. Similar to the Settlement Center in Borgarnes (page 123), admission includes an audio guide, which walks you through the numbered exhibits.

It takes about half an hour. The stories are lively, and kept the kids' interest for most of the time, though there were a few brief periods where they got a little bored. But then

something recaptured their interest; look for the Viking figure that actually moves. It's very subtle!

This is one of the more expensive museums in Iceland; Admission is 2200 krona for adults, and 800 krona for "children"; I was told that means kids 6-12. Under 6 should be free. Very few museums would cost much more.

But, my kids really enjoyed it. The audio guide ensures that they will take their time, and offers a high likelihood that they will get something out of it. The wax figures are very realistic (and some of them are even fairly violent.) All of that makes for a memorable experience.

Matur og Drykkur Restaurant

Matur og Drykkur shares the building with the Saga Museum, and is one of the top-rated restaurants in Reykjavik. The Grapevine is the English Language free weekly newspaper in Reykjavik. In 2016, they selected Matur og Drykkur as the winner for "Best Must-try Dining Experience". They also were the runner up for both "Best Restaurant" (Snaps was the winner) and "Best Place for a Fancy Meal" (Dill was the winner.)

And, Matur og Drykkur has a good looking kid's menu: Three entrées for 1490 each, and all of them are well beyond standard kid's fare. The food was very good, but we found the kid's portion was small, even for a kid's meal. I would have been much better off ordering 2 adult meals for 3 kids to share. Maybe it was just bad luck.

Reykjavik Maritime Museum

Just down the street from the Saga Museum is one of the Reykjavik City Museums, the Reykjavik Maritime Museum. The handful of parking spaces outside of the museum are often full, and the lot at the Saga Museum says you can only park there for the Saga Museum. The best option may be the gravel lot behind the museum. There is an entrance to the museum from this side as well, even though your GPS may take you to the other side with less parking.

The museum is very nice, and the first exhibit (about women in the fishing industry) was very visually striking: darkly lit by design, with a plank floor meant to resemble a boat dock.

Upstairs, there are two more galleries. One talks about the history of fishing in Iceland. This was very well done, though there are many museums in Iceland that cover this topic. They have a nice play area with costumes that kids could try on. And a new exhibit also covers fishing: "Fish & folk – 150 years of fisheries."

The museum costs 1650 krona for adults, and is free for kids under 18. For an extra 950 krona for the adults (or 1300 krona as a standalone), you can take a tour of the old Coast Guard ship Óðinn, which is docked right next to the museum. This ship was heavily involved in the Cod Wars; it was rammed by British ships during the skirmishes. We'll head there now.

A Tour of the boat Óðinn

You can only see the inside of the ship during a scheduled guided tour-- these are only offered at 1 PM, 2 PM, and 3 PM. An 11 AM tour is added in the summers. We were able to come back a different day with our receipts from the Maritime Museum, and only pay the incremental cost for the boat tour. The ship sits right next to the museum on the harbor.

Children under 12 must be accompanied by an adult for the ship tour. But I guess that a kid 13-17 could go by themselves, for free, if the parents didn't want to go? Or maybe not: A warning sign says "High thresholds, uneven floors, steep stairs, and slippery decks. Children must be supervised." This is a real boat.

Óðinn served as a Coast Guard ship in the Icelandic fleet from 1960 until 2006. The ship was used in all 3 Cod Wars, when Iceland and England fought over fishing rights off the coast of Iceland. Óðinn was decommissioned in 2006, and seems to be in exactly the state it (she?) would have been at that time. Many things have been left in place: uniforms still hang in the closets; the kitchen is stocked and ready to use; the helicopter service area is full of tools.

This isn't a must-see attraction, but if you have a child who is into boats, it could be a worthwhile hour.

Þúfa Sculpture

(See picture below)

I'd seen this from a boat in the Reykjavik Harbor, but I wasn't quite sure what it was. Turns out it's a climbable sculpture called Þúfa (or, I guess, Thufa.) You can see the spiraling pathway you walk around to climb to the top of the mound.

The climb up the hill is just a gentle incline; it's a longer walk than I imagined, and it's also a little scary. As you get higher and higher, you realize you're standing very close to the edge.

At the top, you'll be rewarded with a nice view of the harbor, and a small wooden shed with some drying fish inside.

It's a nice piece of interactive art that the whole family should enjoy, at least if the weather is nice. You can find it by getting directions to HB Grandi; the parking lot right next to Þúfa has GPS coordinates of 64.155111, -21.934472.

Omnom Chocolate

First, before we get any further, let's just admit that Omnom Chocolate is a great name for a company. Go ahead and say it out loud. Omnom.

Omnom was founded in 2013, and had a small operation making chocolate bars. But in early 2016 they moved to a much larger location by the harbor. That larger space allows them to offer tours.

This really a tasting tour; by the time you've sampled all of the types of chocolate they've prepared, the tour almost seems like an afterthought. You'll get to taste pure roasted cocoa beans, or cocoa nibs. Then, you'll try some mashed up with sugar added, as well as a cacao tea, made from the husks of the beans. Next come the different varieties of chocolate bars that Omnom produces, and then a tour of the

Þúfa Sculpture

Whales of Iceland
Museum with life-sized models of whales form small to gigantic.

Old Harbour
Whale watching and fising trips, as well as lots of restaurants.

Whales of Iceland O

Reykjavik City Library
The local library-- they have a small selection of books in English.

Saga Museum
An audio guided tour of lively viking scenes.

O **Saga Museum**

The Settlement Exhibition
Interactive Museum on the site of an old Viking house.

Old Harbour O

Alþingi
Active parliament building next to a nice city square.

Reykjavik City Library O

City Hall
On the lovely Tjörnin pond. See the 3D map our get tourist information

The Settlement Exhibition O

Alþi

City Hall O

National Museum of Iceland
Well-orgazied history museum which steps through Icelandic History.

O **National Museum of**

TJÖRNI

Kolaportið Flea Market
Weekend only flea market with clothing, candy, and more.

Bæjarins Beztu hot dogs
The most famous hot dog stand in Iceland-- Bill Clinton was here!

Harpa
Beautiful concert hall on the water. See a show or just walk around!

Laugavegur
Very walkable half-mile long shopping street in Reykjavik.

Skólavörðustígur
Short but nice shopping sreet, leading uphill to Hallgrímskirkja.

Sun Voyager Sculpture
Famous sculpture by the water, just a few minutes from Laugavegur.

Hallgrímskirkja
The famous church. Pay for an elevator ride up to amazing views.

OHarpa

OKolaportið Flea Market

OBæjarins Beztu hot dogs

OSun Voyager Sculpture

OLaugavegur

Skólavörðustígur**O**

OHallgrímskirkja

N

0 feet   1200   2400

Whales of Iceland

factory floor. With more tastings, of course.

Neither the chocolate bars nor the tour are cheap. The tour costs 3000 krona for adults. Kids 7-15 are 1500 krona, and kids under 7 are free. But the tour can be worthwhile and a memorable experience. You'll learn something about how chocolate is made, and you'll get to see a brand new chocolate making facility. And, of course, you'll get to try chocolate in many, many forms.

At least when we were there, the Omnom chocolate bars were cheaper at the Keflavik airport duty free store than in the factory store. So stock up on your way home!

Whales of Iceland

Whales of Iceland museum is a new museum (2015) on Grandi Harbor. This is another very expensive museum; adults cost 2900 ISK, which may be the most expensive museum in the country. Kids 7-15 cost 1500 krona. But, a family pass costs 5800 ISK; that covers 2 adults and 2 kids. And any kids under 7 would also get in free.

So is it worth it? The museum does a good job of building anticipation, as you start with the smallest whales, and then you turn the corner and start to see the giants. These are scale models of the largest animals ever known to have existed, and the reveal is excellent.

Included with your admission is an excellent audio guide, which you can download onto your iPhone or Android phone. Free coffee and tea can be found at the snack bar area at the end of the exhibit, along with a few cakes and other drinks which are for sale.

Both the Saga Museum and Whales of Iceland are excellent museums; they are less than a 10 minute walk from each other. (And the Reykjavik Maritime Museum is between them!) Either or both would be an excellent addition to your time in Reykjavik; you'll have to decide if your family wants to learn more about Icelandic history or whales.

Northern Lights Center.

Near the Saga Museum is Aurora Reykjavik, the Northern Lights Center. There is a gift shop you can peruse for free, or an exhibition that costs 1600 krona for adults, and 1000 krona for kids 6-18.

So is it worth it? I think it's too expensive-- I would have come away with a much more positive impression if they offered a family discount. But my kids enjoyed it. I'd skip it and save the money for other museums, but this may make sense if you have a northern lights fan in your family.

Currency Conversion

Throughout this book, I have avoided using commas or periods when listing Icelandic prices: 5900 krona, not 5,900. That's because in Iceland, the punctuation is reversed! 5.000 means five thousand, and 5,50 would mean five and a half.

Somewhat related, you can use Google to convert prices. To find out how much 5000 krona is in US dollars, just Google:

5000 ISK usd

isk = Icelandic Krona, usd = US Dollars

Reykjavik Old Harbor

Old Harbor is comprised of a couple of sections: Further out on the pier is where most boat tours will leave from: whale watching, fishing, and Viking ships. Closer to land you'll find an area densely packed with restaurants.

Tours from Old Harbor

Let's start with a couple of the tours we did.

Whale Watching with Reykjavik Sailors

(year round; best in summer)

We've been whale watching already on this trip. Twice, actually. The first time was with North Sailing in Húsavík (page 102), and it was an incredible trip. We highly recommend getting to Húsavík if you can, and going with North. But, we realize that many people won't be able to make it way up, um, north to North, and so we decided to try a whale watching trip from Reykjavik to compare.

The other trip was also up north, in Dalvik (page 119) That tour featured some fishing at the end, and it was nice to get to do both on the same trip.

This time, we chose to go with Reykjavik Sailors, a company that just started offering boat tours at the end of 2015. Their ratings on TripAdvisor are slightly better than Elding, the most popular whale watching company in Reykjavik. (But both ratings are just fine.) And Reykjavik Sailors is a little bit cheaper; maybe more than a little bit if you book their family package good for 2 adults and 2 kids up to 15 for 24750 krona. (This was available in mid-2018, but deals like this change frequently.) And kids 6 and under are free.

But, is it as good as the established companies? Maybe not? But almost. Our boat was a little slower than the others, which meant that we got to the whales a few minutes later. I have a lot of pictures of a whale with the Elding boat in the frame. All of the companies share information when and if they find whales, and we were usually behind the Elding boat.

But we got to see plenty of whales up close. Including a humpback, who was "lunge feeding"-- emerging with a wide open mouth. So, the tour was very good. The guide was informative and seemed happy to help out with finding and identifying whales. We saw humpbacks, minkes, and even a happy looking dolphin leaping out of the water repeatedly in the distance.

We were happy with Reykjavik Sailors, though I don't think you will go wrong with any of the major tour operators. If you are ambitious, you could also an Icelandic-only site called hopkaup.is. This is a site like Groupon, and you will sometimes find 30% - 50% discounts on whale watching. Note that I haven't tried it; if you do, let me know how it works!

But still try to get to Húsavík if you can.

Sea Angling with Special Tours

(May – September)

I've said that you can't really go wrong with any of the major companies offering whale watching tours, or other tour activities in Iceland. I really mean that. And I want to mention another company that runs tours out of Old Harbor: Special Tours (https://specialtours.is.) For years, Special Tours has been meticulously documenting every single whale watching trip they take. Click on Daily Diary on the top right of the home page. You see all of the details of each trip: How many whales did they see? How was the weather? It's really quite impressive. (More recently, Elding has also started doing this for every tour. See https://elding.is/whale-diary)

Special Tours, like many other companies, offers whale watching year-round. But having had our fill of whale watching trips, we decided to try something a little bit different with Special Tours: Sea Angling. There are some fishing charter trips in Iceland where you need to know what you are doing. But this tour is for everyone: "If you haven't been sea fishing

Speeding along on the Sea Angling trip with Special Tours

before, don't worry, it is very easy! Our crew will happily show you the ropes, advising you on bait and passing on their knowledge of the seas."

The boat used for sea angling is much smaller than the typical whale watching boat. Whale watching trips typically can take up to 60 or 70 people; Sea Angling with Special tours can take only a maximum of 18 fisherpeople.

Not only is this boat smaller; it's also much faster. This was a really fun and fast ride out to the fishing area. After about 10 minutes we reached our first spot and started to fish. In general, the boat would stay in one place for 15 or 20 minutes or so, and then move on to a different spot. The kids haven't fished much at all, but they got the hang of it very quickly.

From what the guide told me, this was an unusually slow fishing day. Now, we all caught fish, and there was plenty for our dinner. But it sounds like it is more typical for everyone to catch several fish, and for there to be enough for people to take some home with them. Our group of around 16 people caught maybe 20 fish. On a better day, some of the smaller ones would have been thrown back, but today, we kept anything larger than bait-sized.

And that leads me to the staff, especially our guide. I didn't get his name, but he was from Scotland. And he was fantastic-- he was always working hard re-baiting fishing lines, de-tangling fishing lines, filleting fish, and on and on and on.

Everyone on the staff clearly wanted to make sure we all had a great experience. I guess it would have automatically been great if we each caught 10 fish, which supposedly happens sometimes, but we still had a lot of fun.

I should note that our 5 PM tour didn't get back to port until 9 PM! So maybe leave your plans somewhat flexible after the tour. I think we spent extra time trying various spots to see if we could catch more fish. But eventually, we stopped, and the staff started preparing our meal.

The only kind of fish my family caught was haddock; that's almost all anyone caught, though we had some mackerel as well. The meal includes the seasoned fish we caught, along with some potatoes we didn't catch.

It's not fair to call my kids picky eaters, but a couple of them are pretty picky when it comes to fish. But everyone loved one (or both) of the types of fish we had. It was a fantastic meal. There was as much fish as anyone could eat, though there was none left over.

Dinner was ready just as the boat got back to port; you can then hang out on the boat eating your meal for as long as you want, or take off whenever you want. It's a great ending to an enjoyable trip.

The trip costs 13000 krona for adults 16 and older; 6175 krona for kids 7-15 (so less than half price!); and free for kids 0-6. You are paying more compared to whale watching. Whale watching trips with Special Tours are 10900 for adults and 5220 for kids.

But, you're getting a smaller tour, and a delicious fresh fish dinner. That's a pretty good price for a fish dinner in Reykjavik. I guess the dinner isn't guaranteed, but I assume they don't send you home hungry if o one catches anything?

If you can only do one tour, you should probably still opt for whale watching. But if your family loves being out on the water, sea angling can be a great addition to your vacation.

Reykjavik Viking Adventure

Sadly, this fun sailing trip on a replica Viking boat has moved to the town of Þingeyri in the Westfjords. It's a great trip if you're in the area, but most tourists won't be in that area! Check their web site (ReykjavikVikingAdventure.is) for the latest information.

Restaurants on Old Harbor

Now back to the part of the pier closer to the road, and a few of the restaurants (plus one cinema). There are more choices than the few we listed below!

The Sea Baron (Sægreifinn)

The Sea Baron (saegreifinn.is) claims to have the world's best lobster soup, and they also have an assortment of freshly caught fish. I like this place because they show you exactly what you will be getting when you order; the menu is really the refrigerator. Look at the uncooked fish choices, pick one, and they will cook it for you. (See picture below.)

I enjoyed my Plaice (a type of whitefish.) But you only get one skewer for 1850 krona, which isn't really enough for a

meal. And it took 20 minutes to get it, and there weren't many places to sit. When I picked up my order, they were quoting an hour to get your food; I wonder if a whale watching tour had just returned? The fish was excellent, but this doesn't seem like the ideal place for kids.

I'm not really sure where public opinion is on whale; are most tourists avoiding it? If you are interested in trying whale, they have a small tasting option for 300 krona. From what I understand, it has a very strong taste, so this may be a cheap way to see what you or the kids think.

Café Haiti

This is a slightly unusual choice, but Café Haiti (cafehaiti.is/) does a nice job of blending Icelandic food with a Haitian twist. I more or less stole that sentence from their description of their Icelandic Lamb Soup: "Traditional Icelandic lamb soup with Haitian twist."

We tried the Traditional Icelandic Fish Soup, which wasn't overly traditional. But it was very good—it was one of my wife's favorite meals in Iceland. Some of our kids liked it, but it's definitely not for everyone. There are some sandwich options that are less ambitious and also less expensive, such as ham and cheese or salmon and cheese sandwiches.

Salt (Lobster and Stuff)

We didn't eat here, but Salt (verbud11.is) has a nice children's menu. Your kids can choose from the fish of the day, a hamburger, or penne pasta with chicken. The children's menu also states that kids can get a half portion of anything from the adult menu for half price.

Höfnin

It's the same story here: A fancy restaurant with a good kid's menu. The kid's menu at Höfnin (hofnin.is) only offers 2 choices: A hamburger, or fish stew. Both come with homemade vanilla ice cream, and cost 1790 krona.

Dinner entrées start at 3450 krona, and go all the way up to a slow-cooked lamb shoulder for 5290 krona, or about $50. Still, it's nice to know your kids will be welcome if you're looking for an expensive meal.

Cinema No. 2

In with the restaurants, you'll also find a small theater called Cinema No. 2. The full name is The Cinema at Old Harbour Village No2. They show movies about Iceland; most of the films are related to volcanoes or the northern lights. The films are only shown at 5:00, 5:30, or 6:00, so it can make a good option before dinner. It never fit into our plans though, so we didn't see anything here.

The long films are 45-50 minutes, and they are expensive: 1800 krona for adults, 900 for kids 6-16, and free for 5 and under. Shorter movies are 1200 for adults and 600 for kids. You can look at thecinema.is to see if anything catches your interest.

The theater is small, and apparently there are some sofas in addition to the chairs in the theater. Reviews online are generally positive. And prices are a little cheaper than the Volcano House movies across the street in the downtown area (page 135), though kids 11 and under are free over there.

Thermal Pools in Reykjavik

If you have one of the Reykjavik thermal pools close by, find the pool brochure online. Google ""swimming in reykjavik"" (in quotes) to find a link to visitreykjavik.is. If there's a children's pool or two, and / or a waterslide or two, your family will have a good time. Actually, you'll probably have fun no matter what. And they're cheap-- a family of four will pay something like $12 total to swim here in Seltjarnarnes.

See more information about these pools (and other pools around Reykjavik) at the Grapevine's review page. Search for "grapevine swimming Iceland" without the quotes to find the article called "Every Swimming Pool In The Greater Reykjavík Area, Rated."

Drinking water in Iceland

The water in Iceland is some of the best in the world. We drank tap water throughout our trip, and we even drank water right from a glacier (page 82)! Oh, and from Sifra (page 61).

Two tips:

1. Make sure you're drinking the cold water. So, make sure the faucet is pushed all the way to the cold side. The hot water is sometimes naturally geothermally heated, and can have high concentrations of sulfur or other minerals in it.

2. Let the water run for a minute so you're getting water that hasn't been sitting in the pipes. You can sometimes feel when it suddenly gets colder.

But if you follow those tips, you're drinking fresh clean Icelandic water that people around the world pay to drink out of plastic bottles!

Reykjavik Downtown

This is the largest section of Reykjavik we will cover, or at least the one with the most attractions. We're going to cover it in a couple of "layers," starting with the road across from the harbor and working our way back.

Let's start by following one road, named Tryggvagata, from west to east. (On the map on page 130, we're starting just to the west of the Reykjavik City Library.) We'll jump off of this road a couple of times for some attractions and then keep going. This will cover most of the attractions in downtown Reykjavik; then we'll circle back to cover the restaurants, which are generally further south.

Most everything is open year-round in this downtown area, though some places may close for a week or two in late December or early January.

The Volcano House

The Volcano House is the place that is attached to Icelandic Fish and Chips right across the street from the Old Harbor. There's a free museum part that you can visit; I've been there a few times, and it's growing on me. It's a great place to visit before or after a meal, and to maybe buy a cheap souvenir. They have pumice from volcanic eruptions you can buy. The pumice floats!

You also have the option to watch their movie, which is 53 minutes long and plays once an hour from 10 AM until 9 PM. Actually, there are two movies; one about the Westman Islands eruption in 1973 (see page 79), and the other about Eyjafjallajökull in 2010. That second one was nominated for two Emmys in cinematography.

The movies have a little bit of overlap, but otherwise they are both very well done. We enjoyed the movies a lot more than the ones at The Volcano Show (though meeting the creator of that one is still a treat- see page 144.)

The movies may be a little bit long for younger children, but older children, or anyone with an interest in volcanoes, should enjoy these well-made films. It's not cheap though: Adults cost 1990 krona, kids 12-16 are 1000, and kids 11 and under are free. The movie trailer may help you decide? Find them at volcanohouse.is.

Either way, you should check out the free museum part, and

grab a well-priced kid's fish and chips next door at Icelandic Fish and Chips. One commenter on our site said their family wandered through the museum and bought postcards while they waited for their food. It's a good combination!

Icelandic Fish and Chips

Icelandic Fish and Chips has one of the best kid's meal options in town. You won't see the kid's menu on the chalkboard when you walk in, but there are two kid's options on the printed menu.

Those options are a kid's fish and chips, served with potatoes (900 krona) or fisherman's stew (800 krona). We visited a few times, and my kids always opted for the fish and chips. And gobbled up the meal.

The kid's fish has one large piece of fish; the adult portion had 2 or 3 medium sized pieces. Note that you can choose the type of fish that they will fry; the choices of the day are listed on the chalkboard-- cod, tusk, or pollock for one day we were there. We were told that the pollock has a stronger taste, but it's flakier. Ask your server for a description of each.

We also asked for a small mango skyr sauce with the kid's portion; there are a variety of flavors you can choose from. I'm not sure if we were charged extra for this. An extra "Skyronnes" dip normally costs 290 krona, but the one we got with the kid's meal was smaller.

See above (well, left) for information about the Volcano House, which shares an entrance with Icelandic Fish and Chips.

Reykjavik City Library

I always like stopping in places that may be less touristy. And so I'm a big fan of taking your family to the Reykjavik City Library. We actually sent our older son to a computer event sponsored by koder.is. He thought it was a lot of fun, and no one seemed to care where he was from.

Give a quick look at the library's events page- you may find something happening while you are in town, and the events are often free. Go to borgarbokasafn.is/en and click on Events on the menu bar.

While my son was coding (well, and playing some Minecraft too), we explored the library. It's a very welcoming place, with enough children's books in English to keep the kids entertained for a while. And there are a variety of reading nooks and play areas; you're encouraged to stick around for a while. It's a good place to relax, and maybe meet some locals. You can look for the cart that says "Barnabækur á ensku", which mean "Children's Books in English." Or find the shelf of books for younger kids which is labeled in English.

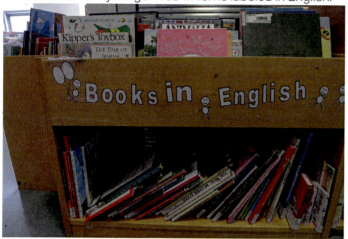

Reykjavik Museum of Photography

The library also houses the Reykjavik Museum of Photography; sadly this museum is no longer free (as of mid 2017). Check the spiral staircase at the back of the library to see if there are some photographs you can sample there. But warn your kids to pay attention to the steps-- spend too much time admiring the photos, and you'll miss a step!

Admission is now 1000 krona for adults, and free for kids.

Reykjavik Art Museum

The Reykjavik Art Museum is either one museum or three museums, depending upon how you think of it. On the one hand, paying for admission to any one of them gets you into all three of them, as long as you go on the same day.

On the other hand, you can't really walk between any two buildings. Take a look at the map "Greater Reykjavik" on page 147. Hafnarhús is in the harbor area; that's where we are right now. Ásmundar is over by the zoo and family park. And Kjarvalsstaðir is in a park in a residential area.

I think that Hafnarhús is what people think of when they think of "the" Reykjavik Art Museum, since it's in perhaps the main tourist area of Reykjavik. It has an interesting collection of art spread across 6 galleries on 2 floors. Just about all of the exhibits change over time, and so you never know exactly what you will see. Go to ArtMuseum.is to see what will be there when you'll be in town. The museum does alway show the works of Icelandic artist Guðmundur Guðmundsson, who apparently is called Erró. The museum says he is "without a doubt the best known contemporary artist of Iceland."

Hafnarhús is a very nice art gallery, but we didn't find anything outstanding for families this trip. (There was an interactive display in 2009 that the kids loved.) We enjoyed the Ásmundur Sveinsson sculpture museum a lot more. See our visit there on page 149.

Admission is 1650 krona per adult, and free for kids under 18. Remember that the one fee gets you same-day admission to all 3 museums .... er, buildings that are part of the one museum.

There is a small restaurant at Hafnarhús, which just opened under new management in the summer of 2016. We didn't eat there, since we had plans to seek out children's menus in the area. But the menu the day we were there looked ambitious for a museum restaurant. Starters included Pork Rillettes and Cod Tartare, and main courses included lamb with kimchi salad and a malt glaze. The snacks were a reasonable 790 krona and the main courses were 2500-3300 krona.

The Settlement Exhibition, aka 871 ±2

Here's our first detour off of the main road; we'll head a couple of blocks south from the Library and Art Museum. The Settlement Exhibition, also called Reykjavik 871 ±2. I don't really like the 871 name, as the main ruins exhibited at the museum are from much later than 871. The 871 ±2 refers to a volcano that erupted around the year 871, and left a distinctive colored layer of ash and rock; this layer makes it easy for archaeologists to determine if a building was built before or after 871. Layers below must be older than 871; layers above are more recent. One of the steps down to the museum is a clever nod to this; look carefully and you'll see one step labeled 871 ±2.

In 2001, a construction project in downtown Reykjavik accidentally unearthed the ruins of a Viking longhouse; this house was built around 930-- the very end of the "Settlement Age." The ruins were preserved where they were found, and are exhibited as the Settlement House.

You walk around the excavated ruins and press buttons to highlight different features of the house. There are also lots of multimedia exhibits around the sides of the museum.

At the far end of the house, there are some ruins that are from before 871 (no one knows how long before); this is the oldest man-made structure ever found in Reykjavik.

The museum also houses a separate exhibit in the same building, and this exhibit varies over time. In 2016, this displayed some old manuscripts from as early as the 1300s. Called the Settlement Sagas, there was an additional fee to get in to this separate room.

But the new exhibit, as of mid 2017, is included with admission. It's called "Viking Animals – The Secret of the Settlement" and shows the importance of animals in the early settlement of Iceland.

Admission is free for kids under 18. For adults, it's 1650isk for the Settlement House. Note that, unlike the Saga Museum (page 127), this is a city museum, and so it is included in the Reykjavik City card; see page 58 for more details.

I think the addition of the new exhibit makes this easier to recommend. The main museum offers a lot of interactive options, and adding in the Viking Animals exhibit makes this a better value. The Settlement Museum is open until 8 PM every night, so it's a good option for an evening in Reykjavik.

Alþingi / Parliament

Still off of the main road, we'll walk a little east to the Parliament building, called Alþingi. What's notable is that Iceland's Parliament has been running continuously from the year 930. It's the oldest continuously running Parliament in the world! Originally, it met in Þingvellir, which is now a national park and part of the Golden Circle; see page 61. There, you can visit the "Law Rock" from where the laws of the country were recited. Now it meets in Reykjavik.

Today, there's a nice public square outside the Parliament building called Austurvöllur; on a nice day, you might see people hanging out, playing music, or juggling. There is also a new statue outside of the building, of Iceland's first female member of Parliament; she was elected in 1922.

The Icelandic Printmakers Association

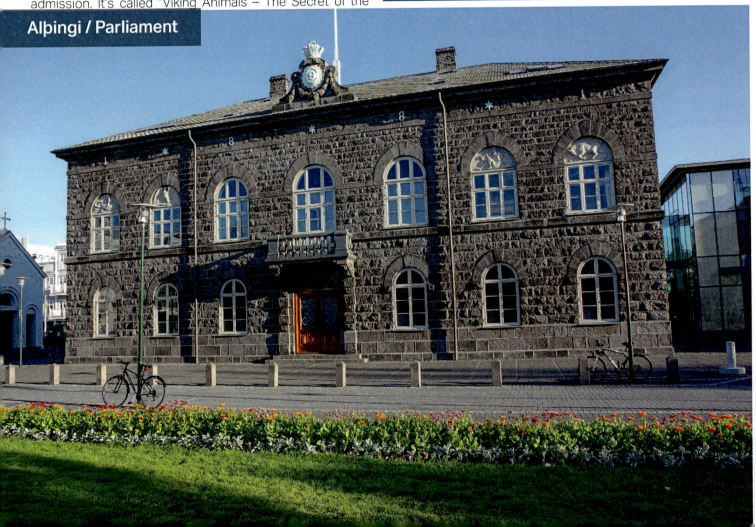

Alþingi / Parliament

We're back on the main road Tryggvagata. You've likely never heard of the The Icelandic Printmakers Association (islenskgrafik.is). I think this is a worthwhile stop if it's open. First of all, it's free. Second, the artist was there when we visited, and she gave us a quick tour of the facility. Third, it's right next to the library, in the back of the Art Museum building. But to get there, you have to go around to the other side—the "back" side of the building which faces the harbor.

The Printmaker's Association is only open Thursday through Saturday from 2-6 PM. If it's a Saturday, you could combine this with the Library and the Flea Market for a free half day of activities in one area.

Exhibits at the Printmaker's Association usually only run in the summer, but there can be some off-season events.

Kolaportið, the Reykjavik Flea Market

On weekends, just down the block from the library is the Reykjavik flea market. It's large enough to browse for hours, looking for the perfect souvenir or Icelandic wool sweater. But we never end up staying that long- I feel like I always want to like this a lot more than I actually do.

They have a few vendors selling wool sweaters (lopapeysas); the prices may be cheaper than you'll find elsewhere. In an article online (search for "hunting lopapeysa" without the quotes) a woman claims you can save about 3000 krona at the flea market-- or about $30 on a $160 sweater. But you have to know what you're doing, and that you are getting the same quality. We recommend buying your sweaters from the Icelandic Handknit Association; see page 141.

There are also stores selling tons of toys and colorful ... stuff. Pajamas and towels and soaps and more. Used clothing too. In the very back, you can buy fresh and frozen fish, fruits and vegetables, and lots of unique food items. And candy, which not surprisingly includes a lot of licorice.

The most interesting souvenir for us has been a vendor that sells Japanese-style kimonos. For around $10, you can get a girl's sized traditional Chinese dress.

It's a loud and crowded environment, which may or may not be a good environment for you and your family. And there were some stalls that seemed to be selling junk at exorbitant prices. I think you can still find some interesting things to buy if you take the time to search. Or, you can just people watch

The hot dog stand line

and sample from fermented shark in the back.

Hours: Saturdays and Sundays from 11 AM - 5 PM.

Bæjarins Beztu Pylsur- Hot Dog Stand

Continuing down the road Tryggvatagata, you'll come to the world famous Bæjarins Beztu Pylsur hot dog stand. It's world famous because Bill Clinton once got a hot dog from here. It's a perfectly adequate hot dog stand, and hot dogs are popular in Iceland (and contain lamb meat!) But you'll sometimes find a line of 30 or more people here. You can find literally the same hot dogs throughout Iceland, with the same toppings. (Seriously, the exact same toppings. It's almost like there's a law stipulating which toppings need to be provided with a hot dog.) Stop here if you're hungry, and definitely try some Icelandic hot dogs. But there's no need to consider this one special.

Arnarhóll

Arnarhóll is the big hill you'll see to your left as you continue past the hot dog stand. At the top is a sculpture of Ingólfr Arnarson, who settled in Reykjavik in the year 874. Legend has it that he threw carved pillars from his ship when he was near Iceland, and decided he would settle wherever the pillars washed ashore. And they washed ashore in Reykjavik.

On nice days, you'll find lots of locals hanging out here.

Culture House Museum

If you're walking in the city center of Reykjavik, you may have seen the Culture House. You can't really tell what it is, but it's a museum.

The current exhibition opened in 2015, and is called "Points of View." I'm not really sure how to describe it. Ambitious? Challenging? The building itself is a fascinating labyrinth of rooms. And each room holds an exhibit about a different, well, point of view. Some of the exhibits are called "mirror", "inside", and "again and again"; the one on the top floor is called "down".

Much of the museum feels like an art museum, with themes in the different galleries. I don't think kids will find it very interesting; adults willing to put in some effort may find it an excellent museum. To the museum's credit, there are many kid's areas and activities scattered throughout. But, these feel a little bit like areas to distract the children while

Culture House Museum

the adults focus on the main exhibits.

The museum costs 2000 krona for adults (up from 1200 in 2016!), and is free for kids under 18. I don't think it's right for everyone, but a subset if families may find it a rewarding visit. The comprehensive web guide may help you decide; find it at culturehouse.is.

Harpa

People call Harpa a concert hall, but it's really much more than that. There are several exhibit halls, multiple evening theater shows, a short movie, and more. Check out harpa.is and see what's going on; some events are completely free.

Let's start with the bad. The exhibits while we were there included one about the Icelandic book of drawings, one about David Bowie, and one from the Icelandic Emigration Center. That first exhibit was in one open room, with a description of the book and some recreations of the pages. But it was disappointing for 1500 krona (free for kids.)

Reviews of the 360° cinematic experience are surprisingly poor; it's a 12 minute movie in a square room for another 1500 krona. Unless they are free, avoid Harpa exhibitions and the movie and spend your money elsewhere.

Now on to the good. Harpa is a beautiful building and I think kids will enjoy exploring it (for free!) There are enormous open spaces with little seating areas by the windows. And there's an ice cream cart by the entrance as well. Find an open couch by a window and enjoy the ice cream while you watch the crowds go by outside.

Icelandic Sagas: The Greatest Hits in 75

minutes

On to one of the nighttime shows in Harpa. Icelandic Sagas-- The Greatest Hits in 75 minutes is inappropriate for children. And my children really enjoyed it. Here are the most important things to know:

• Everything in Harpa is free for kids 12 and under. Therefore, this show is free for kids 12 and under! More on this in a minute.

• The stage is just a long "runway." There are two rows of seats on each side. So you can have front row seats, if you want them. All seats are general admission.

• Everyone needs a ticket, regardless of age. I think there were a few seats left for our show, but I can imagine the show might sell out.

• You are encouraged to take pictures during the show.

• There seems to be no mechanism for getting a free child ticket on Harpa's web site for the show. So I think you need to buy them from the Harpa box office. That's what we did, and it was no problem. Though you do run the risk of the show selling out, so maybe show up 30 minutes early? Then spend some time checking out the cool interior of Harpa.

On to the show:

• You get two energetic performers acting out the Sagas with a clever, witty, funny, high-energy script.

• Audience participation is frequent. Your kids will probably get a job to do; I was onstage for maybe 4 minutes. (I played Donald Trump; it's complicated.)

• The show is funny throughout, and inappropriate in several places. One involves Njal's Saga and the story of Hrut and his wife Unn who complained about ... well, if you're curious, you'll need to search online for "gunnhild" and read footnote 51 on the Wikipedia page you'll find. And ponder the presence of a balloon animal balloon as a prop.

• But it's a funny and well-crafted show. Take the kids! Just remember that balloon.

Laugavegur Shopping Road

So far in Reykjavik, we were generally heading from west

to east; we left off at Harpa and the Culture House Museum. At this point, continuing east, my mental map of Reykjavik changes from "downtown area" to "shopping areas."

Head a block south from the Culture House, and you'll be at the intersection of two major shopping streets: Laugavegur and Skólavörðustígur. Laugavegur is the more famous of the streets; from here, head east and you have a solid half mile of restaurants and shops. You'll find cafes and coffee shops, but also some of the nicest restaurants in Iceland. You'll find clothing shops, souvenir shops, bookstores, and much more. It's a great place to walk and do some browsing or shopping.

Skólavörðustígur heads off southeast. This "shopping district" isn't as long as Laugavegur; it's about a quarter mile, and it's more uphill. But at the end of Skólavörðustígur, you get to one of the most famous landmarks of Iceland: Hallgrímskirkja (Hallgrím's Church). See page 141.

Laugavegur Road

The word Laugavegur means "wash road", and you'll see this root "Laugar" in many other names. The same word, Laugavegur, is also the name of a popular hiking trail. And the word for Saturday in Icelandic is Laugardagur-- wash day.

We're not going to cover everything that is available; as noted above, it's a nice assortment of restaurants, fancy and not-so-fancy souvenir shops, boutique clothing and food stores, and more. Some of the blocks are closed to car traffic; bicycle-shaped gates at some street corners block traffic. But some of the streets do have cars, so be careful.

Parking in Reykjavik

Parts of Laugavegur that do allow cars also have parking. There are 4 zones of parking in Reykjavik, called P1, P2, P3, and P4. P1 are the premium spots, and cost 320 krona per hour. (This has been raised three times since February 2016!) Not surprisingly, all of the parking on Laugavegur, at least in the main shopping area, is the most expensive category, P1. See a nice map at iheartreykjavik.net and search for "parking." Or see bilastaedasjodur.is for the latest prices.

There seems to be an inefficiency if you park in some parking garages. The garage at 94 Laugavegur, called Stjörnuport, cost 80 krona for the first hour, and 50 krona each additional hour. So 4 hours in a parking garage is still cheaper than just 1 hour in a P1 zone. You'll only have to drive on Laugavegur for a block, and you won't have to worry about getting a parking ticket if you stay past your estimated time.

You'll be able to see most everything that is on the main road, and we won't cover those here. Walk and explore! But there are a couple of options that you'll need to head to on a

Sun Voyager Sculpture

side street to find. First is Bókin, Bobby Fischer's favorite bookstore in Reykjavik. In fact, the young girl who was working there, who I assume is the daughter of the owner, has played chess against Bobby Fischer. This place looks like what a good used bookstore should look like.

They have a section of all English books up front, and paperbacks cost 300 krona. There are also some English books scattered throughout the rest of the store. Find it at Klapparstígur 30; it's less than half a block north on Klapparstígur from Laugavegur.

Sun Voyager Sculpture

At around Laugavegur 45, to the north (toward the water) you will be able to see the Sun Voyager sculpture. It will be about a 5 minute walk. You can also drive here; there's a small pull-off parking area. See the location on the map on page 130.

The sculpture is actually called Sólfar, which means Sun Voyager. It is by Icelandic sculptor Jón Gunnar Árnason, and it is by far his most famous work. Because of the metal and shiny base, the sculpture can look very different based on the light and time of day.

Reykjavik Escape

At the end of the shopping district on Laugavegur, you'll

A look down Laugavegur

be about a 5 minute walk from Reykjavik Escape. They have several escape rooms, where your group has 60 minutes to find clues and solve puzzles in order to escape.

I couldn't take pictures of the room, so you'll have to use your imagination. Escape rooms are popping up in cities all over the world; I don't think there is anything special about the Reykjavik site, but the people were nice and the kids had a good time. It's not cheap;, at 5000 krona per person. But it can be a fun activity for the whole family to enjoy together.

Skólavörðustígur Road

I liked the shopping street Skólavörðustígur better than Laugavegur. Maybe it's because at the top you get to Hallgrímskirkja, as well as a sculpture museum? Maybe it's because it's shorter, and more manageable? We let the kids walk around on Skólavörðustígur by themselves.

Or maybe it's because of the Icelandic Handknitting Association store, located at Skólavörðustígur 19. You won't find any bargains here, but you will find sweaters made of Icelandic wool handknitted in Iceland by Icelanders. There has been some uproar in the last few years about this topic; a couple of years ago, the company Icewear sold clothing with the Icelandic flag on it that were not made in Iceland.

It's a store that's appealing because of its chaos. Go ahead and try on a sweater! But don't get too attached until after you've seen the price tag; these sweaters take a long time to knit by hand! See their website at handknit.is.

Café Loki

At the top of the hill, you'll come to Hallgrímskirkja; the area right around the church is very nice, with a statue, a museum, and some dining options. Right across the street from the church is Café Loki. You'll have a great view of the church from the restaurant window as you eat.

Café Loki let kids order a half portion of the lamb soup for half price, so 1100 krona. For adults, a lovely but still fairly

Icelandic Plate Baldur
at Café Loki

small adult meal (Icelandic Plate Baldur) was 2400 krona.

Hallgrímskirkja

After lunch we headed across the street to Hallgrímskirkja. In front of the church is a statue of Leif Eriksson in a large open area. If you let your kids explore the stores on Skólavörðustígur, this is a good place to meet!

You can go inside the main lower part of the church for free. On busy days, there may be a line out the door. This could be the line for the elevator to go up to the top; be sure to see if you can still go into the first floor of the church without standing in line.

The inside of the sanctuary is very nice, with a huge arched ceiling. There is also an impressive pipe organ up above. Check out the church's schedule of concerts over the summer at Hallgrimskirkja.is or listvinafelag.is. We were lucky enough to stumble across someone playing the organ at an unscheduled time.

But the main draw of Hallgrímskirkja is heading up the elevator to get a view of Reykjavik. The church is the tallest structure in Reykjavik, and the 6th tallest structure in Iceland.

The ride up the elevator costs 1000 krona for adults 17+, 100 krona for kids 7-16, and free for kids 6 and under. You buy your tickets in the gift shop and then head back to the front entrance to find the elevator on your right. The elevator only holds 6 people, and it takes a minute or so to go each direction, and so a line can form. If you see a line of people as you walk in, you may want to come back a little later.

The elevator takes you to a landing with some large circular windows, but you can (and should!) also walk up the 4 or so flights of stairs to get to the very top. The views are fantastic in any direction.

You can stay up there for as long as you like; just remember that there may also be a wait to catch the elevator back down! And there's no bathroom up there.

The Einar Jónsson Museum

Hallgrímskirkja, the Leif Eriksson sculpture, and Café Loki are all right on the circle around the church. Also on the same circle, further to the right (when facing the church), is The Einar Jónsson Museum. The sculptor Einar Jónsson lived here, but the building also served as an art museum; he lived on the top floor, used the main floor for exhibits, and the bottom was his studio.

If you head all the way around to the back, you can walk through the free outdoor sculpture garden. You'll find some full sculptures as well as bronze casts of the original sculptures; you'll find many of the originals inside the museum.

The guide at the museum shared some interesting information about Einar Jónsson. One tidbit is that Einar didn't like the neighborhood children viewing his artwork; presumably they weren't very well behaved? And in his will, he specified that kids shouldn't be allowed in the museum. I can't find a source for this, though.

Hallgrímskirkja. Kirkja means church!

Note the Leif Eriksson statue is visible in both this picture and the one below, which is the view from the church.

So maybe I am doing a disservice to Einar's wishes by even talking about the museum in a book called Iceland with Kids? They do have a price for children, and clearly children are welcome; just make sure they don't touch anything! Admission to the building is 1000 krona for adults, and free for kids 18 and under.

You can start in the sculpture garden, and then move on to pay for the museum if your family is interested. We enjoyed Einar's style-- even the kids!

One other free option that the museum kindly provides is an Einar Jónsson statue walk. Go to lej.is/en, click on "works" and scroll to the bottom for a map. This is a nice tour of Reykjavik, with the added bonus of seeing much of Einar's work around town. If your family likes his work, this could be a great outing around Reykjavik.

Below left: My son looking at a sculpture inside the Einar Jónsson museum.

Below: The museum's free outdoor sculpture garden, with Hallgrímskirkja in the background.

Tjörnin pond, with City Hall to the left

Tjörnin

Tjörnin is the name of a pond just south of the downtown / harbor area in Reykjavik. We're going to call this whole area Tjörnin, which again is somewhat arbitrary. It's an easy walk to here from any attraction in the Downtown area, and the Settlement Exhibition (page 136) is just a 2 or 3 minute walk from our first attraction by Tjörnin, City Hall.

City Hall

City Hall sits majestically at the edge of Tjörnin; from the pond side, it looks like it is floating on the water. Inside, you'll find a huge relief map of Iceland. I was excited to show this to the kids, but they were much more excited to go outside and marvel at the building itself and the pond. As of January 2017, the tourist information office has also moved here.

Tjörnin

You can walk all the way around Tjörnin, and we highly recommend this if the weather is nice. On the way, you'll see a good assortment of geese and ducks, walking paths that are right next to the water, sculptures, and a museum.

Starting down the right (west) side of Tjörnin as you leave City Hall you will see a couple of sculpture areas. These are

Einar Jónsson sculpture

only about a 5 minute walk. Actually, you may have already passed the "Unknown Bureaucrat" sculpture, a man with a concrete cube on the upper half of his suited body. He's right by the entrance to City Hall on the pond side. There are a lot of fun sculptures all around the pond, and further south too.

But the large sculpture you'll come to on the west side of the pond is by Einar Jónsson. If you like this, you may want to check out the museum dedicated to his work. It's right by Hallgrimskirkja (Halgrim's church), and there's a sculpture garden outside you can see for free. See page 141.

You should also see the sculpture of the guy on the bench. You can sit next to him for some quality selfies. That's enough sculptures; just know that there are lots of sculptures all around this part of Tjörnin; it's really a fun area.

Hljómskálagarðurinn

Now you have a choice. To your left there's a bridge that keeps you on a strict loop around Tjörnin. But you can also keep going straight south past the bridge, and you'll immediately come to another park called Hljómskálagarðurinn. Yes, that's a long word, but the second part of it, garðurinn, means park (I think). It's also called Hljómskálagarður park.

At the far end of this park is a new sculpture garden. It opened in June of 2014, and features the works of female Icelandic sculptors. You might be tired of sculptures by this point. Fortunately, very close by, you'll find the playground. It's on the east side of the park. In the back, you have a rope climbing structure. In the front, there are 2 trampolines built in at ground level; they are a lot of fun.

There's also a nice play area for smaller children. This is a nice reason to extend your walk around Tjörnin further south, past the bridge, to see this corner of Hljómskálagarður park.

Climbing in Hljómskálagarðurinn

The Volcano Show at Red Rock Cinema

Let's head back up to the southern end of Tjörnin, where we had the option to take the bridge and continue the loop around the pond. A couple of blocks further east and up the hill, you'll find the Volcano Show. If you Google Volcano Show Iceland, you'll get Volcano House (page 135), which is different. Here we're talking about the Volcano Show at Red Rock Cinema. GPS is 64.142834, -21.935974. There's a rock painted red outside.

This is the house of a gentleman is named Villi Knudsen. He, and his father before him, spend their lives (or at least their free time) filming volcanoes. I get the sense that there is a network of people in Iceland who monitor volcanoes. And if one starts to erupt, they all know to call Villi.

Villi is a character. I think he just likes people coming to his house to talk about volcanoes. And the money they pay for the movies helps to fund his hobby. There is a movie theater in his house, and you can choose to watch the 1 hour movie, and then opt to stay for the second hour if you want.

The theater is warm, and the movie is more reminiscent of a travel journal, with Villi telling you about all of the things he had to do in order to get the shot. It's an hour that may not keep your child's attention.

The show runs in English at 11 AM, 3 PM, and 8 PM in the summer. I think there are official prices, but Villi just named a price for our family. Expect to pay about what a museum would cost you.

If you or your child are very into volcanoes, you should go to chat with Villi. Maybe buy a DVD instead of seeing the movie? In my opinion, Villi is the major attraction at Red Rocks Cinema. If you want to see a volcano movie, try the Volcano House (page 135). If you want an experience, go see Villi.

The National Gallery of Iceland

Let's head back up to Tjörnin. As you walk to the left (east) side of the water, across the street you will soon come to the National Gallery of Iceland.

We visited the National Gallery on a Monday. The museum is now open daily in the summer, but closed on Mondays the rest of the year. Check listasafn.is for the current hours.

Admission is 1800 krona for adults, and free for kids 17 and under. Interestingly, this admission price includes admission to two other museums: The Sigurjón Ólafsson Museum (page 150) a decent little sculpture museum on the water, a little over a mile east of the Sun Voyager sculpture; and the Ásgrímur Jónsson Collection (page 145), a small art museum that is less than a 10 minute walk from here.

Happily, you don't have to visit the other museums on the same day. You'll get a ticket that will give you admission to the other museums whenever you want to go. This is different from the Reykjavik Art Museums; your admission there also gets you into two other Reykjavik Art Museums, but only on the same day (page 136). The other museums are open 1-5 every day in the summer; winter hours are extremely limited.

Sadly, I can't really recommend the National Gallery for younger kids. There were a few interesting sights. One was on the lowest level, where you could step on the squares

to change what was displayed on the walls. And there was a Picasso sculpture of his wife which the subject herself donated to Iceland. And a good assortment of very nice paintings, as you would expect from the National Gallery.

But it didn't hold our kids' interests for very long. And the very first exhibit we walked into was somewhat disturbing ... with skinned horses, distorted bodies, and more. This exhibit is no longer there. Check the museum's web site for what's there now. If you do a loop around the pond, you'll be passing right by the museum.

Ásgrímur Jónsson Collection

Let's jump away from the pond to a museum that's just a few minutes away from this area. One of the two other museums that's included with your admission to the National Gallery is the Ásgrímur Jónsson Collection. It's in the middle of a residential street. GPS coordinates are: 64.1400, -21.933056

Hours are 1-5 every day in the summer, and winter weekends, except in December and January when it's closed. We didn't make it here, but perhaps it's worth a quick

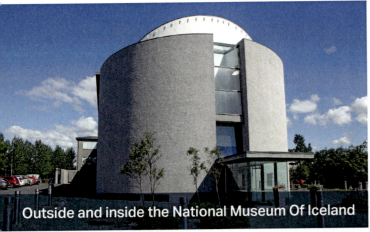
Outside and inside the National Museum Of Iceland

visit if you already have your ticket from the National Gallery.

The third museum is the Sigurjón Ólafsson Museum; see details of our visit on page 150.

The National Museum of Iceland

We spent a fair bit of time at the National Museum of Iceland. (Note the different name-- the art museum on the previous page is the National Gallery.) This is a little off of the beaten path. Okay, that's an exaggeration, since it's less than a 10 minute walk from Tjörnin pond; that's why I'm kind of shoehorning this into this section of the book. But you won't really run into it from another tourist attraction in Reykjavik.

The permanent and main exhibition here (like a few other museums around the country) covers the settlement of Iceland. It's called The Making of a Nation. What makes this one different is the scale of it-- it's huge, and has around 2,000 artifacts. As you walk through the exhibit, you are walking forward in time. Each display tells you what time period you are in. The second floor covers the early periods, and then you head up to the third floor as you get closer to the present day.

The museum costs 2000 krona for adults, but is free for anyone under 18. Given the prices of some museums in Reykjavik (especially by the harbor) 4000 krona for 2 adults and 2 or more kids doesn't seem too bad. A free audio guide is included.

There is a cafe, which was fine, but nothing worth going out of your way for. The soup of the day with bread cost 1300 krona and a quiche with salad cost around 1700. There were also cheaper options for the kids (or for anyone): A bagel with cream cheese or tuna fish is around $6.

So the food is fine if you need a meal while you are visiting the museum, though a walk up to the main part of Reykjavik will provide you with a lot more options. But the museum itself is very very nice, as is the gift shop. And there are typically temporary exhibits as well. The one for 2018 is about Saddlery. The special exhibits aren't of the same caliber as the main museum, but they add a little to the museum overall.

Reykjavik: Beyond Downtown

Nearly everything in the previous chapter about Reykjavik is walkable, or a short cab ride away. But there are some areas further outside of the main downtown area that you may want to explore. Hafnarfjörður (page 158), about 10 minutes outside of Reykjavik, is actually the third-largest town in Iceland. You'll find more museums (many of them free) as well as a beautiful hike up Helgafell mountain (page 159). And you'll run into plenty of locals climbing the mountain too.

Other areas are even more off of the tourist path. You probably won't make it to the neighboring municipalities of Garðabær, Kópavogur, and Álftanes, unless you end up staying in them. Well, unless you want to visit Costco (page 176). We rented a house in Álftanes, and enjoyed looking at the President's House, and visiting Iceland's only wave pool.

East of Reykjavik, you'll find the municipalities of Árbær (home to a great open air museum) and Mosfellsbær (home to hiking trails on Mt. Esja.)

Orient yourself with the map on page 147.

Laugardalur

Laugardalur is an area east of the main downtown harbor area. It's not walkable from too many spots. But there are several attractions here that are great for families. If you're looking to spend part of all of a day in Reykjavik a little bit outside of the downtown area, this is probably your best bet.

One note on the words here: Earlier we talked about one of the main shopping streets in Reykjavik, Laugavegur (page 140). This area is the very similar word Laugardalur.

Here are the attractions you'll find in Laugardalur.

Reykjavik Family Park and Zoo (year round)

The Reykjavik Family Park and Zoo won't compete against some of the large and impressive zoos you may have visited in the United States or elsewhere. But the price doesn't compete either. Adults (anyone 13+): cost 880 krona, kids 5-12 cost 660 krona, and kids under 5 are free.

So a family of 4 with 2 kids who are, say, 8 and 10, can get into both the zoo and the park for around $30 total. You pay one admission price for the whole complex—one ticket gets you into both the zoo and family park.

Let's start with the zoo. The highlight is the seals, who have a large pool an enclosure right in the middle of the zoo area. But you can also see reindeer, sheep, cows, horses, snakes, turtles, chickens, pigs, and more.

At the back of the zoo part, before you cross a bridge to the family park, is a cafeteria. Here they serve basic but reasonably priced zoo food. Examples from the menu include ham and cheese sandwich, ciabatta roll with brie and vegetables, and a waffle with jelly and whipped cream

On a sunny and warm day in June, there was a 10 or so minute line to order food some of the time, so you may want to check back once in a while to find a good time to eat. (Earlier is usually better.)

Past the cafeteria was the bridge to the family park. There

Family park section of the zoo

Grotta
A lighthouse you can walk to, but only during low tide!

AKUREY

Nauthólsvík Geothermal Beach
A free sandy beach with geothermally heated ocean water.

O Grotta

Kvika

SELTJARNARNES

NORDURSTRÖND

Nesvöllur

SUDURSTRÖND

EIDSGRANDI

Reykjavik Family Park and Zoo
An inexpensive family-friendly zoo and playground.

GEIRSGATA

SÆBRAUT

TÚNGATA

HVERFISGATA

BORGARTÚN

SÆBRAUT

BRÚNAVEGU

TÚN

LAUGAVEGUR

O **Zoo**

SÚS

Laugardalslaug
Reykjavik's largest thermal swimming pool- waterslides and more!

BARMAHLID

SUDURLANDSBRAUT

Laugardalslaug

Alftanes Swimming Pool
The longest waterslide in Iceland. And the only wave pool too!

EINARSNES

NAUTHOLSVEGUR

REYKJAVI

O

FOSSVO

Fagrilundu

Nauthólsvík O
Geothermal Beach

KÁRSNESSTIGUR

KÁRSNESBRAUT

NÝBÝLAVEGI

KÁRSNES

ÁLFHÓLSV

Rútstún

DIGRANESVEGUR

HLIÐARVEGUR

HLIÐARH

KÁRSNESSTIGUR

DALVE

BUKASTIGUR

KONGAVEGUR

Fifan

O

SUDURNESVEGUR

O **Bessastadir**

Smáralind

Alftanes Swimming Pool O

BESSASTADIRVEGUR

ARNARNESVEGUR

BREIDASBRAUT

Hlið

ÁLFTANESVEGUR

Gálgahraun

VIFILSSTADAVEGUR

KÁRLDRAUT

REYKJANESBRAUT

Garðahraun - Neðra

PRÝÐI

REYKJAVIKURVEGUR

HÓLSHRAUN

GARÐABÆR

Bessastadir
The President of Iceland's House. The church is open for visitors.

Bali

GARÐAHRAUN

ALHAMRIÐ

REYKJANESBRAUT

Vifilsstaðahraun

Víðistaðatún

HRAUNHOLTSBRAUT

HAMRABERG

REYKJANESBRAUT

KAPTÚN

O **Costco and IKE**

Setbergsvöllur

HÁBARBERG

Hellisgerði

LÆKJARGATA

GARÐABÆR

HRINGBRAUT

HÁHOLT

Costco and IKEA
The largest mall in Iceland. Includes an amusement park, and even child care

Víðistaðatún
A free sculpture park housing 16 sculptures from various artists.

Hvaleyrarvöllur

HVALEYRARBRAUT

SUDURBRAUT

ÁSBRAUT

REYKJANESBRAUT

BREIÐLAS

HAFNARFJORDUR

ÁLFSNES

Tungufoss

Þingvallavegur

Varmárósar

MOSFELLSBÆR

Hlíðavöllur

Álfatangi

Skeiðholt

Baugshlíð

Bjarkarholt

Háholt

Álafoss

VÍKUR

ENGI

Kollafjarðarstaðavegur

Vesturlandsvegur

Langirimi

Víkurvegur

Gagnvegur

HÚS

Fjallkonuvegur

Árbær Open air museum

An outdoor museum-- many old houses have been moved here

Snarfarahöfn

Reynisvatn

Geirsnef

STÓRHÖFÐI

Breiðhöfði

Bíldshöfði

Höfðabakki

teinahlíð

Reykjanesbraut

VESTURLANDSVEGUR

Strengur

Grjóthals

HÁLSAR

Grafarholtsvöllur

Tangarhöfði

Höfðabakki

Árbær
Open Air
Museum

Bæjarbraut

Rofabær

Suðurlandsvegur

Stekkjarás

NORÐURHOLT

Arnarbakki

Suðurhólar

Selásbraut

Sandavegur

BAKKAR

Vesturberg

Austurberg

BERG

Breiðholtsbraut

Búgða

Suðurlandsvegur

Nesjavallaleið

félag Reykjavíkur

VÍÐIDALUR

Seljabraut

Skógarsel

AGARSEL

SEL

Jaðarsel

Breiðholtsbraut

Rauðhólar

Mærastugurinn

Salavegur

Heiðmerkurvegur

ug

Sparkvöllur

Kórinn

Suðurlandsvegur

Samskipavöllurinn

Guðmundarlundur

Suðurlandsvegur

Heiðmerkurvegur

Helgafell Mountain

A mountain climb with lots of different paths and a restaurant at the base.

N

0 feet   1500   3000

Helgafell Mountain

are many activities here that don't cost anything extra, including a water play area, a cool boat / bridge over the water, a zip line, a Viking ship play area, and a swinging tire thing. But other rides require the purchase of extra tickets. You can buy these when you first pay for admission, or you can also purchase them at the snack bar in the family park area. A pack of 10 tickets will cost 2,650 krona, which works out to about $2.50 a ticket. Most rides are 1 or 2 tickets. Given that there are so many free options, I'm not sure it is worth it to pay $5 for a ride, though they certainly look exciting.

There seemed to be a good mix of locals and tourists there. And while this may not be on your list of "must-see" attractions in Iceland, the zoo is a nice place to spend an afternoon. The zoo is open year-round; the availability of the rides and play areas in the Family Park may be limited in the winter.

Reykjavik Botanical Gardens

(year round)

The Reykjavik Botanical Gardens is right next to the Zoo and Family Park, and it's free! Because we wanted to get to the restaurant in the gardens, Florin Café, we parked on the other side of the Botanical Gardens, on Sunnuvegur. GPS of this entrance is 64.1403183, -21.8655612. It felt like we were walking in the back entrance, but parking on the street was easy and free, and it wasn't a long walk to the Botanical Gardens.

The Botanical Gardens are large enough to spend a good amount of time wandering around, exploring the various gardens. You'll find planned gardens with various themes. Some are open areas where the kids can run around, and some have narrow stone pathways through densely planted specimens. This is a great stop on a nice day. And it's free!

Flóran Café

(summer only)

Flóran Café is a restaurant smack in the middle of the Reykjavik Botanical Gardens. It's inside of a greenhouse, and only open in the summer months. And, since cars aren't allowed in the Botanical Gardens, you're walking through the gardens to get to your food.

The inside is spectacular, though I imagine it could get a bit hot on sunny summer days. Flóran offers a regular menu, as well as a weekend brunch. Strangely, they didn't have a brunch menu in the restaurant, at least not one in English. I had to know to ask for it since I had seen it online; very odd. You may have to ask for help with the menu, unless this has been changed.

The food was beautifully prepared, but it's not cheap, unless you get ham and cheese from the kid's menu. As an example, we tried the smoked salmon brunch for 2700 krona. There is a good amount of food on the plate- vegetable quiche, pancakes with blueberry compote, some plain skyr-type thing, smoked salmon, bread, butter, 2 kinds of cheese, and fruit.

A meal here with kids can be pricey, and there are only a handful of things on the menu that kids might enjoy. But this could be a good spot to take a break from walking around the Botanical Gardens and enjoy some hot chocolate (though it's 580 krona!)

Ásmundur Sveinsson Sculpture Museum

Just a 5 minute drive away (or less if you park at the zoo) is the Ásmundur Sveinsson Sculpture Museum, also called Ásmundarsafn. This is part of the Reykjavik Art Museums; if you pay for admission to any one of the three museums, admission to the others will be free on the same day. See our information about the other 2: Hafnarhús is on page 136; see our web site for Kjarvalsstaðir. (Search for "Kjarvalsstadir IcelandWithKids")

We didn't think the "primary" Art Museum, Hafnarhús (the main one by the harbor) had great exhibits for kids. This one was much more kid friendly. Mostly because kids are allowed to climb on three of the biggest sculptures! (I felt a little self-conscious with my kids climbing all over famous works of art.

Laugardalslaug pool complex

I wanted to yell at any onlookers: "The lady at the front desk said this was allowed!")

Outside, the sculptures are by Ásmundur Sveinsson; this was his home and studio. Exhibits inside change; see artmuseum.is/asmundarsafn for what's there now.

Admission to the museum is 1650 krona, but free for kids 17 and under. For families with younger kids, the zoo would most likely be a little cheaper and a bigger hit. But this is in the area, and could round out a nice day at the Zoo and Botanical Gardens.

Laugardalslaug

Laugardalslaug is the city geothermal pool complex in Laugardalur. This is the city's largest pool, but remember that there are a whole lot of impressive pools in and around Reykjavik-- and all over Iceland!

Laugardalslaug is seriously impressive, though. In the picture above you can see the main pool, the children's pool, the big waterslide, and a kid's waterslide. Not shown: The indoor lap pool, a huge hot tub, steam rooms, yet another small kids' waterslide, the sand volleyball area, the rope climbing area ... there's a lot here. And it only costs 980 krona for adults, and 160 krona for children.

I recommend visiting one (or more) of the city pools in Iceland. (See our tips for navigating the Icelandic locker rooms on page 171.) I say "city pool" to differentiate from the much more expensive private pools, such as the Blue Lagoon or Laugarvatn Fontana.

We had a good time at the pool. But this is one of the most popular city pools, and it was crowded-- especially the hot tubs and the children's pool. You should find more manageable crowds either earlier in the day, or at one of the other pools around Reykjavik. But it's still one of the best deals in town.

Laugar Spa

Let's start with the bad news right away: Laugar Spa is only for people 18 and older. We didn't visit, but it looks like a very fancy spa facility that offers massages and other treatments. The facility is right next to Laugardalslaug swimming pool. It doesn't come cheap of course; check out the options at laugarspa.com.

Sigurjón Ólafsson Museum

(Year round except December and January. Hours are seasonal; check Lso.is for current information.)

I hesitated about including this one in the Laugardalur section. It is indeed in Laugardalur, but every other attraction listed here is right in the same area—nothing is more than 2 or 3 minutes from anything else, and some of them are walkable.

The Sigurjón Ólafsson Museum is north, right up by the water. This is one of the three museums that are part of the National Gallery of Iceland (page 144). This gets confusing—there are three museums that are a part of the Reykjavik Art Museums, and a different three museums that are part of the National Gallery of Iceland. Buy a ticket to any of the 3, and you get access to the other 2. (And you can visit the other 2 on a different day with the National Gallery; the Art Museum makes you visit on the same day.)

Back to Sigurjón Ólafsson Museum, part of the National Gallery of Iceland. It's only open from 2-5 PM. In the summer, you get those hours every day; in the winter, you only get weekends.

This is a museum featuring the sculptures of drawings of Sigurjón Ólafsson. There is no permanent exhibit, except for the sculptures outside; check lso.is for what's there now.

If you already have a ticket, this is worth a visit; again, the area around the museum is part of the draw. The museum is right on the water, a mile or so east of the downtown harbor area. It's right on the shore walk that connects to downtown.

But otherwise, we're not sure the National Gallery or these associated museums are worthwhile for families, at least those without a specific interest in art.

Viðey Island

(year-round; daily in the summer, weekends only in winter)

Further east along the shore from Sigurjón Ólafsson Museum is the port from which you can take a short boat ride to Viðey Island. It seems strange to call an island a museum, but it is indeed one of the Reykjavik City Museums. The ferry ride is short-- maybe 5 or 7 minutes? This is a good "starter" trip for a younger child who isn't sure if they like boat rides.

In the summertime, there are actually multiple places where you can catch the ferry to Viðey. You can see the ferry schedule at elding.is. Boats leave from: The Old Harbor; behind Harpa concert hall; or from Skarfabakki pier. Skarfabakki is much closer to the island, and departures are much more frequent. It's also your only choice in the winter.

You can choose to leave from any of the ports, and return to any of them, even if it's not the same one. They don't even check your tickets on the way back-- they assume if you made it to the island, you must have purchased a ticket and now you need to get back! There is only one boat; if there are multiple ports scheduled for the trip, the boat will go from Viðey to Skarfabakki, and then on to the other ports.

The ferry is a small boat as ferries go; it can only hold maybe 20 or 30 passengers comfortably. I was told that the boat almost never fills up; if it does, they will just have it turn around and make a second trip. So you can just get to the port a few minutes early and buy your tickets before you board. (We did this at Skarfabakki, though I assume it works the same way for the other ports.)

What all of this means is that you will probably have 50 or fewer people with you on a large island. It's a nice way to get to a more remote place without having to go very far at all.

The boat docks at the island, and you'll walk up the hill toward the restaurant on the right. There's a church next to the restaurant; feel free to open the door and explore inside. Behind the church and restaurant there are a couple of picnic tables and a small playground for the kids.

The restaurant seems overpriced, though I guess they have to get all of the food out there on a boat. A kid's hamburger was 1890 -- that's about the most expensive I've seen.

Imagine Peace Tower

But you can bring a picnic lunch if you'd like, and just explore the island. There are lots of meandering hiking trails; it's tough to tell where some of them are going, though it seems pretty hard to get lost on the island. The hikes may take longer than you expected; make sure you don't miss the last ferry back!

There are two art installations you can check out if you are interested. The first is far more famous-- the Imagine Peace Tower by Yoko Ono. During the summer, it's just a big round white thing, with "Imagine Peace" written on it in many many languages. But in the winter they turn on the extremely powerful lights inside; the lights shine straight up and are visible from miles away. See the schedule at ImaginePeaceTower.com. It's not something that is a must see, but it's a nice destination for a 20 or 25 minute hike.

The second art installation is called Áfangar, by American artist Richard Serra. It's tough to explain. Basically, there are a bunch of pairs of pillars, each of which goes to the same height above sea level. As the ground slopes, the distance between the pairs changes. It's an interesting and sprawling sculpture, spread over a large chunk of the island.

The ferry to Videy costs 1550 krona for adults 16 and older, 775 krona for kids 6-12, and is free for kids 5 and under. That's the total cost for the round trip. The trip is what you make of it-- don't expect to be entertained on the island! But if you budget a couple of hours to explore the island, it's a great and peaceful getaway. Bring a snack or a picnic lunch!

Icewear Outlet Store

I don't think this is technically in Laugardalur, but it's 5 minutes or less from the zoo. The Icewear outlet store is out in a non-touristy shopping area; it feels like you've found a "normal" part of Reykjavik. The front portion is a regular Icewear store, which merchandise that is sold in other stores throughout Iceland. But in the back there is an outlet section, with merchandise that can be up to 80% off. If you're not picky about what you take home for a souvenir, this can be worth a stop. The address is Fákafen 9 in Reykjavik.

Heading to Viðey Island

Seltjarnarnes

Seltjarnarnes is the furthest west municipality in Reykjavik. This isn't a very popular tourist destination, but there are a few things to see, and it can be a nice break from the more crowded areas of town.

Take a look at our map on page 147. Notice the two land areas jutting out on the upper left side, out into the ocean. The lower land mass is a golf course, though there is a nature reserve just above the golf course. And there's a restaurant in the clubhouse, which we didn't go to.

But the main attraction is the top land mass, where the Grótta lighthouse is located. Here's the fun part: the small bit of land which leads to the lighthouse is only open during low tide. If you get your times wrong, you'll get stuck by the lighthouse for 6 hours as the water rises around you. When I originally posted this online, I downplayed this possibility. Surely someone closes off the road, and no one actually gets stuck. But then we received a comment:

"... the sign with the tides is no joke – the water comes and you will be stuck there for 6 hours and no, no one comes and closes the road. Have been living next to this lighthouse for many years – and there is always someone every year who does not take notice of the sign and get stuck."

Thanks, Freyja! So, before you go make sure you check out the flood table. Google "flodatoflur" and a result from seltjarnarnes.is should be at the top; click through and then click on the month for the flood table you need. It's also posted the parking lot.

It's a short hike from the parking lot, and you end up at the lighthouse. There wasn't much to do here. I think the attraction is two-fold. First, you get to walk to what is technically an island; having to be aware of the tide is cool and interesting. Second, this is a very quiet natural area that's very close to Reykjavik. In fact, you can walk here from the harbor area in about an hour.

Note that the area is closed from May 1 – July 15 because of nesting birds.

If you do walk from Reykjavik, be sure to look for the warm water footbath that you'll find on the way. It was actually made by the same person who made the sculpture Þúfa (page 128)! We didn't see it, as it's out of the way if you drive to the parking lot. Which seems fitting-- we didn't walk far enough to need a warm foot soak!

Grotta Lighthouse

Nesstofa Pharmacy Museum

(Summer only)

Just a minute or two down the road (driving) from Grótta is the Nesstofa Pharmacy Museum. Actually, Nesstofa is the house on the left where the pharmacist lived; to the right is the Pharmacy Museum. Both houses are part of the museum.

The house was built in the 1760s as the residence for the first doctor and pharmacist in Iceland. The house has some art inside of it. Perhaps more interesting for kids is the Pharmacy, which houses lots of old objects related to medicine.

The museum is free, and is worth a stop if you're in the area. You can get here regardless of the tide, but the hours are limited: 1-5 PM, closed Mondays. It's tricky to coordinate those hours with a visit to Grótta lighthouse.

Seltjarnarnes Swimming Pool

As you head back to Reykjavik, but still in Seltjarnarnes, you will find the Seltjarnarnes swimming pool. This is yet another thermal pool in Reykjavik City. This one features a sea water pool, a waterslide, and the usual assortment of hot tubs. There's a tiny cafe next door, with unique sandwiches and smoothies.

If you're in the mood, Seltjarnarnes can be a relaxing place to escape the crowds in Reykjavik.

Sample Grotta tide schedule. Blue is low tide, and the open and close times surround it. So on September 1, you can go between 1:42 AM - 5:42 AM, or 1:59 PM to 5:59 PM. Don't push it until the end of a range, though!

Sept 2018	Opnar	Háfjara árdegis	Lokar	Opnar	Háfjara síðdegis	Lokar
1-sep-18	01:42	03:42	05:42	13:59	15:59	17:59
2-sep-18	02:26	04:26	06:26	14:54	16:54	18:54

South of Downtown Reykjavik

Much of the area south of Reykjavik (beyond Tjörnin) is taken up by the Reykjavik City airport. Remember that this is a local airport; you'll find flights to other cities in Iceland, as well as Greenland. Otherwise, all international flights take off and land at the airport in Keflavik. But there are a few attractions scattered in this area.

Perlan

The Perlan is one of the most recognizable structures in Reykjavik. In many pictures of the Reykjavik "skyline", you'll see Hallgrímskirkja (Hallgrim's church, page 141) on one side, and Perlan up on the hill on the other side.

It's tough to keep up with what the Perlan offers. The Saga Museum moved to Grandi Harbor (page 127) and the revolving restaurant closed in 2017. The artificial geiser is gone too. As of mid 2018, you have:

• A new revolving restaurant, called Út í bláinn. It's open for lunch and dinner. It only rotates from 9-11 PM, though.

• A cafe called Kaffitár that should be a better value than the restaurant

• An outdoor observation deck, with nice views of Reykjavik

• An exhibit called Wonders of Iceland, including a real man-made ice cave and virtual tours.

• A brand new Planetarium

There is now a charge for the observation deck, which used to be free. It costs 490 krona for adults 16 and older; kids 15 and under are free. The exhibit is 3900 for adults and 1950 for kids 6-15 (free under 6.) That 3900 includes access to the observation deck. But families should give serious consideration to the family package. Basically, pay for 2 adults at 3900 each and get 2 kids in free. These prices have increased as new exhibitions are added.

The new planetarium costs just 600 ISK more. Check perlan.is for the latest.

If you don't have a car, there is a shuttle bus that runs from Harpa concert hall in downtown Reykjavik.

Nauthólsvík Geothermal Beach

Nauthólsvík Geothermal Beach is tucked in just below the city airport, and it's not really close to anything else. I had

a little trouble finding it, and there's no way you would just stumble upon it. But let's cut to the chase: It's free, and I think your kids will love it. Note that you'll only find a large parking lot once you get there-- you can't see the beach from the road. But head toward the water, and eventually you'll see it!

Strangely, there is a fee for the locker rooms in the winter, but everything is free in the summer. This is definitely a place where you'll find mostly locals. Well, in the summer you'll still find some tourists, but also a lot of locals. We're really close to the airport here; if the flight paths work out, you'll get some excellent up-close views of planes landing.

Closest to us in the photo above you have a long rectangular hot tub, which is about 38 degrees Celsius, or right around 100 Fahrenheit. This is usually a good temperature for kids to enjoy; any warmer, and they tend to get too hot after a while. Closer to the water (middle of picture) is a round pool which is colder, but still heated. Lots of kids seemed to be frolicking there.

Then you have the ocean water, which is actually heated a few degrees more than normal with geothermal hot water. It was definitely chilly, but also definitely not freezing cold.

There's a snack bar that sells ice cream, drinks, and candy; you can also buy uncooked hot dogs, and grill them on the grills on site.

The changing facilities are not as nice as what you'll find at the other

The Perlan

geothermal pools around town, or around the country. There are no lockers; you just leave your stuff in a crate, which is provided, and slide it onto a shelf. You can do as the locals do and just leave your valuables in your crate, or leave them behind in your car. And the locker rooms are busy and ... fast-moving. You may want to visit another pool before trying this one, though it shouldn't be a big deal. Just remember that, like everywhere else, you have to shower naked before swimming.

Locker rooms aside, Nauthólsvík is extremely nice. And extremely free in the summertime!

Nauthóll

At the far end of the Nauthólsvík parking lot there is a fancy restaurant, Nauthóll. It's open for lunch and dinner every day. I skipped it; I say it's fancy only because the menu looked expensive. Fish soup was 3190 krona, or over $30 But the kids brunch, available only on Sundays. might be a good value. For 1550 for kids (3150 for adults), you get:

"The brunch dish contains leavened bread, serrano ham, camembert cheese, figs, american pancakes and high quality maple syrup, mini-muffin, baked egg, greek yogurt with homemade muesli, Icelandic vegetables and fruit. Fresh orange juice comes with every brunch dish."

Nordic House

I debated where to classify Nordic House; you could just as easily put it at the very southern tip of the Tjörnin pond area, or the very north of this section.

Every Sunday in the summer, the Nordic House hosts concerts in their adorable greenhouse. We listened to Anna Jónsdóttir singing traditional Icelandic Folk music. The concert was about 45 minutes; the kids weren't into it very much, but I thought it was great. The concerts are free; check NordicHouse.is/en/event to see what's happening now.

Every day, you'll find a kid's play area outside (which my kids really enjoyed), and a kid's library inside. There are also temporary exhibitions; check nordichouse.is to see your current options.

After the concert and the exhibit, we tried the Nordic House's cafe for a snack. They had very nice homemade cakes and pies, with interesting crusts. There may have been nuts and/or seeds in the crust? All of the cakes, like our blueberry cheesecake, cost 1100 krona. That's at the high end of what you'll pay for a dessert. They were good, but I don't think the kids appreciated them more than less expensive desserts elsewhere.

If you're in the area on a nice day, at least check out the outdoor play areas!

Kringlan Mall

Kringlan is again hard to classify by its geography. A little bit

Climbing outside of Nordic House

east of the Perlan, this is the largest mall in Reykjavik. It turns out that designation is a bit of a technicality, since Kringlan is 7 minutes away from the larger Smáralind (page 157), which is the largest mall in Iceland. Apparently, Smáralind is just outside of Reykjavik, so it can't be the largest mall in Reykjavik!

There's no special reason to head here, unless the idea of an Icelandic mall interests you or you need to buy something. You'll find a food court that houses some Icelandic quick service places as well as a Subway. There's also the usual assortment of stores, banks, a movie theater, and, perhaps surprisingly, two large grocery stores.

East of Downtown Reykjavik

We visited just a couple of attractions to the east of Reykjavik, in the municipalities of Árbær and Mosfellsbær. These are definitely no walkable from downtown-- you're driving or taking a bus.

Árbær Open Air Museum

(June – August)

First up is another Reykjavik City Museum, Árbær Open Air Museum. Here, they've taken a lot of old houses from around Iceland and moved them to one place. This creates the feel of a village from the mid 19th century, give or take.

Most of the houses are set up so you can see how people used to live. Some have specific exhibits in them. The "museum" is several acres in size, and you can wander around and explore whichever houses catch your interest.

On the day we went, they were playing children's games. There was some rain, and so there wasn't a ton of interest in the outdoor games. But we did play some Koob ("club") with the costumed workers. They'll be happy to tell you the rules of the game; you need to throw your stick and knock down the wooden pieces in a specific order!

Each building has something different going on. One building near the front has an exhibit about toys and life in different years. Kids can explore and play in a room made up with toys from 1968, for example. There's a working Nintendo with Super Mario Bros in the room from the 80's, so prepare yourself if your kids might get sucked into that option ...

Further back, there's an exhibit called "Between the Lines"

which talks about how women used to earn a living in a society that expected them to conform to gender stereotypes.

But most of the houses are just houses, with kitchens and bedrooms to explore. You'll find a blacksmith, a printer, and homes of ordinary people.

If you're lucky, and you're there on a Saturday, you may find someone making scones in one of the kitchens. And on any day you may stumble across other costumed interpreters outside or inside some of the homes.

We let the older kids wander around on their own; the place feels big enough to explore, but small enough that you can always find your way back to the square at the entrance. There's a map on the museum's web site; go to borgarsogusafn.is. This is the web site for the Reykjavik City Museums. Click on "EN" for English, and then choose "Museum Area" from the page for the Árbær Open Air Museum.

You will also find a cafe called Dillon's Cafe. Like all of the other houses here, it was moved to Árbær. In this case, the house was built in 1835 by Arthur Dillon; it was moved here in 1960. We didn't eat here, and the menu appears limited. But you can find several items, both meals (lamb soup is 1700 krona) and sweets (kleina donuts are 500 krona.)

Admission is 1650 krona for adults, and free for kids 17 and under. We enjoyed Árbær, and we recommend it if the weather is nice. I do wish this was more like Colonial Williamsburg in the United States, though the price of admission there is about 5 times more expensive for a family of 4. But it would be fun if Árbær would pick a day in history, and have all of the costumed interpreters pretending to be from that day. I'm not sure what the days would be. June 17th, 1944-- Icelandic Independence Day? The day women got the right to vote in 1915? Someone who knows more about Iceland would have to figure this out.

Anyway, if you have a car, this is a museum where everyone in the family should find something to enjoy.

Mt. Esja

The city of Reykjavik seems to be guarded by Mt. Esja. The mountain is visible from most parts of the city.

Esja is about a 25 minute drive from Reykjavik, and has a complex hiking trail system that should appeal to almost any difficulty level you are looking for.

There is a parking lot at the base of the mountain, as well as a restaurant. We didn't eat at the restaurant, called Esjustofa. They used to have an impressive and inexpensive kid's menu, but that looks like a thing of the past. See the current menu at esjustofa.is.

To the left of the restaurant you will find a very impressive hiking trail map. It's like a subway map, showing you the stops and transfers you can make at each of those points. Take a picture or two of the map to reference as you hike! (Or just bring this book with you!)

But even with a photo, we couldn't really find our way on the paths on the right. Besides the two or three labeled points at the bottom of the mountain, we didn't see any other names. And so we tried to piece it together from the colors that labeled the paths. We eventually found our way, but it was more confusing than I expected.

You will see wooden sticks along the path, with colors on top. But the path we were on was both a green and an orange path? Like I said, it's more confusing than the map implies.

Unless you are an extremely accomplished hiker and climber, you shouldn't go past Steinn, which is a big rock with a sign marked "Steinn"; the last 200 meters or so that lead to the peak seem to be steep and dangerous. Even the hike to Steinn can take an hour or so up; presumably, the walk

Climbing Mt. Esja

The yarn selection at Álafoss

Esja is one of two hikes we recommend within half an hour of Reykjavik; we enjoyed both this hike and Helgafell in Hafnarfjörður (page 159.) On nice days, you'll find a lot of locals at both mountains. Esja has the option of the restaurant at the base, while you won't find any food or drink at Helgafell. And Esja is probably more famous, so it may be your best choice if you only plan to do one of them.

Mosfellsbær

On the way to Esja from Reykjavik, you'll pass right by the town of Mosfellsbær. There are a few places of interest here. By now you probably know that every town in Iceland has a thermal swimming pool. Surprisingly (at least to me), you'll find two thermal swimming pools in Mosfellsbær: The older Varmárlaug, where you'll find more locals and the newer and impressive Lágafellslaug, which is one of the nicest pools in Reykjavik.

We skipped the pools, and stopped by Álafoss, the famous wool store. There's a location in downtown Reykjavik too, but the Mosfellsbær store is much larger.

The yarn selection is impressive; they also had a selection of plans and knitting kits. If you're serious about knitting, this is the place to go. But otherwise, as long as you can handle the crowds and cramped spaces, I thought the Handknitting store in Reykjavik (page 141) is a better place to buy a premium wool sweater or blanket.

I didn't realize that Álafoss is on a quaint street with some other shops. Further back on the left is the Álafoss café; this building used to house the old Álafoss wool factory. You'll find lunch, dinner or cakes here.

Even further down on the left is the Knifemaker-- this was one of my favorite stores in Iceland. You may need to ring the bell to get in. But inside is an amazing collection of handmade knives. Some handles are made from whale bone, reindeer horn, and more.

The knives aren't cheap-- very few of the larger knives were under $300. But they were beautiful works of art, and it's a worthwhile stop if you're already on the street.

Fjallaleiðir
Mountain Paths

F1 Steinn - Varða
7km

F2 Kögunarhóll
6,3km

F3 Fjallaleið um Gunnlaugsskarð
10,6- 10,8km

back down would take less time. The total roundtrip length is about 3.5 miles. If you want to get to Steinn, which can be a gathering place for people doing the hike, stick to the paths on the left and just head straight up.

We were a little lost, but we always knew how to retrace our steps if needed. As you climb higher, you'll get to points where you can turn around and see the beautiful views looking out toward Reykjavik.

Reykjavik's South and West Municipalities

We're now heading outside of the areas of Reykjavik that most tourists go to. But let's take a quick look at a couple of points of possible interest in these neighboring municipalities. Maybe you'll end up renting a house in one of these places, and you're looking for things nearby. Or maybe you want to venture outside of Reykjavik and see what there is to see. You may also not be too far from any of these as you head to or from the Keflavik airport. See the map on page 147.

Garðabær Municipality

Okay, Garðabær is only here because it is home to Iceland's only Ikea and Iceland's only Costco. And they're right next to each other, about 15 minutes south of Reykjavik.

Ikea

Every good Icelandic vacation includes a trip to Ikea. Okay, not really. But if you find you need to buy something— fabric to cover your windows to block the 24 hour sun?— Ikea is the way to go. It's also the way to go if you want a really cheap meal for the kids.

In the United States, you can get a kids meal for $2.49 or so. In Iceland, kid's meals cost 345 krona, or about $2.80. That seems like a better deal than $2.49 in the US, given the higher cost of food in Iceland. And an adult chicken leg meal, with 3 large legs, French fries, and a side of coleslaw, will only cost you 995 krona.

Museum of Design and Applied Art

(year round)

This is a small museum in a strip mall area. The museum shares the building with a grocery store. The main museum is upstairs, and has clothes, furniture, toys, and model architecture. There is a small adjoining room up here, meant for kids. They can pretend to be designers. So for example, kids will be asked to design a fabric for a chair they saw in the main area.

Downstairs, there is a gift shop and a children's play area. Admission for adults is 1000 krona; kids 18 and under are free. honnunarsafn.is

In a neighboring building (the one with the Domino's pizza) there is a restaurant called "Coffee and Sushi". They have great hearty soups for 900 krona: Chicken meatball rice soup with green onion, fresh ginger, and a whole egg.

Costco

The first and only Costco in Iceland opened in May of 2017. The answer to your question is yes: Your membership from the US or another county will work in Iceland too. But you'll have to head to customer service, show your card, and ask for a day pass.

They also sell gas here, which often will be the cheapest in Iceland.

Kópavogur Municipality

Kópavogur is closer to Reykjavik than Garðabær. You can get to any of the places below in 10 minutes or so from downtown Reykjavik.

Smáralind

This is the biggest mall in Iceland. We didn't stop by, though we did pass by many times. Since it's technically in Kópavogur and not in Reykjavik, Kringlan can still call itself the largest mall in Reykjavik, even though Smáralind is both the biggest mall in Iceland and only 7 minutes from Kringlan.

You'll find the same stuff you'll find at Kringlan (page 154): stores, restaurants, a movie theater, and two grocery stores. But here you'll also find an entertainment complex called Smáratívolí, with a "7D" movie, laser tag, mini bowling and more. The activities look pretty expensive (1100 krona for the movie, for example), but this could be something different to try on a rainy day. See smarativoli.is for information on the entertainment complex.

Kópavogur Art Museum

The Art Museum and the Natural History Museum are right next to each other in Kópavogur. Let's start with the Art Museum. Upstairs, you have a strange English word poem exhibit; you'll see a few words of profanity scattered through the poems.

Downstairs there are some wire sculptures that are kind of fun. But what may make this work your time and the admission price (only 500 krona for adults, and free for children) is the play area downstairs. They have hammers, nails, and string. And a wall. If your kids are old enough to hammer some nails into the wall, you may be stuck here for a very long time!

Make your own art!

Kópavogur Natural History Museum

Less impressive than the Art Museum, but also less expensive (free) is the Natural History museum next door; it's inside the town library. You can pay 500 krona for an English guide book, but we just walked around for a few minutes. There is a huge redwood tree chunk, given to Iceland as a gift from the United States. Otherwise, you have several exhibits of animals, shells, and rocks.

If the hammer and nails at the Art Museum sound interesting, you may want to stop by Kópavogur; while you're there, you can explore both museums.

Álftanes Municipality

We spent a month in a house in Álftanes; this municipality is about 15 or 20 minutes from Reykjavik, though it's 10 minutes or less to Hafnarfjörður. If your vacation doesn't take you outside of the Reykjavik area, and you have a car, this can be a nice place to explore. You'll find some quiet black sand beaches, as well as a couple of attractions.

Bessastadir – the President's House

Iceland became an independent country in 1941, and ever since then the president has lived in this house. There are several buildings, all with the same design of white buildings with red roofs. Don't go inside the house, though you can visit the church (which is pictured.) There's not much else to see, though the views of Reykjavik from here are very nice.

Álftanes wave pool

If you're looking for a wave pool in Iceland, you'll need to head out the pool here in Álftanes. It's a great pool overall with lots of friendly locals and very few locals. The waterslide is the longest in Iceland, and the children's pool is large and features buckets that slowly fill and dump warm water a couple of times a minute. In the picture you can see the normal lap pool; the wave pool is off to the right, and is only

Álftanes wave pool

run when an attendant goes over to turn it on. If you hear an announcement in Icelandic, most likely they are saying the waves will be turned on momentarily.

Outside of the pool is a hot dog stand. (That sentence applies to nearly every pool in Iceland too!) This one, called Bitakot, is more like a small restaurant, with hot dogs, hamburgers, sandwiches, a couple of burritos, and more.

Álftanes is an off-the-beaten-path suburb. Given we spent so much time there, I think it's tough for me to judge whether it's worthwhile. But we liked it; a visit to the pool, a black sand beach, and seeing the President's House could be a fun trip if you have some extra time.

Hafnarfjörður

Hafnarfjörður could perhaps be considered a suburb of Reykjavik, but it is a town in its own right. It's about a 15 or 20 minute drive from Reykjavik. I'm guessing most people don't make it out here—they spend time in Reykjavik and exploring nature through the rest of the country. And that's okay. I'm not going to tell you that you have to visit Hafnarfjörður. But it does have a different feel—a little less touristy.

Here is what we saw in town.

Víðistaðatún Sculpture Garden

Víðistaðatún boasts 16 sculptures from artists from 7 different countries. They are spread over several acres, and you may not see them all. But the park had nice walking trails through lava fields, and so it was a nice combination of hiking and art. It's a little tricky to find; it's just a city park in a neighborhood: The GPS coordinates are 64.076389, -21.962778. The park is free to enjoy.

Hafnarfjörður City Museums

The main draw of the museums in Hafnarfjörður is that they are all completely free. The two main museums are next to each other: Pakkhúsið is one; it's a museum about the town of Hafnarfjörður. The other is The Sívertsen´s House, which is the oldest house in town, formerly owned by a wealthy fishing merchant. And behind these museums is a third one, called Beggubúð; it was closed when we tried to visit.

For more information for these and the other smaller museums, go to visithafnarfjordur.is and click on "Art & Culture."

The two main museums in Hafnarfjörður

Viking Village

We stopped by the Viking Village one afternoon, though not much was going on. You can walk around and explore the buildings, most of which are hotel rooms. There's a gift shop in the main lobby, and you'll also find some chickens behind one of the buildings.

A Viking-style dinner is served every evening in the restaurant Fjörugarðurinn. You can try their traditional Viking feast, complete with entertainment from the singing waitstaff. The feast is expensive, though you can also order off of the menu and still get to enjoy the atmosphere.

Viking Village has both hotel rooms and larger family rooms that can work for a family of 5 or 6. But overall, unless you plan to stay here or dine here or attend a special event, I don't think there's a big need to stop by here.

The Hafnarfjörður Centre of Culture and

The Viking Village

Fine Art

(year-round)

One of the buildings in the downtown area is home to Hafnarborg, the Hafnarfjörður Centre of Culture and Fine Art. We started with lunch in the restaurant, which just opened under new management over the summer of 2016.

The new restaurant is Kaffistofan, which was excellent. The food was nothing fancy, but it was very good, and we felt it was very well-priced. A couple of the kids ordered nachos for lunch. They weren't able to finish the portion, which cost

1299 krona. Remember, that includes tax and tip! I ordered BBQ legs, which was 5 large chicken legs in a sauce, with some vegetables on the side. Another good deal for $14 or so. A lunch at Kaffistofan plus some of the free museums in Hafnarfjörður makes for a cheap visit.

Speaking of cheap, while waiting for our food to arrive, the kids checked out the art museum upstairs. It's free! The exhibits stick around for only a few months, so you'll have to check their web site (hafnarborg.is/en) to see what will be there during your visit. The exhibit we saw was called Traces of Water, and featured some interesting sculptures. It's just one open room, but your family should be entertained for at least a few minutes. If you're in the area, it's worth a quick visit, especially for the price (free!)

Ásvallalaug Thermal Pool

(year round)

Of course, you don't have to head out to Hafnarfjörður to swim in a thermal pool. But you do if you want to visit the largest thermal pool in Iceland, Ásvallalaug. Almost all of it is indoors, which is unusual for Iceland. It was nice to have everything inside, since it avoids the cold walks to, from, and between various pools. But somehow it felt less Icelandic to me. (Which is silly, since there will be mostly locals here!)

Like other city thermal pools, it's cheap: $10 or so total for

Ásvallalaug Thermal Pool

1 adult and 3 kids. Again, there's no need to head out just for this.

Helgafell Mountain

Here's how the Visit Hafnarfjörður web site describes hiking on Helgafell mountain: "With an accessible and easy trail, walking on Helgafell is popular for all levels of hikers, including young children."

The parking area can be a little hard to find; GPS coordinates are 64.022917, -21.868306. It's about a half hour drive from the harbor area of downtown Reykjavik; or 15 minutes from

Atop Helgafell

downtown Hafnarfjörður. You're in the right place if you see a Blue sign that says "Helgafell: 2.8 km." (Note that there is another Helgafell in West Iceland; that one is called Helgafell Holy Mountain, but it is over 2 hours from Reykjavik.)

The hike has several sections; there's a lot of walking before you get to the mountain part. First, you're walking along a path to get to a small opening in the fence. The gap in the fence is wide enough for people and bicycles, but I assume it would prevent people from using ATVs. Past the fence is another flat area that leads toward the trail up the mountain. A series of Cairns— stacks of stones— mark the way.

Now you'll finally start climbing the mountain! There are some very steep and slippery sections; good hiking boots help. After maybe 15 minutes, you'll come to the first landing area. You can stop here, or keep heading higher. The views from here are still impressive— you'll be able to see how small your car looks in the parking lot.

But you can also continue up the mountain. Again, not surprisingly, this is steep! At some point, the path more or less disappears, and we just headed one direction: Up. We made it to a landing which wasn't quite the top of the mountain, but it was enough!

From here, you can see Reykjavik off in the distance. After enjoying the view and resting for a little while, we started to head back down. And that's when we had our only non-trivial issue of the day-- we weren't sure where the path was! Heading up, we just walked up. But now, there was no clear path. We were never "lost" exactly, but we did lose the trail.

We eventually found our way; we also could have asked someone, as this area is frequented by locals. Maybe that's the issue-- people come here a couple of times a week to exercise and enjoy the views. There seemed to be dozens of paths, if only we knew where they started and ended.

But it was an enjoyable hike, whether you only make it to the base of the mountain, or to the very top. Just remember how to get back down! Helgafell is a great option if you want to try a hike that isn't too far from Reykjavik, but feels like it's in the middle of nowhere. Another option the other direction from Reykjavik is Mount Esja; see page 155 for our visit there.

Straumur

Let's look at one last place in the area. This wasn't planned: we took a quick stop at a random point of interest sign. As you may or may not know, there is a flower-like symbol on signs that indicates a point of interest. It's called a Looped Square. (See page 33.)

So, seeing one of those symbols, we stopped at a place called Straumur. We had a nice hike, and found some colorful flowers. As you wander, you can see some ruins of the fishing village that used to be here ... in the 1400s! The parking area was just a minute off of road 41, and it will most likely be on your way from the airport to Reykjavik.

Kleifarvatn Lake

Reykjanes Peninsula

Whether you want to or not, you'll start and end your Iceland experience in the Southwest— that's where the Keflavik airport is! Many tourists see it as little more than an inconvenience, since the airport is 45 minutes from Reykjavik. But there's a lot to see here. There are unique museums and sculptures within 10 minutes of the airport. And the natural sites in the Reykjanes Geopark are as good as any you'll see in Iceland. If you want to limit your driving and still see some stunning nature, the southwest can be a good option.

We'd be remiss to not note what must be the biggest tourist attraction in Iceland, at least in terms of dollars spent: The Blue Lagoon (page 169). It's expensive, and somewhat touristy. But we think it's unquestionably worthwhile, especially with kids.

Let's start with the Geopark area and end in the town of Keflavik, right near the airport. You can spend a day here, or just the morning before you head back home.

Reykjanes Geopark

The Reykjanes Geopark. Haven't heard of it? I hadn't either, and I have no idea why. In my opinion, this area should be mentioned in the same breath as the Golden Circle.

The Geopark takes up most of the Reykjanes peninsula, which is where the Keflavik airport is. We approached from Reykjavik-- head south past Hafnarfjörður and onto Road 42. In half an hour, you'll be at Kleifarvatn Lake. If you're starting from the airport, you'll want to reverse the steps (start with the Bridge Between The Continents), and then end up closer to Reykjavik.

Kleifarvatn Lake

Kleifarvatn Lake has a black sand beach, a beautiful blue lake, and interesting mountains. Up the hill behind the lake you'll find some striking rock formations; you can hike up here (across the street away from the lake) to get both a closer view of the rocks and a better overview of the entire lake.

If you wanted to have a day outdoors without too much driving, you could just spend some time here, and also hike Helgafell (see page 159), since you'll be passing through Hafnarfjörður. But we continued south; every few minutes, you'll come to a sign for another attraction. The next one is Syðristapi -- a cliff with a nice view out over the lake and a hidden black sand beach.

There are dozens of different things to see in the Geopark; some of them are listed at VisitReykjanes.is. (Click on "What to See and Do", and pick "Reykjanes Geopark." At the bottom there will be a link for "Geosites.") You could probably look over the list and pick the ones you wanted to see, but it may be just as nice to drive around and see what you see?

Seltún (Krýsuvík)

There are a couple of sites you shouldn't miss, though. The next place we came to, Seltún, is one of them. This is a

Seltún (Krýsuvík)

Saltfish Museum

geothermal area. It doesn't have an erupting geysir, but lots of bubbling pots of liquid and steam. There is a well-marked path to follow, which I appreciate with the kids. It reminded me of Hverir in Mývatn (page 98), except it's much closer to Reykjavik and has a better walkway.

Note that Seltún is a rare example of a place Google Maps might not handle. Search for "Krysuvik" instead, and make sure your destination is right along Road 42.

Grindavik

We skipped a couple of sights on the way to Grindavik, including Krýsuvíkurberg bird cliffs. But it was lunchtime, and Grindavik is your best bet to find a place to eat. We settled on Bryggjan.

Lunch options here are limited, and the main draws are their two soups. They also have bread with smoked salmon or lamb on top. The soups when we were there were a Lobster soup and a vegetable soup. I'm thinking they almost always offer the lobster soup; we were hoping for a lamb soup as the second option. But the price for the vegetable soup is very cheap: 1100 krona for as much soup and bread and butter as you'd like. And it includes coffee or tea. The lobster soup is more expensive (2000 krona), but also includes unlimited refills. There is also a kid's grilled cheese for 1000 krona.

While in Grindavik, we stopped by the Saltfish Museum. It's tough to find; there's just a "Codland" sign outside. Once inside, there are actually two exhibitions. You start off with an energy section, before walking into the fishing section. The

museum costs 1200 krona for adults, 600 krona for 16-20, and is free for kids 15 and under. It's a nice museum, but may not be worth the time or money in the Geopark, which has so many things to see.

I should note at this point that we're only about 10 minutes from the Blue Lagoon. If you're heading to the Blue Lagoon on your way to or from the airport, a stop by Grindavik and some of these Geopark sites could be a good addition if you have extra time. We'll cover the Blue Lagoon on page 169.

For now, if you have more time, continue driving toward the southwest corner of the country. On the very corner, you have many attractions, all within 10 minutes of each other.

Powerplant Earth

NOTE: As of June 2018, Powerplant Earth had a message on their Facebook page that says: "The exhibition is closed until further notice." You'll want to check facebook.com/powerplantearth before you plan to visit.

Powerplant Earth is a nice enough museum; it provides a lot of educational information in and around the displays. It's inside a power plant, and you'll be able to see the working power plant through the windows at the side of the museum. My only concern is that it's expensive for kids. Admission is 1500 for adults, and 1000 krona for kids 14 and younger. Since nearly every museum in Iceland is free for kids, the price to get in here is comparatively expensive for families

with a lot of children.

Note that the hours on their web site are totally incorrect. The museum is open every day from 9-4 during the summer; the rest of the year they are only open on weekends.

A few minutes past the museum you'll come to a sign, offering a choice between heading left to Gunnuhver or right to Reykjanesviti. You should choose … both! You probably saw a sign pointing to Gunnuhver before getting all the way down here, but waiting until you get here means a shorter drive to a closer parking area.

Gunnuhver

Gunnuhver is another geothermal area, but this one is very different. The main attraction is a fierce steam vent. You can hear it from the parking lot-- steam is just pouring out of this thing; it's tough to capture the true power just in pictures.

The only issue with going here is that the blast of steam is so huge that, if the wind shifts, you could find yourself in the middle of a sulfuric rain. Be ready to dart around to avoid this, even if you're on the marked pathway!

Reykjanesviti

The other direction is toward Reykjanesviti, the Reykjanes lighthouse; "viti" means lighthouse. But that's the least interesting thing in this area. It's a lighthouse, and it's nice enough, but I don't think you can go inside. Just past this you will come to a parking area. To your right will be a little statue of an auk, a now-extinct bird. (I think that statue is more interesting than the lighthouse.)

To your left is a big hill, called Valahnúkur. This may have been the highlight of the Geopark for me. It's about a 5 minute hike up to the top; it's not too steep, but it is more or

less a continuous climb. Those of you with a fear of heights may not want to get all the way up to the edge. But you get a great view out over the water. We also *carefully* laid down and peered over the edge; try this at your own risk. But you may see some birds on these cliffs; we spotted a baby bird just a few feet below us over the edge.

Heading out of the Reykjanesviti area, you'll nearly pass by the Powerplant Earth museum again. In the lava field by the parking lot, you may have noticed, well, the sun. This is the start of a scale model of the planets in the solar system! As you pull out of the parking lot, on your left you'll see a tiny dot on a pedestal. That's Mercury.

I loved doing the walking version of this out east in Breiðdalsvík (page 89); this is the driving version. With the larger sizes of the planets (and the sun), the incredible size difference between the sun and Mercury is more obvious-- The sun is almost 300 times larger in diameter than Mercury. As you leave

Bridge Between the Continents

the power plant, assuming you are heading north toward the Bridge Between the Continents (left onto the main road), you'll see the rest of the planets (all on your left) as you drive. Jupiter is over a mile down the road. (See picture on previous page.)

We saw all of the planets except for Pluto. (Okay, I know it's not a planet anymore ...) We later learned that Pluto is in the parking lot of the power plant company. Presumably you can still do the planet hunt even if the museum is closed.

Bridge Between the Continents

Some of the planets are past our next and final stop, the Bridge Between the Continents. But most of them are along the road on the way to the bridge, so it's a nice combination of activities. The land mass of Iceland includes part of the North American tectonic plate, and part of the Eurasian tectonic plate. These two plates fit together like puzzle pieces; there is a dividing line between them across the entire length of the country. Most people associate Thingvellir National Park (page 61) as the main place to see the continental divide, but you can see it other places as well. Like in the middle of a shopping mall in Hveragerði (page 67).

Here is another spot on the divide, and one where you can walk over a bridge between the two continents. The kids always like jumping back and forth from one "continent" to another, and the bridge is a simple but pleasant stop. And you even get a black sand beach area below the bridge; the sand was pleasantly warm on this sunny late-July day.

All of this makes for a very busy day, but there was a whole lot to see. You could do it as a shorter trip, and turn around in Grindavik, or head to the Blue Lagoon just outside of Grindavik. The only downside of the full journey is that the bridge is the furthest out point of the journey, and then you have to get back home; it's about the same amount of time to retrace your drive back, or to go up near Keflavik. (But heading toward Keflavik means you see the rest of the planets!)

Oh, I should mention that you can get a certificate that says you crossed the Bridge Between the Continents. The Visitor's Center in the Saltfish Museum in Grindavik will personalize one for each member of your family, as will Duushus museum in Keflavik.

I think the Reykjanes Geopark should be near the top of anyone's list of must-see attractions in Iceland; I'm not sure why it isn't. You can see some amazing sights in one day, with less driving than a Golden Circle trip. Maybe it needs a catchy name like the Golden Circle has? Giant Geopark?

Keflavik

Airports in Iceland cause some confusion for visitors. Let's recap once more: Reykjavik, the capital of Iceland, is far and away the biggest city in the country. But, the Reykjavik City airport is small—you can't fly from there to any other country, besides Greenland. This airport can be useful if you want to fly to other towns in Iceland in lieu of driving; see ("A domestic flight?" on page 114.) When you arrive in Iceland, you will fly into Keflavik airport. This is the only international airport in Iceland. Keflavik is about 45 minutes west of Reykjavik.

There are a lot of family-friendly options in or near Keflavik that can make a great start or end to your Iceland vacation.

Viking World

Let's start with the Viking World museum, or Vikingaheimar. Viking World, like most of the other attractions in Keflavik, is only about 10 minutes from the airport. But unlike everything else, Viking World opens up at 7 AM. That makes them a good option if your flight arrives in Iceland early in the morning. And, the breakfast special could make this a very inexpensive visit.

Admission to the museum is 1500 krona for adults, and free for kids 14 and under. You can save 10% if you book online, which may not be worth it for the flexibility you lose. But the breakfast specials, available from 7 AM - 10:30 AM, cost 2000 krona and include free admission.

Only people in your party 15 and older would have to purchase these breakfasts (you can get parts of the meals a la carte as well, for you or the kids), and the whole family can get admission to the museum. Or kids 10 and younger can pay 1200 krona for breakfast.

More recently, the museum started offering a lunch buffet,

which costs 2500 krona and also includes admission.

The main feature of Viking World is the replica Viking ship that dominates the building; head upstairs and you can get on the boat. Also upstairs is an exhibit called "Fate of the Gods;" ask for your audio guide when you buy your admission tickets-- or go back for them once you've had your fill of the Viking Boat. The audio guide is included with admission.

The audio is about 22 minutes, and tells stories from Norse mythology. The controls on the audio player are confusing, and there are audio files in 4 different languages. If you want English, make sure the file name displayed on the player ends in "ENG".

There are a few small exhibits downstairs, and a few computers with activities. But if the boat and the mythology part don't interest you, there isn't much left. If you're here in time for breakfast, you can't go wrong. And lunch looks like a good deal too. Otherwise, you'll have to decide whether you want to spend your money and time here, or elsewhere.

The Settlement Zoo

Viking world shares a parking lot with the impressively named Landnámsdýragarður, the Settlement Zoo. During our first visit, there wasn't much going on-- just a few goats wandering around near the Viking Museum. But a little later in the day, we saw a variety of animals, including ducks, rabbits, chickens, goats and more.

The zoo is free, so stop by if you're in the area, Whether you pay to go in to Viking World or not, you can park in their parking lot to see the zoo.

Stekkjarkot

Stekkjarkot is a restored turf house, fully furnished inside, and just a few minutes from the Viking Museum.

The house is only open upon request. We e-mailed the museum (byggdasafn@reykjanesbaer.is) while we were in Iceland, but didn't receive a response. But once we returned, I e-mailed them again; they apologized and confirmed that you can e-mail or call (+354 4203240, or +354 8656160) to set up an appointment. We peered through the windows, and

it looks like a worthwhile visit!

The Icelandic Museum of Rock 'N' Roll

A few minutes down the road toward downtown Keflavik is the Icelandic Museum of Rock 'N' Roll.

To be honest, I very nearly skipped this one. I imagined a museum with a detailed history of rock music in Iceland, with information about a lot of singers and bands I had never heard of. And, there is a fair bit of that.

But there are also several very impressive music stations where your kids, or you, can play music, or sing, or both. There's an electronic drum set, as well as an electric guitar section: just walk in, pick up a guitar, put on the headphones, and start playing. There's also a sound mixer station, where kids can take a song and tweak the volume of different tracks to create their own sound.

All of us spent a significant amount of time in the soundproof karaoke booth, where you can record yourself and e-mail the resulting song to you or friends or family. I imagine this being a big draw, and if the museum is crowded, there may be a long wait. But since it was nearly empty while we were there, we all had our fill of karaoke.

Admission isn't cheap: 2000 for adults 17 and older, and free for kids 16 and under. You can save 15% by booking online. If you're not in town in time for breakfast, or music is more your style than Vikings and mythology, The Rock 'N' Roll museum is a surprisingly good option. And you'll probably get your fill of Vikings over the rest of your vacation ...

Ásmundur Sveinsson Sculpture

About 5 minutes up the road from the museum of Rock 'N' Roll, the road ends. The Duushús museum complex is here, and we'll get there soon. But first, you're going to find a surprising number of interesting things to do and see outside. First you have a sculpture by Ásmundur Sveinsson. We learned about the Ásmundur Sveinsson museum in Reykjavik (page 149), and how kids are allowed to climb on

his large sculptures. This one in Keflavik is huge-- climb away!

If you can pull your kids away from the sculpture, you'll notice a few things off by the water. There's a boat you can walk on, and a few monuments and sculptures as you walk.

Giantess in the Mountain

But all the way up at the end you'll see a tiny house (circled above). That's the house of the Giantess in the Mountain. Feel free to skip any and all of the museums; just let the kids climb on the Ásmundur Sveinsson sculpture and check out the Giantess's house. I can't do it justice with pictures, but there is a Giant who lives in there. She makes snoring noises (and if you wait around for a while, other noises too ...)

She's huge-- 8-10 feet tall sitting down. And you can see her huge bed. And her pacifier tree. I think this is a place you can wean your kid from their pacifier? The giantess is based on a series of Icelandic children's books by Herdís Egilsdóttir. If you're nearby, don't miss this.

Duushús museums

Once we pulled ourselves away from all of the free stuff outside, we headed to the Duushús museum complex. Here, you pay one admission price for access to three different museums. Admission is 1500 krona for adults, but free for kids 18 and under. And, if you visited the Rock 'N' Roll museum on the same day, adults will only pay 1200 krona to get in here.

The three museums are a Maritime Museum, an art museum (no pictures allowed!), and a heritage museum.

There's also a Geopark Visitor's Center with a small exhibition in the middle of the complex, and you don't have to pay to see that.

Given that you get to see 3 museums for one price, it isn't a bad deal. But with so many things to see within walking distance that are free, you may choose to skip this one.

The Icelandic Firefighter's Museum

When you're driving to or from the airport, you may see a fire truck mounted on a sign way up in the air. It's on your left driving from the airport. The museum itself is a little tough to find; you'll only see a small sign at the entrance.

The Firefighter's Museum is back just a minute or two from Viking World (page 164). But, this museum has extremely limited opening hours: Sunday from 1-5. That's it! The owner is a firefighter in Keflavik; he actually served as a firefighter at the US Naval base in Keflavik for many years. A few years ago, he and a friend decided to open up a museum, while still keeping their firefighting jobs

The good news is that the owner was very responsive on the museum's Facebook page; it was very easy to set up a convenient non-Sunday time for us to visit. Search for "icelandic fire museum", and you should find their page: Slökkviliðsminjasafn Íslands Icelandic fire museum.

The museum houses fire trucks and other firefighting equipment from all over Iceland. You start with the oldest stuff: hand pumps!

You'll also see an exhibit about the Reykjavik fire of 1915. Until the moment of the fire, the city thought it didn't need automated water pumps. Apparently, a man tried to sell one to the city, but they refused to buy it. So the salesman left the pump locked up in Reykjavik; it had come over from Denmark, and it was too expensive to bring back.

When the fire broke out, the fire chief remembered the pump, "stole" it to put out the fire, and the immediately purchased it. (I hope I have that story correct!)

You then progress through to more modern fire trucks. For a very long time, nearly all of the trucks were American made; you'll see a whole lot of Ford fire trucks. Almost all of the trucks are still operational, and they may be brought out for parades or special occasions. And, the kids (or you!) are allowed to sit in many of them.

The museum costs 800 krona for adults and free for under 18. This isn't a must see, but if you or your kids are interested in firefighting, this is another nice Keflavik attraction.

Food in Keflavik

Viking World, the Firefighter's Museum, and the Rock 'N' Roll Museum are all within about 5 minutes of each other. Between them and the Duushús area, you'll find at least a dozen restaurants. It seems like most of the restaurants in town are on Hafnargata Street; this is the same street the Rock 'N' roll Museum is on, though its name is Njarðarbraut down there.

We settled on Fernando's Pizza; you can see their extensive menu on their Facebook page; facebook.com/hafnargata28. Everyone enjoyed their pizza; the kid's pizza cost 1395 krona and includes a small ice cream bar for dessert. The more adventurous eaters in the family can choose from a variety of toppings.

Another option is Kaffi Duus, which shares a building with Duushús. They have a fairly extensive children's menu if you're here for lunch or dinner. But we were just here for a snack. And they offer a nice selection of desserts in the display case. For 950 krona, the chocolate caramel cake we tried seemed fairly priced for Iceland.

Other towns near Keflavik: Sandgerði

From the airport, you can also get to the town of Sandgerði in 10 minutes. This town is home to the Suðurnes Science and Learning Center. This is a working research facility, and includes researchers from the University of Iceland. On the lower level you'll find a small art exhibition, and then the main museum is up the stairs.

The museum costs 600 krona for adults 16+, 300 krona for kids 6-15, and is free for younger children. Coffee is only 100 krona; that alone might make the trip worthwhile for some? Note that the hours are somewhat limited, though: Summer hours are 10-4 on weekdays, and 1-5 on weekends. Winter hours are 10-2 on weekdays.

The museum has two exhibitions. The one that was less interesting to our kids was about Jean-Baptiste Charcot, a French scientist and explorer who died in a storm off the coast of Iceland. The exhibition is in French and Icelandic, but the museum can provide you with a binder containing information in English.

The other side is all about animals and marine life. There are lots of animal specimens to see, as well as microscopes you can use to look at a collection of small shells and water samples.

On their web site, the museum talks about programs for school groups, where "students can collect live creatures at the shore or ponds that are close by, bring them to the center and inspect them closely in microscopes." We didn't pursue this, but I assume if you asked, the museum would provide you with the tools for collecting your own samples?

There are two restaurants that are walkable from the museum. Vitinn is directly across the street. This is a seafood restaurant that is known for their fish tanks in the dining area. According to one review on their web site: "The dining area is charming, with tanks of fish and crabs – some pets, some for eating!"

The other restaurant is Pappa's Pizzaria, formerly called Mamma Mia Pizzeria. (Seriously!) Note that both restaurants are visible, and walkable, from the museum parking lot. Of the two, Vitinn seems more interesting, but both are very convenient options.

Garður

Also 10 minutes from the airport, at the very tip top point of the peninsula is the town of Garður, with a folk museum and lighthouse.

Actually, you'll find a museum and two lighthouses. The older lighthouse, right by the shore, has a little tiny restaurant in it. And that restaurant is your ticket to the top of the museum. You can either give them 500 krona to climb to the top, or buy some food. Perhaps you could buy something for under 500 krona? I didn't ask, but there was a kleina for 200 krona, as well as muffins (500 krona), a couple of flatbreads, coffee, tea and juice.

This lighthouse is not associated with the museum, but the taller lighthouse is. This lighthouse was closed when we were there, though the museum was open. Both should now be open. The cost is 1,000 krona for adults and free for kids; hours are 10 AM – 5 PM. This is a typical Icelandic folk museum, with lots of old stuff. There is also a cafeteria upstairs.

The lovely views in Garður

4X4 Adventures Grindavik

The Blue Lagoon (page 169) seems to overshadow all of the other things you can do in Grindavik, or on the Reykjanes Peninsula. It feels like I'm on a bit of a crusade to get people to experience other things in Reykjanes: In particular, I'm a big fan of the Reykjanes Geopark (page 161) which really takes up most of the peninsula.

One more adventurous tour we tried in Grindavik was a buggy tour with 4X4 Adventures Iceland. These tours allow you to explore the Reykjanes Geopark in a very different way. The word "buggy" might not convey the right tone here-- think of an ATV, but one that can hold 4 people.

There was an ATV along with us on the tour, and we covered the same ground. But the buggy can make sense for your family for a couple of reasons. First, all drivers must have a valid driver's license. And the ATVs can only hold 2 people-- 1 driver and 1 passenger. I simply wouldn't have been able to take both boys on an ATV. But the buggy holds 4 (3 plus the driver.)

Also, the ride in a buggy might be a little more comfortable for smaller children. You are sitting IN a vehicle, instead of ON a vehicle. Your kids might like that more. Or they may not, if they are looking for more excitement!

The pricing gets a little complicated. If you want to ride in a buggy with the guide as the driver, it costs 13900. If you want to drive yourself, it depends on the number of people you have: 14900 per person for 4 in a buggy all the way up to 29900 for a single person in a buggy. Kids 6-12 are half price, though I don't know if you can book this discount on the web site for the buggy; you may have to e-mail them.

The office is just outside of the main part of Grindavik; you're less than 5 minutes from places such as Bryggjan restaurant or the Icelandic Saltfish Museum, and maybe 10 minutes from the Blue Lagoon further out of town. When you arrive, you'll sign some paperwork, and be given your outfit-- overalls, gloves, a balaclava (like a think ski mask, to wear under your helmet), and a helmet. Happily, they had no problem finding the right gear for our 6-year-old. After a quick tutorial on how to drive, we were on our way. There's no gear shifting, so it's pretty easy to figure out how to drive. You first head out into a volcanic field with some remnants of a shipwreck.

Then we drove on the main road for a short while-- there might be a little bit of traffic, but it's a fun change of pace. Next came some mountain climbing, including a few sections where I really had to gun the engine to make it up the hill; the guy in the ATV in front of us got stuck! But the guide was by his side quickly to solve the problem.

Eventually, you make it to the top of the mountain to take a break and enjoy the beautiful views. After some time for pictures, we put or helmets back on headed back the same way we came.

There are longer tours as well-- up to 4 hours, or even full day safaris. And when, on a different day, we were eating lunch at the nearby Bryggjan restaurant, we noticed some ATVs parked out front; lunch here is included in the Full day volcanic safari. You'll also get to see a lot more of the Reykjanes Geopark, though that might be a long day for the kids.

Still, we enjoyed the shorter ride. It was loud and fast, so it might not be right if you're kids aren't up for the adventure. My boys said they wished I drove a little slower! But the shorter tours can be a memorable way to spend an hour or two. A buggy ride, a trip to the Blue Lagoon, and maybe a visit to Seltún (page 161) on the way back can make for a memorable day on the Reykjanes Peninsula.

Thanks to 4X4 Adventures Iceland for sponsoring our buggy ride!

The Blue Lagoon

The Blue Lagoon was one of the last places we visited in Iceland. By that time, we'd already been to many pools and spas all over the country. And the Blue Lagoon is much more expensive than any other pool or spa in Iceland. So let's just say that the bar was set pretty high for me to recommend it.

I was just about ready to write off the Blue Lagoon entirely when we got to the front entrance. Or, rather, didn't get to the front entrance. There was a line of people stretching well outside the building.

The Blue Lagoon offers timed tickets. The time specifies the hour during which you are allowed to check in; once you're in, you can stay as long as you like, or until they close (at midnight in the height of summer.) You have to reserve a time in advance. If you haven't visited in the last few years, note that tourism has exploded in Iceland, and pre-booking is new in just the last few years. If you look to reserve a time a week or less ahead, you may only find availability late at night: 9 PM or later, And if there are other time slots, the prices appear to always be much higher than the base price of $65. This works just like airline tickets; as the cheaper tickets are sold, the only ones left are the more expensive ones. Even looking 2 weeks out, you may not find the cheapest tickets available until 8 PM.

And, prices have gone up dramatically in the last year. In March of 2018, the Blue Lagoon eliminated the "Standard" admission, which was the cheapest option. Now the lowest priced option is a "Comfort" admission, which includes a towel and 1 drink. And a higher price, of course.

Outside of the summer season, you may or may not have better luck. But once you know what day you plan to go, book your tickets to get your preferred time and possibly save some money. (Go to bluelagoon.com and choose "Book tickets" in the upper right corner.) Kids 2-13 are free, and they also get a free towel rental. Kids under 2 are NOT allowed to swim; a parent will have to stay with them outside of the lagoon area. I haven't seen this infant policy anywhere else in Iceland-- babies are welcome at just about any other pool or spa in the country. (There is a luxury spa, Laugar Spa on page 150, that is for adults only.)

After a few minutes, we finally made it inside, and saw the line continue to snake around, even for our 8 PM booking. Not the most relaxing part of the experience. One thing that might help minimize the lines is to show up late! There's going to be a rush of people who get there at the exact time their ticket allows for, especially late into the evening. I'm not positive, but I'm fairly certain that had we shown up at 8:30 or 8:40, the line would have been minimal. You could consider booking an earlier time and then showing up toward the end of the hour window. No guarantees, though.

There are a few more expensive ticket options; one of the benefits of the Premium level is that you get a dedicated check-in line. Even though kids who get free admission don't get the upgrades (such as a bathrobe) they can still get in the Premium line with you.

We eventually made it through the Standard ticket line. But with the waiting, and the changing, and the showering, we didn't make it into the water until about 8:45. The locker room was crowded, and not any nicer than some we have seen at thermal swimming pools around Iceland.

And then, after the lines and the changing rooms and the crowds and the showers, there's the lagoon.

It's huge and, surprisingly, not very crowded. I was expecting wall to wall people after all of the waiting, but the lagoon is so big that it handles all of the people quite easily.

One nice feature of the lagoon is that there is a small indoor area, with a door that leads outside. This allows you, and in particular your kids, to avoid the cold walk to get to the warm water. Instead, you can enter the warm water inside (after putting water wings on all kids 9 and under) slowly, and then make your way outside without leaving the warmth. Definitely head left to get to this pool instead of going straight outside. We also saw this design was in Akureyri (page 106); there could be others, but it seems rare.

The water is a perfect temperature; maybe 37 Celsius (99 Fahrenheit)? And just a couple of degrees can be the difference between kids who are done after 15 minutes and kids you have to drag away a couple of hours later. (For example, I thought the Secret Lagoon (page 65) was too hot. The Blue Lagoon was definitely in the dragging-the-kids-away category.)

There are dozens of places you can explore. You can wander around or find a suitable spot for your family and hang out. There's a cave, benches, showers (which are extremely powerful), an area to get mud masks, bridges, alcoves galore, a snack bar, and much more. The mud mask area is back and to the left; the snack bar is all the way back to the right.

Everyone is given a wristband to wear; these can come off fairly easily, and the Blue Lagoon will charge you if you lose one. Make sure you help the kids slide the plastic piece around so the band won't come off. (I'm not really sure why the kids have to wear them, since admission for them is free. I guess it ensures they didn't sneak in without an adult?) These bands are color coded for adults, teenagers, and kids. Adults and teenagers can use their bands to purchase drinks. You'll have to settle each tab at the end; if you are all together, it may be easier to just have one person put all of the drinks on a single wristband and make one payment.

Options at the snack bar include skyr smoothies, juice smoothies and slushies. They also offer beer, with a limit of 3 beers per wristband. The smoothies are premade, and include one with fruit, and one with fruits and spinach (called "Green is Good"). These were very good, but expensive at 900 krona for maybe an 8 ounce serving. The slushies were less expensive at 550 krona (though there's no real fruit), and came in 2 flavors: blue raspberry or cherry. The kids enjoyed drinking the freezing cold slushies while enveloped in the warm water. Any of these can be your one free drink.

So, the question everyone asks, and Googles, is whether the Blue Lagoon is worth it or not. You have to reserve a time well in advance, which limits your flexibility. (By the way, if you have time in the area, we highly recommend you check out the Reykjanes Geopark. See page 161.) You may have to wait in line, or at least optimize your arrival time to avoid the crowds. And it's extremely expensive.

I went in hoping I wouldn't have to recommend a visit to the Blue Lagoon. That I could be a haughty travel writer who tells you to avoid the most touristy spots. (Did you know that the Blue Lagoon is just power plant run-off?) But I won't. Despite the hassles, the Blue Lagoon is incredible. It's huge, it's beautiful, and it's relaxing. Mývatn Nature Baths comes close (page 99), and Mývatn has the benefit of two different lagoons with different temperatures. But it doesn't give you the otherworldly feeling you get at the Blue Lagoon.

So work the Blue Lagoon into your plans, but also be sure to try a thermal swimming pool in Reykjavik, or in any town around Iceland. You'll spend $140 to get your family into the Blue Lagoon, and you'll spend $12 to get into the thermal pool. Both will be worth it.

Navigating the Swimming Pool Locker Room

The public pools in Iceland are beautiful and warm and a great place to take your little ones any time of year. (Swimming outside with snow in your hair is a really cool experience!) It is well worth the effort of getting everyone ready for the pool. But yes, what you've heard is true--you are expected to shower naked (soap, shampoo, and all) before entering the pool. No, you can't skip that part. No, your kids can't skip that part, even if they don't want to be naked in front of strangers. What you need to know, then, is how it all works; that's what we'll tell you here.

With our kids, at least, part of making a new and anxiety-inducing situation more comfortable is talking through it step by step beforehand so that they know exactly what to expect. Kids who feel like experts and who are telling you what happens next are not kids who are worrying! Here's the info you need to let them become experts. All the pictures here are from public pools, not the fancier spas, so they won't be showing the upscale end of things!

When you enter the building, usually the first thing you do will be to pay your entry fee (not usually the children's job!). At this point you should still be in street clothes. When going to the Y at home, it may save you time to put all the kids in their bathing suits ahead of time, but that won't do you any good here--as we noted above, you would have to take the suit off to take a shower anyway. If you are not bringing your own towels, this is also when you can rent towels. You may or may not be given a locker key or token at this point, but almost everywhere we have been, you will eventually have access to a locking locker, included in the admission price. Once all the business at the desk has been taken care of, you will be directed toward the locker rooms.

But before you get to the locker rooms (rarely, inside the locker room), is the shoe area! This is a room/hallway/sectioned off area with benches and shelves where you leave your shoes (and probably socks too)!

Sometimes this area will also have coat hooks for hanging up your cold-weather gear. So everyone sits and takes

The shoe area

off their shoes and then goes barefoot into the gender-appropriate locker room. (I suppose if you are bringing flip-flops, this would be when you would put them on.)

Once you enter the locker room, it is a good idea to scope out the layout before starting to undress--more comfortable to wander around looking lost now than later when you are naked! You will be looking to see where a few things are located. First, the lockers. You may or may not have been assigned a specific locker, depending on the pool/spa you are at. Next, the showers and the towel/swimsuit cubbies.

There should also be a bathroom somewhere. Sometimes there are two: One between the lockers and the showers and one between the showers and the pool. Finally, look for any

baby-related supplies you may need. There is always a diaper changing area, usually a lot more sturdy than the plastic fold-down ones in the US. Unfortunately, the one locker room where we asked to take pictures was the one where they had the standard US-type!

The men's locker room will also have a baby changing area, though not always as nice. In the men's locker room at the same pool, there was just a pad sitting on the counter.

There is usually also at least one high chair. These are small and easily moved high chairs, typically near the towel cubbies.

Why would you need a high chair in a locker room? Well, it is a handy place to stash the baby when you are changing into or out of your swimsuit or drying off--much nicer than a towel on the floor. I've not tried to bring it into the shower with me, but it is very difficult to shower with a baby on one hip and the high chairs aren't the kind to be damaged by water, so that might not be a bad plan, either!

Once you have the layout figured out, it is probably best to send everyone to the bathroom before you really get started. Then everyone undresses, putting your bags/clothes/etc. into the lockers, but keeping your swimsuits and towels (and goggles or any other supplies you need *at* the pool) with you. Ideally, you won't come back to the locker after this until you are leaving! You all head to the towel/swimsuit cubbies and put your towels and swimsuits (and swim diaper if your child needs one) there. Note that occasionally these may have numbers that correspond to your locker on them, but usually they are unnumbered, so you can choose whichever one(s) you want.

The showers are usually all in one open room, as you may remember from gym classes in high school (if you are old like me!).

You do not have to bring soap with you, as every one we have seen has had shower gel at a minimum. The fancier spas will also have shampoo and conditioner, though you

can't count on that. To minimize the stuff I need to carry, we usually just use the shower gel to wash our hair as well, and worry about conditioning (if necessary) when we get home. So once your suits and towels are stashed, take your showers as the signage directs--usually there is a visual (to avoid the language barrier) indicating that you must wash your hair, underarms, crotch area, and feet. (You can see an example of this on the wall in the picture at right.) After showers, you go back to the cubby area-- not the locker area: they try to keep the floor there dry-ish--to put your swimsuit on. You can leave your towel in the cubby while you swim or you can take it outside with you if you are worried about the temperature. At many pools you will be encouraged to leave your towel inside, as sudden rain would not be an unusual event, and you don't want to emerge from the pool to a cold, wet towel.

You might wish to give some thought ahead of time to the mechanics of showering and suiting up with your children. Since I have an infant with me, but also older daughters, we can trade off who is holding the baby so that I don't usually have to shower with a baby on my hip or pull on my swimsuit while holding a slippery wet baby. The high chair is invaluable for the times when I have been there without one of my older kids.

Another useful thing to know is that on the way from the locker room to the pool, you

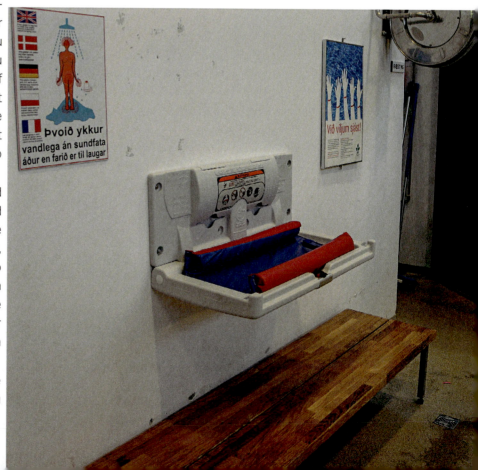

can usually find a box of water wings that are free for children to use. That was a hit for us on our last trip seven years ago, and the seven year old still uses them at some pools---even the 10-year-old occasionally. (Most pools have very shallow areas, but one spa was almost uniformly 4 feet deep, which was slightly deeper than she liked.)

As far as entering the locker rooms with a child of the opposite gender, I am not sure of the cut-off age. I have certainly seen little boys of 3 or 4 with their mothers. At the other end of the range, my 10-year-old went to the women's locker room by herself when she went swimming with just Dad and brothers.

When exiting the pool, we will sometimes rinse off with a warm shower on the way in, just to minimize the amount of whining about how cold the air is! Pick up your towels at the cubbies, and then reverse the whole process until you are back outside with your shoes on. Remember to dry off near the cubbies where you pick up your towels to keep the floor dry near the lockers!

The first pool we went to, I heard some complaints from my kids about having to undress in front of people, but given how much they enjoyed swimming in the nice warm(!) pools, I haven't taken much flak for it since then. Hopefully, with a little preparation, the locker rooms won't seem scary to your kids either, and they can just look forward to splashing in the pools!

Whale watching Tips and Tricks

We spent nearly 3 months in Iceland; when I ask the kids what their favorite thing was, the answer is immediate. "Whale watching!" Well, that's the answer from some of them; some of them didn't go. They were too worried about getting seasick on the 4 hour ride. But the rest of us tried 3 different trips; here are the tips and tricks we have learned. Knowing what I know now, I think everyone in our family could have enjoyed whale watching!

Check the Weather

Many of the bad reviews you'll find online involve rough seas. I can't imagine many worse things on a vacation than a sick kid stuck on a 3 or 4 hour boat ride. One way to help your chances is to check the wind forecast. The Icelandic Meteorological Office provides forecasts for the next 6 days. (It's easy to remember the web site: en.vedur.is. "Veður" is pronounced "vethir", which sounds a whole lot like weather. Oh, and it also means weather.)

Click on the city you're whale watching in. (Reykjavik and Akureyri are listed on the main page; find Húsavík by clicking on the whole country map first.) I personally wouldn't go if the wind is 5 m/s or higher, but I admit that's somewhat arbitrary. 5 meters per second is 11 miles per hour.

One day I looked, and the forecast for Reykjavik was for winds of 8 m/s, or 17 mph. Elding, the biggest boat tour company in Reykjavik, happened to offer a whale watching tour at that exact time. Here is their report about that trip:

"We sailed out in the bay, facing also some rocky waves. The conditions were not perfect to spot the wildlife. Still we counted with the bravery of our passengers who decided to stand in the outside part of the upper deck, challenging a sea that, unfortunately, kept going worse."

To be clear, this isn't anything against Elding-- I love that they have a detailed description of every single trip they take. And they canceled their 7 PM tour on the same day, and gave free vouchers to everyone on the 2 PM tour to come back a different day. The lesson here isn't that Elding did anything wrong-- but when I'm traveling with kids, I feel like I'm responsible for ensuring a smoother ride.

So my advice here is to not book ahead of time-- wait until a day or two before your trip, and see what the weather looks like. You may get sold out, but I think a sold out whale watching tour is too crowded anyway.

Consider the Time of Year

You'll have a better chance of success in the summertime. Nearly all whale watching your companies offer a guarantee regardless of the time of year. Here's what North Sailing says:

"In the unlikely event that you don't see whales on your trip, we'll offer you another trip, free of charge."

Because of these guarantees, the companies keep excellent data on whether each trip spotted a whale or not. North success rates are strikingly different in the summer vs. the winter. In 2014, they saw whales on 97% of trips during the summer, but only 60% in the winter.

Yes, if you don't see a whale, you get a second trip for free. But it's rare that you would have the time (or energy) for another trip during your vacation. You also don't want to be on a trip with just a single whale over 3 or 4 hours; a summer trip is more likely to result in multiple sightings.

Find Less Crowded Whale Watching Trips

For almost every other part of your trip (airfare, hotels, car rental, etc.) we recommend booking ahead. But for whale watching, I think waiting is better. First, as we just covered, you can keep an eye on the weather. But also, I don't think a sold-out whale watching trip is much fun. The boats can hold 60 or 70 people, and all of those people might be running to one side of the boat to see the whale that someone just spotted. There can be some jostling as people scramble, and it just won't be much fun with kids (or without, honestly).

In general, tours in the late afternoon seem to have fewer people on them. The big tour group companies tend to book tours that last from, say, 9 AM until 7 PM. For example, there is a big bus tour on Grayline called Whale Watching and Golden Circle afternoon. They do a 9 AM whale watching trip; a whale watching trip that starts at 5 PM wouldn't fit in their schedule.

With some companies, their reservation system allows you to see exactly how many people are booked on a given trip. When you choose the number of people for your trip, scroll to the end and see how many tickets are left!

Consider Húsavík for Whale Watching

Húsavík is in the far north of Iceland, about a 6 hour drive from Reykjavik. I don't think it makes sense to head out there just for the whale watching; you'll most likely see whales from Reykjavik too. But if you are going to be up north, we recommend North Sailing in Húsavík. The guides we had were far and away the best we had on any boat ride. The boat was quiet, and the whales were plentiful. Yes, that last one is luck, but the other two are not!

See more about North on page 102, or NorthSailing.is

Check the Whale Watching Diaries

Two of the Reykjavik whale watching companies publish daily posts with updates about their whale watching trips. Here you can find out about both the weather conditions as well as the types and quantity of whales they are seeing. In general, the different whale watching companies share information, and so most trips see nearly the same whales. So check out the Special Tours Diary (specialtours.is, "Daily

Diary") and/or the Elding diary (elding.is, "Whale Diary").

For Húsavík, North Sailing has a diary (northsailing.is, "Whale Watching Blog"), but it's not updated quite as frequently.

If you're on the fence about whether to try whale watching, you can use the diaries see if it seems like they are spotting a lot of whales. If they are giving a lot of refunds, and it's not just the weather, there may not be too many whales in the area right then.

Think About the Type of Boat

You have a few options for the type of boat you'll be in. In Húsavík, you're likely to be in a traditional oak fishing boat, like the ones North Sailing uses. In Reykjavik, you'll probably be on a more traditional fishing boat, like the boat from Reykjavik Sailors.

A couple of companies also offer much smaller, and much faster RIB boats. RIB stands for "Rigid Inflatable Boat." RIB boats have some potential advantages:

• The RIB boat is faster, and lessens the travel time to and from the whales.

• You may see more stuff. Tour operators can more easily add in quick detours to see puffins.

• You may be less likely to get seasick. The trip is shorter, and the faster boat can cut through the waves a little more.

• You can get closer to the whales. The fast, maneuverable boats can move as soon as there is a whale sighting; a good captain can estimate the place where the whale might surface next.

Of course, there are some downsides:

• They are more expensive. The price for adults is nearly twice as much in a RIB boat.

• The RIB boats are not recommended for kids under 7.

• The RIB boats might be less safe. This is anecdotal, but there have been some recent issues- two people broke their backs on a RIB boat. Now, this wasn't a whale watching trip; it was more of an adventure ride. I would be cautious, though it's tough to tell if there's an issue here or not.

Bring Medicine / Sea Bands

The first trip we took, we loaded up with both Dramamine and Sea Bands. As we did more boat rides, and learned to pick the calmest days, we realized we didn't need anything at all. Still, the medicine did seem to make a difference, so you may consider having some on hand.

Many of the tour companies will provide you with anti-nausea medicine, but I'm happier to have my own. Children's Dramamine is inexpensive, chewable, and half of the adult dose. (Read the label to make sure-- typically the children's dose is 25mg and the adult dose is 50mg.) So that one children's package could cover your whole family-- 1 per child, and 1 or 2 per adult.

We also purchased Sea Bands, which are wristbands that put pressure on an acupressure point on your wrist. There is one size for kids and another for adults. Remember, though, that you want these to be fairly tight to make sure it's putting pressure on the right spot.

You may not need any of these, but it might provide some comfort to kids who are afraid of getting sick. Or you could also learn the spot where the Sea Bands put pressure (see sea-band.com), and teach the kids to put pressure on that spot with the fingers of their other hand.

Bring the Right Clothes

Most of the time, if you're going to be outside in Iceland for several hours, you want to wear lots of layers. Our kids might wear 4 layers (wool base layer, shirt, sweater, fleece) to keep warm and keep the wind out. But most whale watching trips give you very warm overalls to wear. And my kids ended up being too hot if they wore the overalls with more than 2 layers.

The hard part is that, if it's warm enough, they may not break out the overalls, so ironically you may need more layers in warm weather than cold weather. (You can bring a bag or backpack on board to store any layers that you or the kids end up shedding.) And in either case, you may want a hat or gloves, since the overalls don't help those parts of your body to stay warm.

Iceland Whale Watching Recommendations

North Sailing in Húsavík is our top pick; we had a great tour with them. The tour guides on the boat were fantastic. And their customer service is excellent-- I get prompt responses to all of my e-mails. See our write-up of North on page 102.

To be fair, all of the tour groups will do a good job. All of them get good ratings overall; complaints mainly relate to rough seas or crowded boats. The cheapest option in Reykjavik is with a new company, Reykjavik Sailors. See our write-up on page 132

But you really can't go wrong with any tour from any city. Just check the weather, try to find a less crowded trip, and go find some whales!

Seeing and Riding Icelandic Horses

Icelandic horses are unique, and their history is amazing. Here's a quick summary. In the year 982 (yes, nine eighty-two!) a law was passed in Iceland forbidding any horse from being imported into Iceland. A horse can leave the country, but it can never come back. And this law has been in place continuously for over 1,000 years.

These Icelandic horses have a unique characteristic. Most (all?) horses can walk, trot, and gallop. But Icelandic horses have two more gaits: The Tölt, and Flying Pace. Both of these gaits are considered to be extremely smooth for how fast they are.

Seeing and Petting Icelandic Horses

You may or may not want to go on a horse riding tour while in Iceland, but a quick stop to see them can be an enjoyable experience. You'll see cars stopped by the side of the road to pet random horses they come across, though I don't think it's ideal to visit strange horses on private land.

I used to recommend a place called Fakasel, where you could pet the horses and see a short but entertaining show, but sadly they seem to be out of business.

The Icelandic Horse Center

So I am switching my recommendation to a brand new place, The Sólvangur Icelandic Horse Center. Their web site is IcelandicHorseCenter.is, which redirects to hesturinn.is. Sólvangur is about 40 minutes outside of Reykjavik, and 10 or 15 minutes south of Selfoss. So it's not far out of the way if you're on your way to the Golden Circle.

I shouldn't really call this a brand new place. They've been breeding horses and offering riding lessons for 17 years. But what is brand new is a stable tour and the café and gift shop.

The stable tour is the reason to come out of your way to get to Sólvangur. The 20 minute tour is a nice option for families with children too young to ride, or if some people simply don't want to ride. The cost is 1800 krona for adults, 1000 krona for ages 3-15, and free for kids 2 and under.

Before or after (or instead of) the stable tour, you can also visit their horse-themed gift shop, as well as the café, which is open from 11 AM – 5 PM. You can just drop by and see and pet some of the horses, but if you'd like to take a stable tour, it's best to e-mail and make a reservation; e-mail them at IcelandicHorseCenter@gmail.com

Riding Icelandic Horses with children

Sólvangur now offers 20 minute children's horse rides for 3500 krona. If you have 3 or more children, ask about a "package deal" for a stable tour combined with a children's horse ride. I've found them very responsive to e-mails:

IcelandicHorseCenter@gmail.com.

Lots of companies offer horse rides of an hour or two, and just about all of them are reviewed favorably online. Just like with guided tours, you can't go wrong with smaller group tours in Iceland.

We enjoyed our ride up north at Hestasport in Varmahlíð (riding.is). They are west of Akureyri, in an area where there isn't as much to do as you will find, say, on the south coast. If you're traversing the entire Ring Road, Hestasport is a nice stop on a long driving day. The minimum for their "Pleasure in Every Hoofstep" tour is 6 years old. See page 109.

Note these names are all sounding similar: hesturinn, hestasport. "Hestur" means horse in Icelandic!

Riding horses near Reykjavik

If you are looking for options closer to Reykjavik, make sure you look at the minimum ages different companies have. Almost all of your options have excellent ratings online, but only a few offer tours for younger children.

One good option is Íshestar. (There's that Icelandic word for horse again!) They are about 20 minutes south of Reykjavik, near Hafnarfjörður. It's just a few minutes out of your way if you are heading to the airport. Or, if you want to make a day of it, see more options in Hafnarfjörður (page 158). If you don't have a car, Íshestar will pick you up for an extra 1500 krona per person.

Íshestar offers a tour called Family Adventure for kids as young as 6: "Our trained guides take you and your whole family on a quick ride on calm horses allowing both you and the youngest ones to experience the breathtaking nature and the excitement of riding a horse." It's a 30 minute ride. Kids under 6 can go for a ride around the paddock. Longer tours (as well as an expensive stable tour) are also available.

If you plan to ride with a company not listed here, you will still more than likely have an amazing experience! Horses are a respected part of Icelandic history, and companies offering riding tours all seem to offer excellent service. The companies above just offer options for younger riders or non-riders that you are less likely to find at other horse farms.

Food in Iceland

Airfare to Iceland can be surprisingly cheap. Lodging can be very reasonable, especially if you're willing to use Airbnb. But everything else is really expensive. Hopefully, you won't need to buy clothes while you're here, or a camera. But you will need to buy food. As a very general rule of thumb, expect to pay about twice as much for food as you would at home. But there are some exceptions to this rule, so let's take a look.

Quick service food in Iceland

There are lots of restaurants in Iceland that serve a "fast food" type menu. Hot dogs, hamburgers, fish and chips, and ham and cheese sandwiches are the standards here. You'll find places like this in many gas stations, and in most towns and villages. For me, the price shock was the highest at these types of places. Hot dogs (Pylsa) seem okay, at 350-400 krona. But everything else is just plain expensive. A hamburger with various toppings might cost 800 or 1000.

A hamburger meal with fries and a drink might cost 1300, even at a gas station. A fish and chips meal might be 1800. The food will be fine, but it won't be anything memorable.

Full service food in Iceland

Full service restaurants have had the lowest price shock for me. Fish and chips might only be a couple dollars more than our quick service fish and chips, at 2000 krona. Nicer entrees (fish or steak) can cost 2700-4000 or more.

But look for children's menu. A 1000 krona kid's meal at a fancy restaurant can save you a lot of money. (See some examples in "Restaurants on Old Harbor" on page 133.)

Remember that tax is built into the price, and there's generally no tipping.

Buffets in Iceland - take the kids!

Buffets continue the trend of more reasonable prices and great deals for kids. We had a buffet lunch at Café Nielsen; see page 91. The all you can eat price was 2,100 krona for adults 14 and over, 1,050 krona for kids 7-13, and FREE for kids 6 and under. 2,100 is the exact same price as fish and chips from our quick service place above. But here, we had a salad bar, vegetable soup, and 3 entrees to choose from: An even better deal was a lunch we had at Tjöruhúsið in Ísafjörður in the Westfjords. See page 119.

Many buffets seem to have similar pricing, where they are free for little kids and half price for older children. You can see a list of some of the Reykjavik buffets that offer discounts for kids by looking online for: "Eating Out: Free Food for Kids!".

Grocery stores in Iceland

Of course, cooking for yourself will always be less expensive. If you don't have a kitchen, you can always buy bread, sliced cheese, or peanut butter and jelly. (Most stores will only have small containers of peanut butter.) Some larger grocery stores will have baby carrots, and most will have apples or bananas. Prices here will be higher than at home, but nothing is too painful. For example:

Bread	$3.50 for a loaf
Peanut butter	$3 for 12 ounces
Apples	$2 a pound
Bananas	$1.50 a pound

If you're going to eat soon after your grocery store, trip, Kronan and some other chains will have has a warm ready-to-eat whole chicken deal for about $15.

With a kitchen, things open up even more. Examples:

Pasta	$1.50 for a large box
Eggs	$6 a dozen
Small frozen pizza	$4 or $5 each.
Frozen chicken legs	$2.50 a pound

Surprisingly, lamb is much more expensive, given that there are more than twice as many sheep as people in Iceland. You'll pay $8 - $10 a pound for most lamb meat. Beef is also expensive.

Note that you will need to pay for your plastic shopping bags in Iceland. Almost all places will charge you 20 krona, though a few charge 25. You'll need to estimate how many you need, and tell the cashier.

Grocery store brands and hours in Iceland

Kronan and Bonus have the largest sized grocery stores in Iceland. Kronan is found only in and around Reykjavik, though you will also find Bonus stores in Akureyri, Egilsstaðir, and even Ísafjörður. Outside of those areas, you'll find a Netto, Kjarval (in the south) or something from Samkaup (which actually owns Netto too.) There are two types of Samkaup stores: Samkaup Strax and Samkaup Úrval. Strax means fast or immediate, and these are going to be smaller convenience-type stores. Úrval means ... maybe selection? These Úrval stores won't be as big as a Bonus or a Kronan, but they will be a little bigger than a Strax store.

Hours will also vary with size. Some Bonus stores in Reykjavik and Akureyri are open 24 hours; some Samkaup Strax stores are closed on Sundays and may close at 6 PM on weekdays.

Costco

If you have a car, and you're staying in Iceland for more than a few days, and you have a Costco membership at home, you could consider stocking up at Iceland's only Costo, which opened in 2017. See page 157.

See our web site for some pictures and more details. Look for "Food in Iceland - Iceland with Kids." or "Monday, July 11 update: Art museum and children's menus in Reykjavik"

Emergency Stuff

U.S. citizens who have an emergency and need to reach the U.S. Embassy during normal working hours, 0800-1700 Monday through Friday excluding US and Icelandic holidays, should call the U.S. Embassy switchboard at (354) 595-2200.

SafeTravel.is

- safetravel@safetravel.is   +354 570-5929
- Check for alerts and warnings
- Submit your travel plan if you're heading to remote areas by yourself, but we never felt the need to use this. Submit your plan using the "112 Iceland app" or the web site.
- Download the 112 Iceland App

en.vedur.is

- Weather and weather warnings.
- If there's an alert of any color (yellow, orange, or red) pay attention!

road.is

- Detailed road conditions
- Also see "Weather and Road Conditions" on page 26.

Medicine in Iceland

Like grocery stores, pharmacies in Iceland have very limited hours. The pharmacy with the best hours we have seen is next to a 24-hour(!) grocery store in Reykjavik. This was out next to the Hagkaup store in Garðabær.

Their hours are Mon.-Fri. 9-6:30, Sat. 10-4, and Sun. 12-4. More typical hours are during the workday during the week, and possibly for a few hours on Saturday. And you need a pharmacy to buy *any* medicine: so far as I can tell, you can't even buy Tylenol (acetaminophen) at the grocery store! (Vitamins are available at most grocery stores.)

Because you are in a foreign country, remember that the drug brand names you know are not necessarily the brand names that will be available, and once you figure out the brand name you need, the dosage may be different per pill or per teaspoon. Or your normal dosage may not be available over the counter. If you know you are going to need medicine, bring it with you!

If you know the generic chemical name for the drug you need, the process is much easier because the pharmacist likely knows that name, too. If, however, you only know the brand name, you are likely to be reduced to trying to explain your symptoms (or mime them). It took us quite a while to get a bottle of Pektolin (Benadryl!) for our daughter—we needed Benadryl, not Claritin or Zyrtec, equivalents of both of which were readily offered. And when we did figure out the right name, it was only available as a liquid over the counter. For pills or tabs, we would have needed a prescription.

The easiest way I've found to get the Icelandic brand name is to first Google the US brand name to get the generic chemical name. Then Google the generic name plus "Iceland." A result on drugs.com/international/ is usually good, though Wikipedia is sometimes surprisingly helpful. Either way, the list of brand names is likely to be very long, so you may have to search on the page for the word Iceland as well. Below is a list of some of the more common drugs you might need.

Note that some of these have additional active ingredients that I have not included—so they are not necessarily direct equivalents! I am not a doctor or a pharmacist. I am not guaranteeing that any of these medications are exact equivalents—so please use your own judgment—research and talk to a doctor or pharmacist about any medicine you intend to take!

Pain/fever/analgesics:

Ibuprofen (Advil): Íbúfen

Acetaminophen (Tylenol): Panodil, Paratabs, Pinex

Aspirin: Hjartamagnyl, Alka-Seltzer, Aspirin Actavis, Treo (also has caffeine)

Naproxen (Aleve): Naproxen Mylan

Diarrhea relief:

Loperamide (Imodium): Imodium, Loperamid Portfarma

Bismuth subsalicylate (Pepto Bismol): De-Nol (confirm active ingredient is Bismuth subsalicylate)

Itch relief:

Hydrocortisone cream: Ciproxin-Hydrocortison, Daktacort, Mildison, Plenadren, Locoid, Solu Cortef, Fucidin Hydrocortisone

Antihistamines:

Diphenhydramine HCl (Benadryl): Benylan, Pektolin

Loratadine (Claritin): Clarinase, Loritin

Cetirizine (Zyrtec): Cetrizin ratiopharm

If over the counter medicine isn't enough, then you will have to find a clinic. Thankfully, we have avoided needing that so far, so I do not have any direct experience with going to the doctor, urgent care, or emergency room here in Iceland. There is a post on a different blog that has a little information and may be helpful if you do need a doctor. To find it, search for:

"Doctors, Clinics, Medicine" Iceland

Let's hope you don't need to use this section!

Made in the USA
San Bernardino, CA
22 March 2019